How To
Maximize Your
Unemployment
Benefits

COMPLETE INFORMATION FOR ALL FIFTY STATES

Raymond Avrutis
Geraldine S. Wulff

Avery Publishing Group
Garden City Park, New York

In the course of writing this book, the authors and editor have attempted to simplify complex matters and tables in order to make this information accessible to you, the reader. Although we have relied on state and federal publications, the interpretations are our own and should not be considered points of law. Because the laws that regulate unemployment insurance benefits are constantly changing, it is important to contact your local unemployment insurance office whenever questions arise regarding specific state regulations and dollar amounts.

Cover designers: Rudy Shur and Ann Vestal
In-house editor: Joanne Abrams
Typesetter: Bonnie Freid
Printer: Paragon Press, Honesdale, PA

Library of Congress Cataloging-in-Publication Data

Avrutis, Raymond.
    How to maximize your unemployment benefits : a practical guide to avoiding the common pitfalls to getting what is rightfully yours / Raymond Avrutis, Geraldine Schepker Wulff
      p. cm.
    Includes index.
    ISBN 0-89529-568-7
    1. Insurance, Unemployment—United States—States. 2. Insurance, Unemployment—United States—Territories and possessions.
    I. Wulff, Geraldine Schepker. II. Title.
HD7096.U5A82 1994
368. 4'4'00973—dc20   94-1709
                                 CIP

Printed in the United States of America

10 9 8 7 6 5 4 3 2 1

CONTENTS

ACKNOWLEDGMENTS

This book is dedicated to my late parents, Adelaide Sofrance Avrutis and William J. Avrutis, in fond memory. I also dedicate this book to my high school headmaster, Alex Rode Redmountain, and to the late Paul S. Weisberg, M.D., both of whom taught me to appreciate the gifts my parents gave me. I shall miss Dr. Weisberg's wise counsel.

I sincerely thank John H. Hall, William H. Jackson, Edward C. Smith, and Martin Wenglinsky—my outstanding teachers. And I acknowledge my friends who were there at the right time: Lynne Seaborg Cobb; Christopher J. Kuppig; David Kusin; David McD. Lee; Dorothy McGhee; and Christopher Simpson. I also thank the late Beverly Anne Moore, Raphael Perl, Dianne Lancaster, Elaine English, and Gilbert Navarro. Without their help, this book might never have been published.

Three other people have had significant influences on the writing of this book: Glenn T. Seaborg, chemist and educator, whose outstanding creative example I chose to emulate at age sixteen; the late Abbie Hoffman, whose *Steal This Book* was an inspiration; and early twentieth-century chess grand master Aron Nimzovich, whose *My System* was an inspiration in its own way.

Also deserving of thanks are Avery Publishing Group's managing editor, Rudy Shur, who realized the great need for this book, and Joanne Abrams, Avery's executive editor, who made hundreds of necessary editorial changes.

Finally, I wish to thank the personnel of the United States Department of Labor, Employment and Training Administration, Unemployment Insurance Service, for their time and technical assistance in the preparation of this book. The opinions expressed herein—as well as any errors—are solely my own.

R.A.

I would like to thank my husband, Roger Wulff, who promised and gave full support while I worked on this book. I also thank the many former coworkers who responded to questions on technical matters. And I acknowledge the encouragement and confidence given me by the good folks at Avery Publishing Group.

G.S.W.

PREFACE

I felt angry after I was terminated from my job with the National Council on Crime and Delinquency. I hit the streets looking for work, but couldn't find a job. I was frustrated. I knew that, to survive, I had to collect unemployment insurance.

It was mid-May. The unemployment office told me to apply in July. In July, I was told to reapply in October. I barely made it on my savings. I do not wish this semi-starvation on anyone.

Unfortunately, my experience was not unique. In good economic times as well as bad, at least 2 million people each year do not receive their rightful unemployment insurance (UI) benefits, often because they don't believe they are eligible. Still others get less UI benefits than they should because they are "late filers" who wait until they've exhausted their savings before applying.

Certainly, the newly unemployed person is faced with a maze of complex rules and regulations—an intimidating maze that prevents many people from getting their rightful benefits. That's why *How to Maximize Your Unemployment Benefits* was written—to help you move through this maze as painlessly as possible, and to insure that you apply for and *get* the unemployment insurance and related assistance that can sometimes make the difference between disaster and survival.

Each chapter of this book familiarizes you with the UI system or gives you practical information that will help you maximize your benefits. In Chapter 1, you'll get a brief look at the history of unemployment insurance—how it developed, why it developed, and why the system is structured the way it is. This chapter will give you insight into the workings of the current system.

In Chapter 2, you'll find out what you can expect during your first visit to your local unemployment office—and beyond. When's the best time to file your claim? What forms of identification must you bring with you? How will you file for subsequent weeks of benefits? All of these questions will be answered. Plus you'll learn how to successfully file an appeal, and how to trouble-shoot any problems that may arise during the claims-filing process.

Many people wrongly believe that they are not covered by unemployment insurance, and therefore fail to claim benefits. In Chapter 3, you'll learn what types of employment are covered and what types are excluded. You may be pleasantly surprised to learn that 97 percent of wage and salary work *is* covered by UI!

Claimants who have been disqualified for certain actions—such as quitting a job without good cause—may have their benefits postponed, reduced, or denied. In Chapter 4, you'll learn about possible causes of disqualification, and find out how you can often avoid the pitfalls that prevent many claimants from receiving their UI benefits.

To receive UI benefits, claimants must meet specific eligibility requirements or have their benefits reduced or denied. Chapter 5 takes a close look at the factors that affect eligibility.

Once you know if you qualify for UI benefits, you'll most certainly want to find out exactly how much you're entitled to receive. Chapter 6 will lead you through the computation process. You'll learn about the factors that affect your benefit amount, and you'll learn how you can calculate your weekly benefit amount and your maximum potential amount. You'll also find out if you are eligible for a dependents' allowance, and you'll see how your benefits may be affected by earnings from part-time work and other sources. Throughout the chapter, tips are provided to help you get the greatest benefits that you are eligible to receive.

Chapter 7 takes a brief look at programs that can extend your benefits, provide job training, or furnish other types of assistance. If your regular benefits have been exhausted, or if you have lost your employment due to trade adjustments, disaster, or technological changes, this chapter may provide a much-needed lifeline.

Throughout the book, tables provide detailed state-by-state information that will allow you to accurately determine your weekly and total benefit amounts, any penalties that may be imposed in your case, and much more. Finally, you'll find a glossary designed to clarify those terms that you'll want to understand as you learn about the UI system.

For most of us, a period of unemployment is a difficult time. Certainly, unemployment insurance benefits should make this period a little easier. Yet for many people, the process of claiming these benefits is often intimidating and frustrating. I hope that this book will take the "sting" out of the process. I hope that the information presented here will answer many of your questions, and will assist you in framing your remaining ones in a way that will provide you with the facts you need. I believe that this book will give you a firm understanding of what you are eligible to receive, and—most important—of how you can go about getting what is rightfully yours. I wish all of our readers the best of luck!

Raymond Avrutis

Surviving Your First Visit to the Unemployment Office

If you've ever been in an unemployment office, you have a good idea of what you'll face during your upcoming visit. If this will be your first time, though, you may be in for an unpleasant surprise! Long lines and maximum inconvenience may await you. Is there any way to make your initial visit to the office a little more comfortable? Of course there is! These suggestions may help.

❏   *Use public transportation if you can to avoid the hassle of parking in a metered lot. If you take your car, be sure to bring along plenty of change for the meter.*

❏   *Bring along reading material–an engrossing novel, a newspaper, or a magazine. It will make the time pass much more quickly. (And it's not a bad idea to bring along this book, too. You may need it!)*

❏   *Take along a pen or pencil for filling out forms. It may be difficult to borrow one when you need it.*

❏   *Bring along a few snacks–granola bars, nuts, juice, or whatever. You may get hungry, and if you leave the office to pick up lunch, you may lose your place in line.*

❏   *If you have to leave the line you're standing in for any reason, make sure to ask the person in front of you or behind you to save your place.*

Finally, try to be patient, and don't be discouraged by the long wait. If you've decided to do everything possible to get the maximum benefits you're entitled to receive, you'll want a clear head. Anger and frustration can only lead to making mistakes during the claim-filing process.

INTRODUCTION

Some part of the American labor force has always been unemployed, even if only 4 percent in any one month. Since 1936, when the State of Wisconsin paid the first benefit check, people have lined up to sign for unemployment insurance (UI) benefits. Certainly, the practice of paying compensation has proven to be a good social policy. UI benefits help lessen the anxiety and financial distress that unemployment routinely caused before compensation became the right of workers who had lost their jobs through no fault of their own. Often, these payments make the difference between subsistence and destitution. And for those living well above the subsistence level, UI makes it possible to avoid drastic, adverse adjustments in the standard of living.

Despite the important role played by UI—and although more than $400 billion have been paid in unemployment compensation since that first benefit check was presented to a claimant—the federal government has never written a book for the unemployed person, explaining his or her benefit rights. The small "claimant's handbook," known by different names in different states, has often been the only source of information for those out of work—and an inadequate source, at that. This book attempts to fill that gap by providing state-by-state information on how to apply for benefits, how to appeal if your claim is denied, how to avoid errors that might lead to disqualification—in short, how to obtain the benefits to which you are entitled.

At this time, you probably have many questions about unemployment insurance. Especially if you have never applied for UI benefits before, you want to know if you're eligible for benefits, and how the UI system works. Let's take a closer look at each of these questions.

DO YOU QUALIFY TO RECEIVE UI BENEFITS?

In order to receive UI benefits, two requirements must be met. First, you must have worked in covered employment. Second, you must be eligible.

If you have worked approximately six months in the past and you are now unemployed—or have suffered a substantial reduction in employment—through no fault of your own, you may be eligible for UI benefits. Each state has its specific eligibility requirements with regard to how long you must have worked and/or how much you must have earned in covered employment. In addition, you must have a continuing attachment to the labor market—that is, you must be able to work, available to accept work, and actively seeking work.

The term "covered" actually refers to the employment or the employer, rather than the worker. Most employment is covered, because most United States workers are employed by an individual or corporation that pays the tax which makes unemployment insurance possible. The employment of individuals who work for municipal, county, and state governments is also covered. And the services of civilian employees of the United States government and persons who are honorably discharged from the United States Armed Forces are covered. Although federal civilian employees and military service members are covered under different laws, the process is administered and the benefits are paid under the same state programs that serve private-industry employees. Indeed, about 97 percent of all wage and salary jobs are covered by unemployment insurance!

On the other hand, the earnings of most people who are self-employed are not covered; nor are the earnings of people who work on a commission-only basis; nor are the earnings of people who work illegally. And certain types of work are excluded from coverage or exempted from taxation by federal or state statutes. But chances are, if you are an American worker, your employment is covered. Even if your employer has failed to register and pay taxes to the state unemployment offices, has gone out of business, or has declared bankruptcy, you could be eligible for benefits if

---

TIP: *If you have worked steadily at full-time employment for at least one year, you don't have to worry about wage and employment requirements. You have met the requirements for a maximum-duration claim!*

your employment *should* have been covered and you meet the eligibility requirements.

Later in this book, we will speak more specifically about coverage and eligibility. At this point, we advise you to proceed on the basis that your employment was covered and that you are eligible to receive UI.

HOW DOES THE UI PROCESS WORK?

Employers are required by federal and state unemployment insurance laws to cover their employees by paying taxes based on their payrolls. The UI taxes paid to state governments are used to fund benefits to workers. The taxes paid to the federal government are used to cover the administrative costs of the UI system. In wage record states, employers are required to report the wages of their employees to the state UI system on a quarterly basis. In wage request states, employers report these wages within a specified period of time after a claim application is filed. State unemployment insurance agencies collect the state unemployment taxes and deposit them in the UI trust fund, maintain each employer's account, and determine employer liability rates based on each account's claims "experience." These agencies then accept, compute, and pay unemployment insurance claims. UI rates, details of coverage, and eligibility requirements vary from state to state; however, all state unemployment insurance laws must be in compliance with the Federal Unemployment Tax Act. Because of this requirement, there are more similarities than differences between state systems.

Individuals usually file unemployment insurance claim applications (called initial claims) by visiting a local unemployment office in person. Local offices are found throughout the fifty states, the District of Columbia, Puerto Rico, and the Virgin Islands. In some instances, such as mass layoffs, applications are accepted on the job site or through other arrangements. In the not-too-distant future, applications may be taken by phone, by mail, or through personal computers.

Once the initial claim application has been filed, a computation of eligibility is made based on past employment. Then, if needed, interviews or meetings are scheduled to resolve any questions of eligibility. Usually, though, such interviews are unnecessary, and the claimant is able to file for specific weeks of benefits. With increasing frequency, individuals file for each week by mail rather than reporting in person, and payments are sent to the claimant by mail. In some cases, it's even possible to file continued claims by touch-tone phone! Once an individual returns to work, he or she simply reports that fact on a mail claim or during a visit to the unemployment office.

HOW DO YOU FIT INTO THE PROCESS?

In some occupations, periods of unemployment are expected and recurrent, and workers can plan and budget for these times. For most people, however, unemployment is totally unexpected and causes a range of emotions from mild embarrassment to anger.

For many, jobs are an integral part of personal identity and self-worth, and the sudden loss of a job leaves the individual in shock. Some may blame themselves and feel useless. They may try to get another job right away and pretend that the layoff or firing never took place. Others may lash out at their families, their communities, or even their prospective employers.

Fear is a typical emotion associated with unemployment. Everyone has financial responsibilities, and to have the means of fulfillment taken away is indeed very frightening. Certainly, unemployment insurance can help meet these needs and make the situation less frightening. Yet, some people are too embarrassed to ask for help by applying for benefits. They believe that doing so will label them failures or bums. In the vast majority of cases, this is far from the truth. It's important to remember that you must have *worked* to be eligible for unemployment benefits. And you must be trying to regain employment to maintain that eligibility. As anyone who has made a concentrated attempt to gain employment will tell you, this is hardly the occupation of a bum. Employers are required to pay taxes on *workers* so that during periods when unemployment is unavoidable, the impact is lessened on both the worker and the community. It is only in this very broad sense that unemployment insurance can be called welfare.

Yes, you may experience embarrassment, anger, and fear—and all of these emotions are very real and legitimate. Our purpose in mentioning them is to help you recognize and deal with them in constructive ways. Don't carry your anger, your fear, or your frustrations to the unemployment office, to the job service, or to interviews with prospective employers. Instead, discuss your emotions with your friends and family. Many community organizations have self-help groups for people who are unemployed or seeking work, particularly during recessions or in times of plant closures or mass layoffs that affect entire communities. You might find such groups in churches, community colleges, adult education centers, or public libraries. If you can't find such a group, consider starting one.

Finally, consider the possibility that your period of unemployment is a valuable opportunity to investigate other career options and explore new directions. Many people discover unexpected resources and talents during times of unemployment—possibilities that never would have occurred to them while they were employed.

HOW TO USE THIS BOOK

Until you again gain employment, unemployment insurance will provide a valuable means of support. This book was designed to enable you to successfully navigate the UI maze and obtain the assistance that is rightfully yours.

Chapter 1 of this book provides a brief look at the history of our unemployment insurance system, giving you valuable background for information presented in later chapters. If you're curious about the roots of the current system, this chapter is sure to be of interest.

If you're just about to make your first visit to your local unemployment office, Chapter 2 will guide· you through that initial contact. You'll learn the best way to file claim applications—as well as the best time and the best place to file them. You'll learn how to keep the claims process running smoothly so that you can continue to receive benefit checks throughout your period of unemployment. And if you've already made that first contact, and have run into some problems, you'll want to turn to the latter part of the chapter. There, you'll learn how to trouble-shoot small problems and how to successfully file an appeal in the event of adverse determinations.

We've already mentioned that in order for claimants to receive benefits, they must have worked in covered employment. If you're worried that your employment was not covered, turn to Chapter 3. There, you'll learn exactly what types of work are covered, and what types are excluded from UI coverage. Did you work for a nonprofit organization? Were you employed in agricultural work? Did you work in a family-owned corporation? Chapter 3 will tell you if you're entitled to UI benefits.

If you suspect that you may be disqualified for benefits or that you fail to meet eligibility requirements, Chapters 4 and 5 will tell you about actions that may lead to disqualification or ineligibility, as well as about the resulting penalties that may be imposed in each of the fifty-three states and jurisdictions. Throughout both chapters, guidelines are provided for avoiding the pitfalls that can prevent claimants from receiving their benefits.

In Chapter 6, you'll learn how to compute your benefits for each

---

TIP: *Even if your calculations show that you don't qualify for UI benefits, don't hesitate to file a claim application. You may, in fact, qualify!*

---

week of unemployment, as well as for the full benefit year. You'll also learn how a dependents' allowance may add to your weekly check. And you'll see how worker's compensation, earnings from part-time employment, pensions, and many other types of income can affect your benefit check. The many tables in this chapter show exactly how each state makes its computations to determine each of these amounts. If you feel comfortable with math, this is the chapter for you. If math scares you—and you're in good company if it does!—feel free to skip this chapter. The unemployment office will, of course, make all of these calculations for you.

Chapter 7 will tell you about programs that can extend your benefits beyond the usual benefit year or furnish other types of aid. If your benefits have been exhausted, if you need job-training or job-search assistance, or if you've lost your employment due to trade adjustments, disaster, or technological changes, this chapter may have the information you're looking for.

The unemployment insurance system has been set up for specific purposes: to determine employer liability and collect the taxes that finance the system, and to determine claimant eligibility and distribute payments to eligible unemployed individuals. The system may not seem user-friendly to either party, and to you, the unemployed person, it may seem especially daunting. At a time when you may already feel vulnerable, you find yourself in a seemingly uncaring, unyielding bureaucracy. Increasing automation of various UI systems, particularly of those having to do with claim computation, wage records, and weekly claimant reporting, has decreased the time spent waiting in lines. But automation has also diminished staff, and requires greater self-reliance on the part of the claimant. The truth is that if you have worked in covered employment, have become unemployed through no fault of your own, and are able to and available for work, you are exactly the person for whom the system was designed. This book will help you get each and every dollar that is rightfully yours.

Feel Free to Ask

Right now, you probably have a lot of questions about unemployment insurance. We hope that this book will answer many of these questions. To guide you in finding the answers as quickly as possible, some of the questions most commonly asked by UI claimants have been listed below, along with the numbers of the pages on which the relevant discussions begin. But because each claimant's case is different, you may have questions that are not answered in this book. If this is the case, don't hesitate to seek answers from the staff of your unemployment office. To help you understand their answers, carry this book with you. Use the glossary for "translations," and the index to zero in on the topic in question.

❑ *What type of identification or documentation do I have to bring to the unemployment office? (See page 19.)*

❑ *Do I have to report to the unemployment office in person every week in order to file continued claims? (See page 27.)*

❑ *I was just laid off from work, and I'm hoping that the layoff will last only a week or so. Should I file for unemployment insurance right away, or should I wait to see how long the layoff will last? (See page 18.)*

❑ *I recently moved from one state to another, and most of my employment took place in the first state. Will I be able to file a claim in my new state of residence? (See page 17.)*

❑ *I left my job because my employer decreased my hours, resulting in a reduction in pay. Can I collect unemployment benefits without penalty? (See page 74.)*

❑ *I left my job to care for my children. Can I collect unemployment benefits without penalty? (See page 77.)*

❑ *I attend school. Am I eligible for unemployment insurance? (See page 75.)*

❑ *How often and where do I have to register for work? (See page 24.)*

❑ *I sometimes do odd jobs to supplement my income. If I take part-time jobs during my period of unemployment, will I still be eligible for benefits? (See page 119.)*

❑ *I have two young children. Am I entitled to greater benefits because of these dependents? (See page 171.)*

❑ *My spouse is also out of work. Will this entitle me to greater benefits? (See page 171.)*

❑ *What's the largest amount I can expect to receive in my weekly benefit check? (See page 46.)*

❑ *For how many weeks can I expect to receive benefit checks? (See page 170.)*

❑ *If I'm told that I'm ineligible for benefits because of insufficient wages or an insufficient period of employment, what options do I have? (See page 37.)*

1. WHAT IS UNEMPLOYMENT INSURANCE?

While it is certainly possible to get the unemployment insurance (UI) benefits you are eligible to receive without any knowledge of the UI system's background, even a superficial understanding of the origin, founding philosophy, and structure of the UI program provides insights that may prove helpful as you navigate the system. In this chapter, you'll learn about the circumstances in which unemployment insurance was first established in this country, the intended purpose of compensation, and the federal-state relationship that makes the UI system work.

THE HISTORY OF UNEMPLOYMENT INSURANCE

While unemployment may have always been a fact of life for Americans, unemployment insurance is a relatively recent phenomenon. The practice of paying benefits during periods of unemployment based on prior periods of employment originated in Europe in the late 1700s. Early programs were privately financed by guilds of skilled workers, and coverage was limited to guild members. The first public program was established in Berne, Switzerland in 1893, and by the early 1900s, the concept and practice had spread to several European cities. Great Britain enacted the first national UI law in 1911.

A few years after these public programs began sweeping European cities, state legislatures on this side of the Atlantic began struggling with the impact of unemployment on their economies. The State of Wisconsin was the first to actually pass an unemployment insurance law. Wisconsin began collecting employer contributions in 1934, and in 1936, the state paid the first benefit check.

The Great Depression was the single most influential catalyst for a national American UI system. In 1934, President Franklin D. Roosevelt appointed the Committee on Economic Security to study the growing problem of unemployment. The committee feared that if it created a completely federal UI system, the program would be struck down by the Supreme Court, as had happened with other aid programs initiated by the Roosevelt administration. The solution to this problem was the "Federal-State" system—a system that operates now. The UI program became law as part of the Social Security Act of 1935.

In the beginning, the program required employers to pay a payroll tax to the federal government on each employee. This tax was fairly steep—3 percent of each employee's total wages. But employers who contributed to a federally approved *state* unemployment system were given a credit of up to 90 percent of their federal UI tax. This provided the states with an incentive to start their own programs. It worked. By 1937, every state had enacted a federally approved unemployment insurance law. In 1939, the federal unemployment tax provisions of the Social Security Act were codified as the Federal Unemployment Tax Act (FUTA).

THE THEORY AND PURPOSE
OF UNEMPLOYMENT INSURANCE

Since its inception, the theory and purpose of unemployment insurance have remained very much the same. In addition to the central concepts of basing unemployment benefits on past earnings and taxing the employer to finance the program, there has always been the belief—codified in each state's laws—that benefits should be temporary, that benefits should be partial, and that benefits should be paid to workers who experience unemployment through no fault of their own. Workers contribute to their benefits only in Alaska, New Jersey, and Pennsylvania. Even in these states, the amount contributed by the worker is very small—from 0.1 percent to 1.125 percent of his or her taxable wages. The remainder of the UI benefit payment is financed by employer contributions to either the state or federal UI tax funds.

The components just mentioned did not come to be part of the system accidentally. It was believed that having employers contribute would spur employers to prevent unnecessary layoffs and to avoid discharging workers for trivial reasons. At the same time, unemployment insurance would not be so attractive as to discourage workers from seeking employment. So benefit payments are partial, ranging from less than 25 percent to slightly more than 50 percent of an employee's gross wages, and benefit payments are temporary, generally lasting for no more than twenty-six weeks, or about six months. In most states, the claimant must serve a waiting period—an unpaid week of eligibility after filing the claim application—before benefits can be paid. Benefits are payable only to workers who are unemployed through no fault of their own, that is, workers who have not voluntarily left, who were not discharged for misconduct, and who have not declined suitable employment. Further, recipients must have an attachment to the labor market—they must be able and willing to accept employment, and must demonstrate that availability by actively seeking suitable employment.

The unemployment insurance system is described as protection for the individual worker, but it also protects the employer, because it promotes a stable work force, and the community, because it promotes economic and social balance. Workers are less likely to move from a community because of temporary or cyclical unemployment when they have compensation to provide basic needs until recovery can occur. So the employer can depend on having a stable, trained work force available for recall, and the community can depend on the revenue generated by a stable and secure population.

HOW THE UI SYSTEM IS ORGANIZED

Just as was true in 1935, when the Social Security Act established unemployment insurance, the UI system is now controlled by both the federal and state governments, each of which plays a clearly defined role.

The Role of the Federal Government

Although the system of UI funding has changed somewhat over the past sixty years, the relationship between the federal government and the states has remained essentially the same. The amount of wages subject to taxation for each employee within a specific calendar year is called the *tax base,* and the percentage of that base which must be paid is the *tax rate.* The federal UI tax base now amounts to the first $7,000 of each employee's wages, and the tax rate is now 6.2 percent. However, since employers can be given a credit of up to 5.4 percent of the UI taxes they pay to the state, the net federal payment may be as low as .8 percent of the $7,000 base. State tax rates vary according to the experience rating of each employer's account and the condition of the state UI fund. More than half the states have higher tax bases than the federal tax base.

The federal UI tax money collected by the Internal Revenue Service is deposited in the Department of the Treasury. There, the money is maintained in three separate Federal Unemployment Trust Funds, which pay for state and federal administrative costs, finance federal extended benefits during periods of extended unemployment, and advance money to those states whose trust funds have been depleted. The allocation of funds from these accounts to each state is made by the Department of Labor based on various factors, including the population of the state, the ratio of covered employees to uncovered employees within the state, and the relative cost of administering the program within the state. The method of allocating funds is based on several statistical factors having to do with workload, time needed to process specific work items, and salary and benefit costs.

There are historical reasons for the Department of Labor's control of the trust funds. President Roosevelt's Secretary of Labor, Frances Perkins, chaired the Committee on Economic Security that devised the system. And because the purpose of the UI system was, and is, to promote employment security and economic stability, it seemed logical to invest this authority in the agency whose primary concern is the American worker and work place.

Now, the responsibilities of the Department of Labor are to maintain control over collected taxes, to oversee and fund sound administration of state programs so that the overall system is protected, and to establish and maintain performance standards, insuring conformity of state laws and practice.

The Role of the State

Each of the fifty states—as well as the District of Columbia, Puerto Rico, and the Virgin Islands—has its own unemployment insurance law, and each of these laws is in conformity with the Federal Unemployment Tax Act. Each state's responsibilities remain that of maintaining a complete unemployment insurance program and administering the program through state laws and by state employees. The states must register liable employers; collect the state UI tax, the source of the benefit payments; maintain employer accounts by notifying employers of claims filed against their accounts and assessing rate changes based on claims experience; accept claims; settle issues of eligibility; and pay benefits both for claims based on employment within the state system, and for claims filed under federal programs and interstate agreements.

Our unemployment insurance system grew out of a social need to protect not only the worker who loses employment through no fault of his or her own, but also the employer and the community. While funding of this system is controlled partly by the federal government, each state is responsible for the administration of its own UI program. In the next chapter, you'll learn more about the day-to-day workings of the system as we lead you through the claim-filing process.

2. WHAT TO EXPECT AT YOUR UNEMPLOYMENT OFFICE

As an unemployed individual, you have the right to file a claim for unemployment insurance (UI), to receive help in finding a job, to receive timely benefit payments, and to appeal any determination that you believe is incorrect or unjust. This chapter will take you through the process of filing an initial claim, from your first screening at the unemployment office to the receipt of your monetary determination and the resolution of issues based on factors other than wages. Information is also provided on the filing of continued claims, the appeals process, and follow-up interviews.

FILING YOUR INITIAL CLAIM

Where—and Against Whom—to File Your Claim

Generally, you must appear in person at a state unemployment office to file your *initial* UI claim application. Usually, your wages will have been reported to the state in which you worked, and if you worked in only one state, your claim must be filed *against* that state—that is, it will be subject to that state's eligibility rates and requirements. Since most people live and work in the same state, they also file in that state. However, you may apply for UI benefits at *any* unemployment office in the fifty states, the District of Columbia, Puerto Rico, or the Virgin Islands, and you may even apply for U.S.-based unemployment benefits in Canada. Any unemployment office will accept claim applications for another state or jurisdiction, and will forward the paperwork to the state against which you are filing.

Of course, individual circumstances vary considerably. If you have worked as a civilian for the U.S. Government, have recently served in the military, have worked in more than one state, or have worked in one state and then moved to another, the information below will guide you in choosing both the state *against* which you should file your claim and, when restrictions apply, the state *in* which you should file your claim.

Federal Civilian Claims—Unemployment Compensation for Federal Employees (UCFE)

Because civilian employment for the U.S. Government is not subject to regular state UI taxation, in 1954, Title XV of the Social Security Act provided UI coverage for such employment.

If you have worked as a civilian for the U.S. Government, your claim should be filed against the state of your last duty station, which is usually the state in which your services were performed. There are exceptions, though. If you earned subsequent covered wages—that is, wages covered by a state UI program—in your state of residence prior to the time of the initial filing, wages from your federal civilian employment will also be assigned to your state of residence. The claim, therefore, should be filed against that state. If your duty station was outside the United States, your civilian wages will, again, be assigned to your state of residence at the time of filing, and the claim should be filed against that state.

Once you have filed a claim based on federal civilian wages and the wages have been assigned to the correct state, the state unemployment office will report the use of the wages to a U.S. Government data control center, and all wage credits from that period of employment will remain assigned to that state.

Federal Military Claims—Unemployment Compensation for Ex-Servicemembers (UCX)

Because service in the Armed Forces is not subject to regular state UI taxation, in 1958, the Ex-Servicemen's Unemployment Compensation Act provided a permanent UI program for discharged servicemembers. Claims filed under this program are processed and paid by state unemployment offices according to each state's eligibility requirements and rate of compensation, but under federal regulations. Since "wages" paid to servicemembers are not considered to be directly equivalent to private-industry wages, the Department of Labor provides state unemployment offices with equivalency charts that convert the salaries at various service ranks to civilian salary rates. Each state uses these charts to determine the weekly benefit entitlement at that state's rate of compensation. The Department of Labor also regulates and monitors the assignment and use of UCX wages for UI purposes.

If you are filing a claim based on service in the United States military, you can actually choose the state against which you will file, but you must submit your claim application in person in that state. Once you have filed a claim based on military service, your wages from that period of service will remain assigned to that state.

Combined Wage Claims

If you have worked in covered employment in two or more states during the base period of the state against which you are filing your claim, you should file a combined wage claim in order to maximize your benefits. When filing a combined wage claim, your benefits and the eligibility requirements you must meet will be those of the state *against* which you file. This usually must be the state *in* which you submit your application. Note that you do not have to have covered wages in the filing state.

In most cases, the work must have been performed for two different employers if you are to qualify for a combined wage claim. However, it is also possible to file a combined wage claim when you worked for only one employer but performed the work in two different states—as long as your employer reported your wages for each work period to the state in which the work was performed. Generally, of course, employers are *required* to report wages to the state in which the work was performed. However, if the work was incidental to the usual work assignment, or if the work regularly required employment in more than one state, the employer may be permitted to report the work to the employer's base of operations. For clarification, let's look at two examples. First, let's consider the case of a construction worker who worked primarily in State A but was temporarily assigned to a project in State B, and whose employer reported all of his wages to State A. In this case, the worker would not be permitted to file a combined wage claim, simply because his wages were reported to only one state. Similarly, if a salaried sales agent worked for one employer in several states, it is unlikely that he would be permitted to file a combined wage claim, because his employer would probably have reported all wages to the state in which the employer was licensed.

Federal civilian (UCFE) and federal military (UCX) wages can be combined with private-industry wages. For example, let's say that an individual worked in private industry in State A, followed by employment by the federal government in State B. He then became unemployed. As long as both periods of employment were in the base period of the filing state, the worker could file a combined wage claim. (See page 134 for an explanation of base

---

TIP: *When filing a combined wage claim after working in two or more states, maximize your benefits by filing against the state with the highest benefit amounts.*

---

periods.) But if we change the example so that the worker was employed first by the federal government in State B and then in private industry in State A, his state of residence, the situation is very different. As discussed on page 14, the state of assignment of UCFE wages is altered by subsequent covered employment in the state of residence at the time of initial claim filing. So, in this case, all wages would be assigned to State A, and a combined wage claim would no longer be possible. It should be noted that the reverse is not possible. Federal civilian and military wage-assignment regulations have no effect on the assignment of private-industry wages, as the taxation of private-industry employment is the right of the state in which the work is performed.

If you have worked in more than one state in the last twelve to eighteen months—nineteen months in California—it may benefit you to do a little research before filing your claim. To maximize your benefits, you should file your claim against the state that has a base period which includes your employment in at least two states and has the highest weekly benefit amount. If you have dependents, you should also find out if the states you are considering are among the fourteen that pay a dependents' allowance, and, if so, what limitations each state places on the dependents' allowance. For example, in the Washington, D.C. area, it generally pays to file combined wage claims against the District of Columbia, because D.C.'s rate is so much higher than that of neighboring states. Moreover, the District of Columbia has the most frequently used base period, so if an individual has wages in two or more of the neighboring states, some or all of the wages will be in D.C.'s base period as well. D.C. also pays a dependents' allowance, whereas most neighboring states do not.

Interstate Claims

If you have earned wages in two or more states, it is not necessarily advantageous to file a combined wage claim. Sometimes, you can qualify for the greatest benefits by filing an interstate claim against a single state—a claim based on wages earned in only one state. For instance, if you have earnings sufficient to qualify you for the maximum weekly benefit amount in a state that has a relatively high benefit entitlement, and you have base period earnings in other states with lesser entitlement rates, you should file a claim against the state with the highest entitlement. If that state is too distant for daily commuting, you should file an interstate claim. (In Chapter 6, we will show you how to compare base periods, benefit amounts, and qualification requirements so that if you have worked in more than one state, you can maximize your potential benefit entitlement.)

If you have worked in one state and then moved to another, you then *must* file an interstate claim against the state in which you worked. All state unemployment offices, as well as offices in Canada, will accept interstate claims for other states. Claim applications and accompanying documentation are both sent by mail and transmitted electronically to the state in which you worked. Your entitlement and eligibility requirements will be those of the state in which you worked, and payments will also be issued by that state. The filing state will serve merely as an agent by accepting your application and assisting you in its completion. You may also change a previously established claim to an interstate claim if you move after filing a regular claim.

Interstate Combined Wage Claims

In our discussion of combined wage claims, we stated that, in most cases, a combined wage claim must be filed in the state that the claimant is filing against. Therefore, an interstate combined wage claim is a rarity. But by agreement between the states, an individual can file an interstate combined wage claim if, and only if, he or she would not qualify monetarily for a claim in and against the filing state. In this instance, the first option would be to file an interstate combined wage claim against the state in which the last period of employment occurred. If that did not result in monetary eligibility, the claimant would file against another state in which he or she worked. Only if the claimant failed to qualify for benefits in every state in which he or she worked would it be possible to file an interstate combined wage claim against *any* state whose base period and monetary eligibility requirements would result in eligibility.

When the Unemployment Office Comes to You

In some states and in some situations—before a mass layoff, for instance—staff from the unemployment office take claim applications at the employer's place of business, a union hall, or another designated location. In a case such as this, you will be notified in

advance regarding where the applications will be accepted and what materials should be brought with you.

When to File Your Claim

To insure that you will receive your first UI check as soon as possible, you should file your claim application the first week you are unemployed. Your benefit entitlement will be based on earnings in previous covered employment of a specified time period called the base period. The base period will be determined by the week in which you file your claim, so if you wait too long to file, you may include periods of unemployment in your base period, which may reduce your monetary entitlement. On the other hand, if you experienced a substantial increase in earnings shortly before becoming unemployed, you may wish to delay the filing so that the period of increased earnings will be included in your base period.

In all states but New York, your unemployment compensation claim becomes retroactively effective the Sunday of the week in which you file the initial claim application. (In New York, the claim becomes effective the Monday of the week in which you file.) Mondays are the busiest days at most state unemployment offices, so if you can, it would be best to file your claim on another day of the week. If you attempt to file a claim on Friday, and you are told that you have arrived too late in the day and that you should return the following week, be sure to request a note stating that you reported on that day. If you have already received the claim application form or an identification card, ask to have the document date-stamped so that your eventual application can be "backdated" to the week you originally appeared. UI office workers are understandably reluctant to backdate claims, as this practice makes it difficult for them to meet their timeliness standards. In fact, some state laws do not permit backdating. Remember that you will be able to appeal the effective date of your claim once you receive the initial determination of eligibility. Generally, though, it's a good policy to avoid filing on a Friday so that you will not be faced with this problem.

Some states have specific requirements regarding the day on which claimants may file applications. In Michigan, for instance, claimants must file claims on the first "reporting day" after they are laid off, as determined by the last digit of their Social Security number. For instance, if the last digit of your Social Security number were 0 or 1, you would report on Monday; 2 or 3, on Tuesday; and so on. It may be worth your time to make a phone call and ask if your state has such specific requirements. Most offices serve those claimants without appointments on a first come-first served basis.

Preparing for Your First Visit to the Unemployment Office

During your initial visit to the unemployment office, you will be required to supply certain information about your previous employment. Depending on the state in which you are filing and the type of work you have performed, you may need certain documents, including specific forms of identification. By familiarizing yourself with the claims process and knowing what to bring, you'll be able to prepare yourself, and therefore will avoid unnecessary delays or problems.

What to Bring With You

When filing your initial claim, be sure to bring your Social Security card or other pieces of identification that contain your name, Social Security number, and picture. For instance, a driver's license or passport will be accepted by many state offices. However, in some states, like New York, the staff will not authorize benefit checks until you present your Social Security card. If you are filing for UI in such a state and you don't have your Social Security card, you may continue to sign up for checks anyway. However, all checks due you will be released only after you have presented your Social Security card. Certainly, you should never delay filing your claim simply because you don't have a Social Security card or other necessary records. File as soon as you lose your job, and obtain the records as soon as you can. Your unemployment office cannot backdate your claim simply because you delayed filing. Also be aware that if you don't provide the unemployment office with your Social Security number, you will not be eligible for benefits because your wage records will not be accessible for the computation of your claim.

In *wage record* states, all you may have to do is give the name and correct address of your last employer. The unemployment office should have records of wages from all covered employment performed in that state. (For information about covered employment, see Chapter 3.) In *wage request* states, where the unemployment office

---

TIP: *Even if you don't have all the documents you need, file for benefits as soon as you lose your job.*

must request specific wage data from the employer, it is important to list *every* employer worked for during the base period. Failure to do so may result in receiving less benefits than you are entitled to, and possibly no benefits at all. There are only two states in which the unemployment office must request all wage data: Michigan and New York. It is probably best to prepare a written employment history for the past eighteen months—nineteen months in California, and twelve or twenty-four months in New York State—including the addresses and phone numbers of all the employers for whom you worked during that period. You will then be able to transfer the information to the forms at the unemployment office as needed.

In many states, when you are separated, your employer is supposed to give you a slip stating the company name, address, and UI account number. Presenting such slips when filing your claim will help the unemployment office accurately compute your benefits. Regardless of what state you've worked in, it is a good idea to take along with you some proof of your wages for the past eighteen months. Pay stubs, W-2 forms, or other payroll records are adequate proof. In the event that your wages are stored under an incorrect Social Security number or your employer has failed to report or pay the UI tax, you will have provided the unemployment staff with the information necessary to correct the error and promptly process your claim.

If you have been employed as a civilian for the United States Government, you should take along *Standard Form 8,* which shows the address to which the UI office must send claim inquiries, and *Standard Form 50,* which shows your pay rate. Federal personnel offices are required to give employees Standard Form 8 at the time of separation. They are required to issue Standard Form 50 each time there is a personnel action—such as promotion, demotion, transfer, change of duty station, or separation—that causes a change in employment status. The official duty station for federal employment is shown on Standard Form 50. Whereas Standard Form 8 is supposed to be issued in person, Standard Form 50 is often issued by mail.

Many unemployment offices will help federal civilian employees complete an affidavit while they file the initial claim. The affidavit permits the state agency to process the claim in a timely manner even if it does not receive the employing agency's reply. Standard Form 50, which shows your pay rate; pay stubs; or a W-2 form is usually adequate proof for this affidavit.

If you are filing a claim based on service in the United States Armed Forces, you must take your *DD-214,* which is the official discharge document given to you when you are discharged from the armed forces. The DD-214 contains the information—length of service, nature of discharge, and rank at discharge—on which your eligibility will be based.

If you are not a citizen of the United States, you should bring your Alien Registration card (green card), work permit, or other proof that you were legally employed. If you are a U.S. citizen, you may be required to sign a statement to that effect.

If you are going to claim a dependents' allowance, and particularly if you are legally required to pay child support, it is a good idea to prepare a list of the names and birth dates of your dependents. This suggestion may sound patronizing, but many people do not remember the birth dates of their dependents when required to list them. (See page 171 to find out if the state you're filing against pays a dependents' allowance.)

When you file your initial claim application, you will be asked to state the reason for the separation from your employment. Usually, a copy of your statement will be sent to your employer. It is a good idea to have a brief explanation of the separation ready before your visit. If you don't write well, you might want to ask a friend to help you compose it and write it down.

Again, if you don't have the various documents mentioned here, you should still file your claim application as soon as possible so that you will not lose the benefits that you would have otherwise received. Then be sure to supply the necessary documents as soon as you can. Remember that it's a crime to use someone else's Social Security card or number, or to knowingly misrepresent your Social Security number. It is also a crime to knowingly misrepresent any facts that are necessary for the processing of your claim.

Finally, because you may be registering for work immediately before or after filing your initial claim application, be sure to take along any records you have regarding your educational qualifications, job experience, and job training or licenses.

Be Prepared to Wait

Be aware that you may encounter long waiting times, so plan accordingly. It's a good idea to bring a book to read while you are waiting. Because few urban offices offer free parking, use public transportation if you can. If not, you will probably have to park your car in a commercial parking garage or metered lot. It's not unusual for claimants to lose their place in line because they left the office to feed a meter. If you do have to leave and wish to retain your place, speak to the receptionist to see how close you are to

TIP: *During your first visit to the unemployment office, be sure to ask for the "claimant's handbook," which explains your rights and responsibilities as a claimant in that state.*

being called, and ask if your place in sequence can be protected. Try not to be discouraged by the long lines. Most claims processing is routine, and if you are eligible for benefits, you will get them— but only if you file the application and complete the process.

Many unemployment offices are multi-service offices. When the doors are opened, there may be people who want to file a new claim, make a check inquiry, reopen an existing claim, or file an appeal. Still other clients may not even know what their need is, because they don't know whether they have an existing claim. So the staff will log in clients, making an initial inquiry as to the service needed, and then try to arrange staff and resources to provide the services as efficiently as possible. If you are there to file a claim application, it is likely that you will be asked to wait until your Social Security number is "screened." This means that the staff will check your Social Security number on the computer to see if you already have a claim, or to see if your wages are on file for a claim. As soon as you have been logged in, ask for the "claimant's handbook." Known by different names in different states, this booklet or pamphlet explains claims processes, as well as your benefit rights and responsibilities, under that particular state's laws. Read the pamphlet carefully for any information that's not included in *How to Maximize Your Unemployment Benefits* (there's always some). Such information may be very important, and you will be responsible for knowing it.

Completing the Claim Application

During this first visit, you will be given forms to complete. Be sure to answer every question you can, as errors or omissions will cause delays in the processing of your claim. In some states, an interviewer will record your answers for you. Whether the claim is being filled out by you or by someone else, make certain that all spaces on any claim form have been filled in *before* you sign your name. If an item does not pertain to you, draw "X's" or lines through the space so that it cannot be completed by someone else after you have signed. This is particularly important when completing affidavits on which you state that the information contained in the form is correct. Remember that once you have signed an affidavit, you will be held responsible for any overpayment caused by an incorrect estimate of wages—regardless of whether you or someone else made that estimate. Incorrect estimates are a frequent cause of overpayment on federal civilian claims. Often, the claimant does not pay attention to the estimate of wages, or the claims taker fills in the blanks after the claimant leaves the office. Fortunately, such overpayments are rarely attributed to willful misrepresentation (fraud). Nevertheless, the overpayment may be deducted before further benefit payments are made, or you may be required to repay the money. Clearly, it is a good idea to pay attention to each detail of your application.

In all states, you will be asked to provide the name and address of your last employer and the date on which you last worked. (Some states need a complete record of all employers for whom you worked in the past twelve to eighteen months or more.) As mentioned on page 21, you will also be asked to state the reason for your separation. This is not the point at which the determination of eligibility will be made. However, it is important that your statement be accurate and brief. If you were involuntarily separated for reasons other than misconduct on the job, you might want to ask your employer for a written statement. If your separation was for alleged misconduct, briefly explain that you were involuntarily dismissed and that you would prefer that the employer supply the reason. You see, it is the responsibility of the employer to establish that an involuntary separation was due to misconduct. Also, it is not wise to incriminate yourself—to imply that you committed a wrongful act—especially since your employer may not choose to raise the issue. By allowing your employer to state the reason first, you will give yourself the opporunity to later refute any accusations he or she might make.

If you resigned from your job rather than being laid off or fired, you inititated your own job separation, and the burden of proof will be on you to show that you quit for good cause. Having a good *reason* to quit a job is not always the same as having good *cause*, and therefore you may be disqualified. (See page 67 for more information on good cause.) But even if you suspect that your reason for leaving your job may result in disqualification, you still should file your claim application. Once you receive the notice of disqualification, you will learn the terms of the disqualification and the requalification requirements. Also keep in mind that this determination is the responsibility of the claims staff, and that you *could* be eligible despite your suspicions.

Other than the statement regarding your separation from employment, the minimum information needed to complete your form includes data regarding your personal identification (name, Social Security number, and mailing address), your ability to work, and your availablility for work. Other information that may be requested includes the names, ages, and relationship of any dependents you are claiming; any status you may have as a veteran; your educational attainments; and your pension status. Still other items on the claim application involve coded demographic data that you claims taker will complete.

REGISTERING FOR WORK

One of the eligibility requirements for unemployment benefits is that the claimant be actively seeking work. In most cases, you are required to register with the public employment service immediately after you file your claim. In fact, many states have a joint application process. Although they perform two separate functions, the unemployment and employment service offices are often located in the same building. Since you will be registering for work, it will be helpful if you bring with you any records regarding your educational qualifications, your job experience, and any special training or licenses. The employment service may immediately refer you to job openings, so it is important to be able to describe all of your talents, abilities, and skills. You should report dressed as though you were going for a job interview or to work, because you could be referred to either.

Many people believe that, rather than drawing UI benefits, a person should take any job he or she finds. They see the condition of being unemployed as less worthy than that of being employed at *any* job, no matter how menial or unsuitable. But keep in mind that no state says that an unemployed person must take any job! So be careful to specify the kind of job you are looking for and to aim as high as you reasonably can. After you make this specification, you will be classified as looking for this kind of work, and may be forced to take a job that meets the description you provided. And you may find through bitter experience that although the employment service lists some fairly good jobs, it also lists some with poor pay and bad working conditions.

As you file for subsequent weeks of benefits, you may be referred to other jobs, and you may be immediately disqualified

---

TIP: *No state says that you must take any job! Carefully specify the kind of job you're looking for.*

for UI benefits if you refuse to accept the referral. Be prepared to explain the reason for your refusal. Remember that you cannot be required to take unsuitable work. It goes without saying, though, that should you receive an offer of suitable work, we strongly recommend that you take the offer and count yourself among the lucky.

Finally, be aware that there are exceptions to almost every rule. In the case of a mass layoff, especially one of known duration, registration with the employment service and work-search requirements may not be applicable. However, don't make that assumption. The unemployment office will tell you whether or not you have to register for work.

THE NOTICE OF MONETARY DETERMINATION
or, getting the official word on your payments

If you were laid off due to lack of work, you may not be scheduled for another unemployment office visit. However, if there is a question regarding your eligibility, you may have to return for a predetermination fact-finding proceeding. (A discussion of this proceeding begins on page 35.) But whether or not you are required to return for issue resolution, the processing of your claim application will continue. Your application will be entered into the computer, and the computation of your monetary eligibility—that is, your eligibility for benefits—will be made.

Monetary eligibility is based on the wages you earned or length of time you were employed during a specified period of time called the base period—a period defined by state law. The most common base period of the fifty-three "states" includes the first four of the last five calendar quarters that are completed at the time the initial claim is filed. (See page 134 for a detailed explanation of base periods.)

In some states, the UI staff is able to determine monetary eligibility during the initial visit—provided that the applicant's wage records are in the computer system. In most states, though, the computation of your eligibility and your benefit amount can be made only after the application has been entered in the automated system. Subsequently, a formal appealable Notice of Monetary Determination is mailed to you or, if you have been scheduled for a future appointment, the notice may be hand-delivered to you when you return.

The Notice of Monetary Determination is the statement of benefits to which you are potentially entitled. It must show your weekly benefit amount; your maximum benefit entitlement, which

is the total amount you will receive if you remain unemployed and continue to meet eligibility requirements for the entire potential duration of your claim; and the wages that were used to make these determinations. Usually, the Notice of Monetary Determination also shows any dependents' allowance to which you are entitled and the base period for which your claim was computed. It is very important that you review this notice for accuracy. Make sure that the notice includes all of your covered employment during the base period, as well as the correct wages for that period. Also make sure that employment or wages that are *not* yours are *not* shown. (If someone else's wages are shown, you could be overpaid. Later, when the error is discovered, you will have to return the overpayment.) If you believe that an item on your Notice of Monetary Determination is incorrect, follow the directions on the notice to request a reconsideration and/or appeal. Usually, a reconsideration request or appeal of a monetary determination should be accompanied by wage records that support your assertion. Such wage records would include pay stubs, W-2 forms, or other payroll records. If you submit original documents, they will be returned to you only upon request. Ask the staff at your local office to make photocopies for their files, as you may need your originals at another time. Be aware that there is usually a specified time limit for requesting reconsideration or appeal of any type of determination. Often, the time limit is ten days from the date the notice is mailed or delivered to you. It is important that you make your request within the time limit. (See page 37 for a discussion of the appeals process.)

The first Notice of Monetary Determination that is mailed or delivered to you may be based only on those wages that appear in the filing state's wage records. Do not be alarmed if wages from another state—or from employment with the federal government—are not shown on your initial notice. As we have explained, these wages are not part of your filing state's wage tax records. The filing state must request these wages and then include them in the computation before your final monetary eligibility is determined. If your private-industry wages are sufficient to qualify you for UI benefits, you may initially be paid benefits based only on these wages. When the federal or out-of-state wage reports are received,

---

TIP: *As soon as you receive your Notice of Monetary Determination, make sure that the information on it is accurate. If not, immediately request a reconsideration or appeal.*

the state will re-compute your claim. If this results in a higher weekly benefit entitlement, you will be paid an adjustment for any back weeks. However, as we mentioned before, many states will process a federal civilian claim or the federal portion of a claim based on the affidavit that you complete at the time of the initial filing. Moreover, the *Internet System*—a system of electronic interstate claims application, wage transfer, and information exchange begun in 1983—is increasing the processing speed of combined wage and interstate claims.

Once the final computation of your claim has been completed, your weekly benefit amount and potential maximum benefit amount will remain the same until your benefits are exhausted or your benefit year expires. In most states, the *benefit year*—that is, the period during which you may draw your total potential entitlement—is the fifty-two-week period that begins the week you file a valid initial claim. (See page 144 for a detailed discussion of the benefit year.)

If you do not receive a Notice of Monetary Determination within ten days of submitting a claim application, and you have not been notified of a potential delay, it is advisable to contact your unemployment office to find out the cause of the delay and to determine if any additional action is necessary.

CONTINUED CLAIMS
or, filing for your weekly benefit checks

After you have filed your initial application, payment for subsequent weeks of full or partial unemployment will be applied for through a process called *continued claiming*. If you file a claim against a state that has an automated mail-in continued claim system, you should receive your first continued claim form in the mail shortly after filing your claim application. Most of the time, each claim form contains certification for two weeks. During your initial visit, you will receive instructions on completing the continued claim forms. Procedures vary from state to state, and also depend on any eligibility issues that may be connected with your application.

If eligibility issues have arisen, a fact-finding interview will be scheduled to resolve the issues, and you may be asked to bring your first mail claim with you to the fact-finding interview. (See page 34 for more information on the fact-finding interview.) In some states, all claimants must return for a review of eligibility before UI payments can be authorized.

If you do not receive your continued claim form within ten days of your initial filing or if you have any questions regarding procedures, you should contact your unemployment office. Be aware that you will be held ineligible for benefits for any weeks for which you fail to file timely continued claims.

Only fifteen states require that claimants appear in person to sign for benefit checks. These states are Alaska, Arkansas, Delaware, Indiana, Kentucky, Massachusetts, New Hampshire, New York, Oklahoma, Pennsylvania, South Carolina, Texas, the Virgin Islands, West Virginia, and Wyoming. All but Indiana, Massachusetts, and New Hampshire allow some claimants—those living in rural areas—to sign up by mail. All states issue benefit checks by mail.

In some automated mail claim systems, your first benefit check will include a stub that will serve as your mail claim for the next filing period (usually two weeks). Your continued mail claim card will be input in the computer pay system, causing the computer to issue a check—as long as everything on your claim is acceptable. Thereafter, each time you receive a UI check, whether for one week or for two, your mail claim for the next filing period will be attached. In the other states, the claims office's receipt of the mail claim will cause two separate actions—the issuing of a benefit check and the issuing of the mail claim for the next filing period. In either case, you should contact your local office if you have not received a check or some communication from the unemployment office within ten days of the return of your last continued mail claim. Automated mail claim systems—particularly those using optical scanners—require that the claimant pay special attention to the completion of the mail claims. Such things as creases, stray marks, or misplaced or incomplete responses can cause a delay in payments.

Each mail claim will ask you to respond to specific questions on specific weeks. In some states, you will also be asked to report your work search on the claim form. If your answers to the questions on the mail claims raise doubts regarding your eligibility—or if you have information or documentation that you wish to submit to the unemployment office—you will be told whether you must report in person, send a written statement, or respond by phone. In the case of interstate claims, the paying state usually contacts the claimant by phone when there is any question or discrepancy, and the claimant is directed to mail any documentation directly to the state's unemployment staff, as it has the task of making eligibility determinations. In some instances—for example, when a document needs the signature of a state representative or witness—the paying state has the claimant report to the agent office in the filing state.

The states of Colorado, New York, and North Carolina now allow at least some claimants—probably those who have no issue with regard to eligibility—to file continued claims by touch-tone phone. The claimant simply phones a special number and then enters his or her Social Security number and a personal identification number in response to the promptings of a tape recording. As the tape presents each of the questions, the claimant enters a response.

The questions asked on the mail-in claims and in phone claims pertain to eligibility, and are basically the same as those asked in states in which claimants must appear in person to sign for checks. Following are explanations of those questions most commonly asked. Should you want further information on any of the issues raised in these questions—availability for work, for instance—see Chapter 5.

❑ *Have you worked this week? Are you unemployed?*

If you are not working and are not being paid, you are unemployed. If you are working part-time, you may still be considered unemployed—or partially unemployed and eligible for partial benefits—depending on how much money you are making and the amount of time you spend on the job. The mail claim will have a space in which you must enter any earnings. You may be required to give the identity of your employer, as well. *You must report such work.* If you do, you may still get full or reduced benefits. You may also be eligible to file an unemployment claim in a second consecutive benefit year. If you don't report your earnings and the unemployment office learns about your employment, you can be charged with fraud.

When reporting employment, be sure to report 100 percent of your gross wages—your wages *before* taxes. Do not wait until the wages have been paid to report them; rather, report all wages as they are earned. Waitresses and waiters must report tips. And in some states, you must report other forms of remuneration—such as the value of meals, housing, etc.—if earned in lieu of wages. If you do not know the exact amount of your gross earnings and your employer cannot tell you how much you earned, you may estimate your earnings. If your estimate is later found to be incorrect, you must promptly submit a written statement of correction, or risk charges of fraud. Be sure to submit proof of actual earnings. If you find that you have overestimated your earnings, be sure to ask for the money you did not receive as a result of your overestimate. Again, the unemployment office must know your total earnings, not your take-home pay. Be sure to contact your local office if you are not sure if the money or other remuneration you received should be reported as earnings.

❑ *Are you able to work?*

Unless you cannot work, always say that you are ready, able, and available for work. If you were previously ill and unable to work, or if you must limit your activities for some reason, bring a doctor's statement to show that you can work now, or that you can work within certain limitations. Make sure that the doctor's statement is clear and pertains to work-related activities such as sitting, standing, lifting, and reading, as well as to environmental factors such as noise, dust, lighting, etc. Poorly written doctor's statements can cost time and cause confusion.

All states require you to be physically able to work in order to be eligible for unemployment insurance. However, some states, such as Alaska, Idaho, Massachusetts, and North Dakota, have provisions in their laws that allow the payment of benefits when a claimant becomes ill or disabled *after* filing the unemployment claim and registering for work, as long as there is no interruption of the period of unemployment and the claimant doesn't refuse suitable work because of the illness. In other words, if you just happen to get sick while you are claiming benefits but there is no work for you nor any work offer refused by you, you could still receive benefits. The State of Massachusetts limits such periods during which benefits will be paid to three weeks, and the State of Alaska limits them to six consecutive weeks. The purpose of these provisions is to allow benefits when a person's illness is not relevant to the reason that he or she is unemployed or to his or her chances of regaining employment. Regardless of what state you are filing against, you should answer the question regarding your ability to work honestly, and allow the unemployment office staff to make the correct determination.

❑ *Are you available for work?*

This question pertains to your willingness to work, and to any unreasonable restrictions or activities that will prevent you from seeking or accepting employment. An unreasonable restriction is one that you cannot or will not change to gain employment. Examples of restrictions on availability are a lack of child care during regular work hours; a lack of licenses, tools, or special clothing needed to perform in your customary occupation; school attendance or other activities that prevent you from working during the usual hours for your occupation; and an unwillingness to work the customary hours for your occupation. Of course, you will not be asked about every possible restriction, but you should advise your unemployment office of any restrictions that prevent you from seeking and accepting employment. You won't necessarily be held ineligible, and the staff may help you find a solution to your problem.

You may be required to demonstrate your availability by listing the places you looked for work. In some states, you must list your job-search contacts on the mail claim. In other states, you are required to show the contacts periodically, on request by the unemployment office. Some states have specific requirements for the work search. For instance, Maryland advises that it is acceptable to seek work through a union hall if this is the customary way for union members to gain employment. Most states, though, require in-person contact with prospective employers.

If you are filing against a state that requires you to list job-search contacts on the mail claim, be sure to supply the exact details requested. Use a notebook to record all the places at which you have applied, including the dates, the names of the people to whom you spoke, the phone numbers, whether you were offered a job, and whether you accepted a job. If no job was offered, be ready to state why—for instance, that there were no openings for new employees.

❑ *Are you in school or training?*

Certain activities can restrict your availability to accept work. If you are in approved training—usually vocational or basic-skills training—you may be allowed to draw UI benefits even if you are not immediately available for work. Claimants in Massachusetts and Michigan, for instance, may have their benefits extended up to eighteen weeks while in training. Such training is usually voluntary. However, in Washington, D.C. and Michigan, you can be disqualified for benefits if you refuse the approved training to which you were referred by the state. Regularly enrolled full-time students are not usually eligible for UI benefits, as their course of study restricts their availability to seek and accept employment.

If you are attending school or training or considering doing so, speak to the staff of your unemployment office regarding the rules in your state.

❑ *Are you receiving a pension or severance pay?*

Certain types of income are deductible from UI payments, and when the amount of deductible income is greater than the UI entitlement, the deduction causes total ineligibility. Information regarding these types of income is usually requested on the initial claim application, but because some types of income may take effect later in the benefit year, this information is also requested on the continued claim form. The continued claim may also have a space in which you must enter the amount of the pension or severance payment.

Again, state laws vary regarding the types of income that are deductible and the way the deduction is made. In some states, all pensions, including Social Security benefits, are deductible; in others, only pensions contributed to by base-period employers are deductible. Severance payments may be deducted as paid—that is, for the week in which the actual severance check is issued—or they may be deducted for the whole period of time for which the severance payments are made.

❑ *Have you returned to work (full-time)?*

As we have stated, it is the purpose of unemployment insurance to tide you over until you can find suitable employment. It is assumed that you will eventually find employment, and that when you do, you will report it. Since this often occurs without the intervention of the employment service or unemployment office, your only means of notifying the unemployment staff of your job may be the continued claim form. Remember that you must report your employment as soon as you return to work—not when you get your first paycheck.

It may seem that this question asks for the same information requested by the first question, "Have you worked this week?" However, the first question was designed to determine your *degree* of unemployment—that is, whether you are you are fully or partially unemployed, and therefore claiming full or partial benefits. This last question was designed to determine whether your period of unemployment has entirely ended.

These are the basic questions that are asked on continued claim forms, whether you are filing in person or by mail, manually or by automated systems. There may be state-to-state variations in the language and format. In the future, when claimants will file via computer modem, they still will be required to answer these questions, as this information is needed to determine continued status and eligibility.

FILING ADDITIONAL CLAIMS

If you return to full-time employment and become unemployed

again in the same benefit year, you may file an *additional claim.* By definition, an additional claim is the reopening of an existing claim following a period of one or more weeks of employment. But even if only *one day's* earnings make you ineligible for unemployment compensation for that benefit week, you will have to file an additional claim after that week.

The filing of an additional claim does not usually require as much information as that needed to file an initial claim, because the benefit year, monetary entitlement, and other determinations have already been established. In states that have a waiting period, you will not be required to serve another waiting period on an additional claim, as it will merely "restart" the continued claim series. (We briefly explained in the first chapter that many states have a one-week waiting period—a period of eligibility that must be served before benefits can be paid. The waiting period is meant to prevent claims from being filed for one-week layoffs and vacation periods.)

Of course, you must have a balance remaining on your monetary entitlement in order to draw benefits on the additional claim. And if there is any issue with regard to your sepaparation from this new employment, you may be subject to the same disqualification faced by initial claimants who separated under unacceptable circumstances.

THE ELIGIBILITY REVIEW PROGRAM

Periodically, your unemployment office will conduct a review of your eligibility. The frequency of this type of interview will depend on your job classification, the condition of the local labor market, and, possibly, the workload in your unemployment office. You may be asked to fill out a form stating where you have looked for work. Some states require claimants to have such a form signed by the employers whom they contacted regarding possible jobs. In most cases, eligibility reviews result in the continuation of benefits; however, they can result in suspensions.

If you are called in for an eligibility review and you fail to appear, your benefits will probably be discontinued until you visit your unemployment office. However, keep in mind that it is better to go to a job interview or, if you are filing on the basis of partial unemployment, to work, than it is to take time off to attend a review. If and when such a time conflict occurs, be sure to notify your unemployment office as soon as possible before the scheduled review or, failing that, as soon as possible after the missed review.

THE QUALITY CONTROL PROGRAM

In addition to the eligibility review program, there is also a quality control program. The U.S. Department of Labor has 30 percent of its unemployment insurance staff—about 50 out of 170 people—working in quality control. Each state has its own quality control staff as well, and some staff members are assigned to local offices. The purpose of the quality control program is to insure that claims are being correctly processed, and to recommend changes and improvements of the claim system. In the course of these activities, staff members sometimes detect errors, eligibility issues, and evidence of fraud, but this is not the main purpose of the program.

In the quality control program, claims are selected at random by computer, and claimants are asked to fill out detailed questionnaires about their claims and to meet with a quality control investigator in person. In addition, former employers are visited in person to insure that wages were reported accurately. And if you are filing against one of the fourteen states that have a dependents' allowance, you may be asked to furnish proof that you have all of the dependents you claim to support. These quality control interviews differ greatly from the eligibility reviews because they examine every facet of eligibility for a computer-selected week, and because while nearly every claimant has at least one eligibility review, only a small fraction are selected for quality control interviews.

THE FACT-FINDING PROCESS
or, how questions of your eligibility are solved

If you were laid off simply due to lack of work, and there is no reason to initially question your ability or willingness to work, you should be given all instructions regarding the filing of continued claims, your benefit rights, and your responsibilities during your initial visit. In a case such as this, you will not be scheduled for a fact-finding interview. However, if an issue—that is, a question of eligibility—arises as a result of your responses on the initial claim application, your responses on continued claim forms, an eligibility or quality control review, or an employer inquiry, you may have to attend a fact-finding interview.

To clarify the terms "fact-finder," "claims examiner," and "adjudicator," let us explain that in nearly all states, unemployment systems are organized into central offices and local offices. Usually, the central office—the location of the main frame computer—is responsible for UI tax collection, employer registration, monetary computation, actual benefit payments, and related matters. The local offices, found throughout each state, are responsible for taking claim applications and interviewing claimants. In some states, local offices also make the determinations of eligibility based on nonmonetary issues such as separation, ability to work, and availability for work. In such cases, the local office has "claims examiners," also called "adjudicators," and these staff members may be responsible for conducting the interview as well as making the determination that results from the interview. In other states, particularly ones with remote rural claim-filing offices, as well as in instances in which there are mass claim filings, the nonmonetary adjudication is a function of the central office. In these cases, however, local office staff members are still responsible for fact-finding—the interviewing of both claimants and employers to get the facts upon which the examiner in the central office will base his or her determination. In such instances, the interviewer is a "fact-finder," and the person who makes the determination is the claims examiner or adjudicator. Be aware that staff members often use these terms interchangeably, and that, sometimes, appeals examiners are also referred to as adjudicators.

The Predetermination Fact-Finding Proceeding

At the time you file your claim application, either you or your employer may raise an issue regarding your separation from your job, your ability to work, your availability for work, or any other eligibility requirement. If and when this occurs, you will be scheduled for a fact-finding proceeding. This interview is also called a "predetermination" proceeding because the fact-finding should occur before any determination of eligibility is made.

Most predetermination proceedings involve separation issues, because they generally result from the filing of an initial or additional claim. For instance, sometimes an employee will say that he or she was laid off, when in fact the employee quit. In a case such as this, both the employer and the employee have the right to appear at the proceeding to present their positions. Your former employer may present evidence by phone or by mail. Indeed, in some states, all fact-finding proceedings are performed by phone, including the claimant interview.

During the predetermination proceeding, be sure to correctly and concisely present the facts. Don't mislead, and don't lie. Provide complete information, but don't volunteer information. And remember that the fact-finder is your judge and jury—not your friend.

Other Fact-Finding Interviews

As stated earlier, issues can arise at any time during the claims process, so not all fact-finding interviews are predetermination interviews, nor do they all involve two parties, such as the claimant and the employer. For instance, an interview on the applicant's availability for work may take place simply between the claimant and the claims examiner.

As was true of the predetermination interview, during other fact-finding interviews, you should try to provide concise, factual, and complete information. The amount of information you should volunteer depends partly on the issue or issues under consideration. A look at two examples will give you a clearer idea of what you may face at a fact-finding interview.

Let's say that issues arise regarding your ability to work or your availability to accept employment. In this case, it is your responsibility to provide information—as well as possible documentation, such as medical or child-care certification—that would establish your ability or availability. In a case in which you have restrictions, try to focus your statement on your abililties rather than your limitations.

If you have refused a job referral or work offer, it is again your responsibility to justify your action. The U.S. Department of Labor's Employment and Training Administration states that there are three factors that must be considered in the adjudication of a work refusal. First, was the job offer bona fide—that is, did the opening actually exist, and was the job to be filled? Second, was the work suitable to your abilities, skills, and salary level? Third, did you have good cause to refuse the offer? It is the responsibility of the employer—or of the party making the referral—to establish the first factor. If you refused the offer because you did not think it suitable, it is your responsibility to show why the job was not suitable. If you refused the offer for another reason—because it would have required you to relocate, for instance—you, again, have the responsibility of establishing good cause.

During any fact-finding interview, a written record of the proceedings is made. The record includes each party's signed agreements and that of any witnesses, as well as any documents submitted in support of each position. Often, claims examiners or fact-finders write these statements in order to save time, to focus the interview records on the facts that are most relevant to the issues, and to state regulations. If your statement as summarized by the fact-finder is accurate and reasonably complete, and especially if it supports your eligibility for benefits, by all means, sign it. If, on the other hand, your statement has not been summarized fairly or accurately, you should be prepared to write your own statement, or, at least, to explain the problem to the fact-finder. Ideally, prior to the fact-finding interview, you will have prepared a written summary of the sequence of events or of your position on the issue. The fact-finder can accept your statement as part of the interview records. He or she may still be required to summarize the facts or to request your signature to affirm that what you have submitted is true and correct.

The Determination

Once the necessary information has been gathered, the claims examiner or adjudicator makes a determination of the claimant's eligibility or ineligibility. Sometimes, this is completed at the interview; in other cases, a notice of determination is mailed.

When an employer is involved in the issue, he or she must be notified in writing when the determination is made in the claimant's favor. The claimant must be notified in writing when the determination is *not* made in his or her favor. (The purpose of the notification is to allow either party to file an appeal of the decision.) Some states notify both parties of any determination. If your state is one that does not notify all parties of all determinations, you will know that the determination has been made in your favor when you receive your benefit check in the mail. The written notice of determination—particularly one that is not favorable to the claimant—should contain a brief summary of the facts upon which the determination was based; the result of the determination—that is, eligibility or disqualification; the terms of any penalty and the means by which the claimant can requalify; and instructions for requesting an appeal.

All states must make determinations within specified time limits. If you have not received your check or a notice of determination within ten days of the fact-finding interview, be sure to contact your unemployment office about the delay.

Occasionally, benefit payments are made in error, and a determination of disqualification results in overpayment. Some states may waive such an overpayment, particularly when the error was not the claimant's fault. Often, however, the claimant is required to repay the amount regardless of where the fault lies.

THE APPEALS PROCESS

Benefit determinations are of two types. The first type determines the amount of benefits to which your base-period earnings entitle

Avoiding & Solving the Twelve Most Common Claims Problems

No matter how carefully you fill out your claim form and how conscientiously the unemployment staff processes your claim, mistakes can be made and problems can occur. Fortunately, you can take steps to avoid many common pitfalls and to solve any problems that do develop as quickly as possible. Here are a few tips that may help.

1 When visiting the unemployment office to file your initial claim application, be sure to take all of the necessary documents with you, including your Social Security card and any other records that may be needed in your case. (See pages 19–21 for details.)

2 When filling out your claim application–or any other form–be truthful and accurate. Before signing the form, be sure to draw a line through or "X" through any questions that have been left blank because they are not relevant in your case. This will prevent the claims taker from filling in the blanks–possibly with incorrect information.

3 Whenever you receive a determination from the unemployment office–for instance, the Notice of Monetary Determination, which lists your benefit amount–be sure to check it for accuracy. If any of the information on the determination is incorrect, immediately follow the instructions found on the determination for requesting a reconsideration or appeal.

4 If you receive a verbal determination instead of a written one, and you disagree with the determination, be sure to request it in writing so that you can file an appeal.

5 If you must appear at any fact-finding proceeding, be sure to correctly and concisely present the facts. Provide complete information, but don't volunteer information. If you have any documents that support your case, bring them with you to the proceeding.

6 *Prior to attending a fact-finding proceeding, prepare a written summary of the facts involved in your case so that this statement can become part of the interview record.*

7 *When filing an appeal, carefully follow the instructions on the determination regarding where, when, and how an appeal must be filed in your state. If you have any doubts about the proper procedure, immediately contact your unemployment office for information.*

8 *Be sure to attend your appeals hearing even if you have resumed employment. In some cases, an adverse ruling may make it necessary for you to repay any UI benefits you have already received.*

9 *Be sure to present all of the necessary facts–including all documents–during your appeals hearing. Chances are, this will be your one and only opportunity to state your case.*

10 *While waiting for your hearing or for any decision, be sure to continue filing claims even if you are not receiving benefit checks. If you win your appeal but have not filed claims for the weeks under appeal, you will not be paid benefits for those weeks.*

11 *If you fail to receive a mail-in claim, a benefit check, a determination, or any other expected document within a reasonable amount of time–usually about ten days–immediately visit your unemployment office in person to make an inquiry.*

12 *Be sure to include your Social Security number on all UI-related correspondence, as all transactions at the unemployment office are based on that number.*

Most important, at each stage of the claim-filing process, and throughout all related procedures, make sure you know what is expected of you. If you don't understand any instructions, don't hesitate to ask for further explanations. And if you don't receive the help you need from a staff member, ask to speak to a supervisor or manager. Keep in mind that you earned these benefits during your period of employment. Be sure to get all the benefits that are rightfully yours!

you. The second type affirms or denies your eligibility to collect your benefits. (Sometimes, both determinations are issued on one form.) Either the claimant or the employer may appeal either type of determination.

A large number of claimants have been able to reverse adverse determinations through the use of the appeals process. In 1993, for instance, about 752,664 claimants who, for various reasons, had been denied benefits by state UI programs, appealed these adverse decisions. About 231,544 of these claimants—or 30.8 percent—had the decision reversed through a first-level appeal. About 125,234 of the remaining claimants went on to appeal at the second level, and about 18,610, or 14.9 percent, won at the second level.

A UI appeal is, in many ways, different from a trial or other court proceeding. A UI appeal is designed to be simple, speedy, and inexpensive. (The first appeal is free, and most appeals take place within four weeks of the request.) The parties involved must be told their rights in nonlegal language. Formal and technical procedures are kept to a minimum. It is not necessary for the involved parties to have a lawyer present, but they are permitted to do so. All parties have the right to subpoena witnesses free of cost. And all parties have the right to receive assistance from agency personnel when completing appropriate forms to request the appeal.

Yet, an appeal is an administrative hearing, and so must follow certain guidelines that rule such hearings. Evidence is given under oath. A written and/or recorded transcript of the proceedings is made. There must be an orderly presentation of evidence, and this must be explained at the beginning of the hearing. Above all, the entire appeals process, from the request stage to the written decision, must be fair to all parties.

Where, When, and How to File an Appeal

Notices of determination must include instructions for filing an appeal. Usually, you are allowed to file an appeal in person at your local office, but you may also file by letter. Depending on the state, the time limit during which you may file an appeal ranges from seven to thirty days from the date the determination was issued.

It is vital to read and follow the instructions regarding where, how, and when you may file. In some states, you may simply write, "I disagree with the determination and wish to file an appeal." In others, you must provide a substantial reason for your appeal—that is, you must specify why you think the determination is in error. If the written notice of determination does not specify what is needed, the appeals request form will. If you are in doubt, ask your local unemployment office for clarification. Of course, you must also include your Social Security number, address, and other identifying information. In some states, your letter is all you need

---

TIP: *If you disagree with any determination, always ask for the determination in writing so that you can file an appeal.*

---

to file an appeal. Other states provide an appeals request form if you file in person. Whether or not it is required, it is a good idea to enclose a copy of the determination you want to appeal, or to make reference to it by citing the date and issue of the determination. This is particularly important when more than one issue has been raised. Also include photocopies of any documents that will support your position. For instance, on an appeal of a monetary determination, you should include copies of pay stubs, W-2 forms, or other wage records.

If you are filing an appeals request on an interstate claim, you may submit your appeal to the agent state that accepted your claim application, and that office will forward the request to the appeals unit in the state against which you are filing. Or you may mail your request directly to the state against which you are filing. In the case of an interstate claim, it is likely that the actual hearing will take place over the phone, as you no longer live in the state you're filing against.

Never wait until the deadline to file an appeals request. If you have any doubts about the justness or accuracy of any written determination, file your appeal immediately. If you receive a *verbal* determination that you don't understand or agree with, ask for the determination in writing so that you can exercise your right to appeal. Once you have filed an appeal, continue to file claims, whether by mail or in person. If you do not file continued claims for the weeks under appeal, even if you win the appeal, you will not be paid benefits for the affected weeks.

Once an appeals request has been made by either the claimant or the employer, all parties are notified of the appeals hearing. The notice of the appeals hearing will provide specific information regarding the time and location of the hearing, as well as the proceedings that will be followed at the hearing. You may bring anyone you like—including a lawyer, a friend, or a witness—to the hearing. The employer, if one is involved, will also be allowed to bring legal counsel or witnesses. Be aware that anyone whom you wish to testify must have firsthand information regarding the matter under appeal.

Keep in mind that even if you resume employment before an appeals hearing is held, you should attend the hearing. If your employer appeals and wins, you may be required to repay all or part of the UI benefits that you already received. In some states, any overpayment that has not been repaid will be offset by the withholding of benefits if and when you once again become eligible for UI payments.

The Hearing

Appeals hearings are supposed to start promptly, so be on time. If your hearing is to be conducted by telephone, be sure to be at the phone number you have specified—and to have submitted any necessary documentation—at the scheduled time. If you have been instructed to phone the appeals office, be sure that you do as instructed. If the filing party fails to appear at the scheduled time, or—in the case of a telephone hearing—if that party cannot be reached by phone at that time, the appeal will be dismissed.

An appeals examiner—also called a referee—should state the order of the proceedings at the start of the hearing, and will reserve the right to ask questions or otherwise expedite an orderly and fair process. Appeals examiners may assist either party in developing evidence or framing questions. These hearings follow general rules for administrative hearings, and, although they are informal, they are meant to be conducted impartially and in an orderly manner, with all parties having the opportunity to testify, cross-examine, and summarize their cases.

Usually, appeals hearings are "de nova"—that is, they start anew—so don't be surprised if you are required to repeat testimony you gave to the fact-finder. Appeals hearings are always conducted under oath, and must be taped or transcribed, as in most states the findings and decision of the first-level hearing are subject to review at a higher level. The examiner may read from your claim record into the appeals record, and parties may submit written evidence or documentation, as long as they can show that it is applicable to the issue under consideration. The appeals examiner will mark exhibits with an identification code and describe them for the record.

Remember that this hearing will be your one and only chance to present any testimony, witnesses, and documents that you deem necessary, so be prepared to present your entire case at the hearing. You will probably not be permitted to supplement the

---

TIP: *Once you request an appeal, keep filing claims. If you win the appeal, this will allow you to receive benefit checks for those weeks.*

record after the hearing. Hearings are seldom continued, and are postponed only when a compelling need for a postponement is demonstrated.

As when speaking at a fact-finding interview, you should answer all questions asked by the appeals examiner—or by the other party during cross-examination—as honestly and concisely as possible. Avoid arguments, and do not interrupt others when they are speaking. Be prepared to present facts—not opinions or rumors. If you do not understand a question, ask for clarification. If you are interrupted by the other party, pause, and allow the appeals examiner to correct the party. It is the responsibility of the appeals examiner to conduct and control the hearing.

The Decision

The appeals decision must be issued within thirty days of the hearing, and is sent to all parties, as well as to the unemployment office from which the determination under appeal originated. This document should state the issues that were heard; a summary of the facts—called the finding of facts—upon which the decision was based; and the examiner's decision. It should also provide information regarding the next step in the appeals process in the event that either party chooses to appeal at the second level.

While you are waiting for your hearing—and later, when you await the decision—be sure to follow the instructions provided by your unemployment office with regard to the filing of continued claims. As long as you are unemployed, you should continue filing claims even if you are not receiving checks, because if you win your appeal but you have not filed continued claims for the weeks under appeal, you will not be paid benefits for those weeks.

The Second-Level Appeal

Either party may appeal the decision of an appeals examiner or referee—except in Hawaii, Nebraska, and the Virgin Islands, where there is only one appeals level within the state's unemployment agency. Again, the directions for proceeding with a second-level appeal will be included on the decision of the first-level appeal. Be sure to follow these instructions regarding how, when, and where the appeal is to be filed. Usually, the second-level appeal is an administrative review of the original appeals record and proceedings. Often, this review is performed by a panel. If additional testimony or documentation is needed, the appropriate party may be asked to supply it. When the appeals review officer or panel completes the review, a written decision is issued. This document

---

TIP: *If you don't receive the help you need from an unemployment office staff member, don't hesitate to ask for the supervisor or manager.*

---

contains both findings of fact and the final decision. It also states the right of either party to appeal to the next level—that state's civil court—and specifies the directions and time limits for doing so.

Once you have exhausted the appeals rights in the state civil court system, your case could be carried to the U.S. Supreme Court if that court chooses to honor your petition. Be aware that the Supreme Court honors only about 5 percent of the petitions it receives, but that the court has heard some notable unemployment compensation cases.

One Supreme Court decision—known as the Java Decision—deserves mention because it had such far-reaching consequences. Prior to the Java Decision of 1972, if the unemployment office made an initial determination of eligibility for benefits, but the employer appealed, the payment of benefits was withheld pending the outcome of the appeals hearing. Some employers filed meaningless appeals merely to stop former employees from receiving UI benefits that would, of course, be charged against the employer's account. Because of the Java Decision, once the unemployment office decides that you are eligible for benefits, it must issue payment for any weeks of unemployment you have claimed, and must continue to pay benefits as long as you meet eligibility requirements until the appeals decision reversing the determination has been issued. Of course, if the appeals decision does reverse the initial eligibilty determination, you will be required to repay any benefits that you received.

HOW TO TROUBLE-SHOOT CLAIMS PROBLEMS

Throughout this chapter, we have advised you to pay close attention to the instructions given to you on various claims forms and by the unemployment office staff. At each stage of the process, make sure that you know what is expected of you, as well as what you should expect of the unemployment staff. If you don't understand any instructions, don't hesitate to ask for clarification. If terms are too technical, ask for an explanation. People who work with a program every day develop a verbal shorthand, and often don't realize that most people are unfamiliar with the specialized terms that have become second nature to them. If you don't receive appropriate assistance from a staff member, ask to speak

---

TIP: *If you don't receive a mail-in claim, a check, or any other document in a reasonable amount of time—usually ten days—contact your unemployment office.*

---

to a supervisor or manager. Very often, even if the manager can't solve your problem, he or she will be able to direct you to someone who can. Every state is supposed to have an Interstate Coordinator who resolves and coordinates interstate inquiries, as well as a Federal Programs Coordinator who resolves and coordinates matters on claims involving federal wages. These coordinators are located in the central office, and you may have to contact them through your local office manager or supervisor.

If you do not receive a mail-in claim, a check, a determination, or some other document in a reasonable amount of time, visit your unemployment office in person to make an inquiry. There is no advantage to waiting for the problem to resolve itself; in fact, there may be great disadvantages involved. Most of the time, you will be told what the reasonable waiting time is in each case. As a rule of thumb, allow ten days from the last action you took. For instance, after sending off a mail-in claim, you should expect to receive your benefit check within ten days.

If the unemployment office takes too much time to process your claim, and you have not yet received a benefit check, call or visit your local or state representative, or write to your congressional representative. Be sure to include your Social Security number on all correspondence, as all transactions at the unemployment office are based on that number. Sometimes, the only way to get paid is to contact your elected officials. But be certain that you have taken all the appropriate steps before you seek outside intervention, and try to be as specific and factual as possible when explaining your problem.

To a first-time claimant, the workings of the unemployment office may be intimidating and confusing. However, the procedures followed in your unemployment office were designed to help you obtain the benefits that you have earned. In this chapter, you've seen when, where, and how to file the various types of claims; how to handle continued claims; and how to use the appeals process to reverse any incorrect determinations. In the next chapter, you'll learn more about the UI system as we see which types of employment are covered by unemployment insurance, and which types are excluded from coverage.

Your Maximum Expectations

As you'll learn in Chapter 6, many factors are considered when your weekly benefit amount–the amount of money you can expect to receive in each benefit check–and your potential benefit amount–the amount of money you can receive during the benefit year–are calculated. However, no matter how much money you earned during your employment, you can receive only a certain amount from each state. That's what the following table shows–the maximum weekly and maximum potential benefit amounts you will receive if you meet all the requirements. A claim that provides these maximum benefits is sometimes referred to as a "Max-Max" claim.

Column 2 of the table shows the minimum amount of wages you must have earned in the highest quarter of your base period to qualify for maximum benefits. (Don't worry! You'll learn about high-quarter wages and base periods in Chapter 6.) As you'll see, some states–Alaska, for instance–don't have high-quarter requirements.

Column 3 shows the minimum total amount of wages you must have earned in your base period to qualify for maximum benefits.

Column 4 shows the maximum amount of benefits you can receive each week. Where two figures are shown, the higher figure includes the maximum dependents' allowance–a special allowance provided in some states for claimants with family support responsibilities.

Column 5 shows the maximum number of weeks a claim can last. As you'll see, in most cases, the maximum duration of a claim is twenty-six weeks.

Finally, column 6 shows the maximum total amount of benefits you can receive. Again, where two figures are shown, the larger figure includes the maximum dependents' allowance.

You might not be eligible to receive the maximum benefits listed in this table. In Chapter 6, you'll learn how to compute the benefit amounts you're eligible to receive based on your particular employment history. Make sure you get every penny that is rightfully yours! This book will help you do just that.

The "Max-Max" Claim

State (1)	Minimum Required High-Quarter Wages (2)	Minimum Required Base-Period Wages (3)	Maximum Weekly Benefit Amount (4)	Maximum Duration of Claim (5)	Maximum Potential Benefit Amount (6)
AL	$3,948.01	$12,868.51	$165	26 weeks	$4,290
AK	None	$22,250.00	$212–$284	26 weeks	$5,512–$7,384
AZ	$4,612.50	$14,428.51	$185	26 weeks	$4,810
AR	$6,604.00	$19,812.00	$254	26 weeks	$6,604
CA	$7,633.34	$11,958.01	$230	26 weeks	$5,980
CO	$6,786.00	$27,144.00	$261	26 weeks	$6,786
CT	$8,242.00	$12,680.00	$317–$367	26 weeks	$8,242–$9,542
DE	$6,095.00	$12,190.00	$265	26 weeks	$6,890
DC	$8,710.00	$17,420.00	$335	26 weeks	$8,710
FL	None	$26,000.00	$250	26 weeks	$6,500
GA	$4,625.00	$19,238.01	$185	26 weeks	$4,810
HI	$7,056.01	$8,762.00	$337	26 weeks	$8,762
ID	$6,110.00	$19,857.50	$235	26 weeks	$6,110
IL	$6,142.50	$12,285.00	$235–$311	26 weeks	$6,110–$8,086
IN	$4,550.00	$15,785.71	$170–$192	26 weeks	$4,420–$4,992
IA	$4,853.00	$16,458.00	$211–$259	26 weeks	$5,486–$6,734
KS	$5,882.36	$19,500.00	$250	26 weeks	$6,500
KY	None	$19,282.72	$229	26 weeks	$5,954
LA	$4,525.00	$17,427.77	$181	26 weeks	$4,706
ME	$4,356.00	$15,444.00	$198–$297	26 weeks	$5,148–$7,722
MD	$5,328.01	$8,028.00	$223	26 weeks	$5,798
MA	$8,450.00	$27,083.33	$325–$487	30 weeks	$9,750–$14,610
MI	None	$19,810.00	$293	26 weeks	$7,696
MN	$7,930.00	$23,790.00	$305	26 weeks	$7,930
MS	$4,290.00	$12,870.00	$165	26 weeks	$4,290
MO	$3,888.89	$13,650.00	$175	26 weeks	$4,550
MT	None	$21,700.00	$217	26 weeks	$5,642
NE	$4,250.00	$12,009.00	$154	26 weeks	$4,004
NV	$5,750.00	$17,940.00	$230	26 weeks	$5,980
NH	None	$24,500.00	$196	26 weeks	$5,096
NJ	None	$20,241.90	$347	26 weeks	$9,022
NM	$5,122.00	$8,536.67	$197	26 weeks	$5,122
NY	None	$11,980.00	$300	26 weeks	$7,800
NC	$7,332.00	$21,996.00	$282	26 weeks	$7,332

State (1)	Minimum Required High-Quarter Wages (2)	Minimum Required Base-Period Wages (3)	Maximum Weekly Benefit Amount (4)	Maximum Duration of Claim (5)	Maximum Potential Benefit Amount (6)
ND	$6,032.00	$19,302.40	$232	26 weeks	$6,032
OH	None	$12,376.00	$238–$319	26 weeks	$6,188– $8,294
OK	$5,925.00	$15,405.00	$237	26 weeks	$6,162
OR	None	$22,720.00	$285	26 weeks	$7,410
PA	$8,163.00	$13,080.00	$329–$337	26 weeks	$8,554– $8,762
PR	$3,432.00	$5,320.00	$133	26 weeks	$3,458
RI	$6,709.95	$22,388.88	$310–$387	26 weeks	$8,060– $10,062
SC	$5,278.00	$15,834.00	$203	26 weeks	$5,278
SD	$4,368.00	$13,104.00	$168	26 weeks	$4,368
TN	$4,810.01	$19,240.00	$185	26 weeks	$4,810
TX	$6,100.25	$23,588.89	$245	26 weeks	$6,370
UT	$6,448.00	$23,881.48	$248	26 weeks	$6,448
VT	None	$9,405.00	$209	26 weeks	$5,434
VA	$5,200.00	$20,800.01	$208	26 weeks	$5,408
VI	$5,486.00	$16,458.00	$211	26 weeks	$5,486
WA	$8,500.00	$30,600.00	$340	30 weeks	$10,200
WV	None	$26,500.00	$280	26 weeks	$7,280
WI	$6,075.00	$15,795.00	$243	26 weeks	$6,318
WY	$5,500.00	$18,333.34	$220	26 weeks	$5,200

3. COVERAGE AND EXCLUSIONS

WHAT TYPES OF WORK ARE COVERED BY UNEMPLOYMENT INSURANCE?

Many people wrongly believe that they are not covered by unemployment insurance (UI), and therefore fail to claim the benefits that are rightfully theirs. It is important to remember that the matter of coverage refers to the employment and the employer, rather than the worker. *All* work is covered if the employer is required to pay taxes on it. Nevertheless, it is beneficial to you, the claimant, to understand how coverage works and what the exclusions are.

In this chapter, we will review basic coverage and exceptions under FUTA—the Federal Unemployment Tax Act—as well as any related exclusions that might apply in the various states. We will also look at coverage under statutes other than FUTA. Finally, we will discuss general categories of exclusions.

Be aware that although we have tried to examine coverage on a state-by-state basis, we may not have covered all aspects of each coverage issue or exclusion in every state. If after reading this chapter you are still unsure as to whether your employment is covered, please check with your local unemployment office for further information.

WHO IS COVERED BY UI?

Earlier in the book, we stated that 97 percent of wage and salary employment is covered by UI. We also explained that both federal and state laws affect coverage for benefits, as state UI laws must comply with FUTA specifications and requirements, but may differ from one state to another in specific details.

Employers are required to pay 6.2 percent FUTA tax—that is, federal tax—on the first $7,000 (the tax base) paid to each worker in each calendar year. The money is actually collected by the Internal Revenue Service (IRS), and is used to administer the UI program. FUTA defines what is considered covered employment on a federal level, but does allow some exceptions to coverage requirements for specific services. FUTA also requires the states to cover some employment that is exempt from FUTA taxation.

In addition to paying the FUTA taxes, employers covered under state laws are required to pay state UI tax on their payrolls. It is these funds that are used to pay UI benefits. The state rates and tax bases can differ from those stated in FUTA. In fact, more than half of the states have higher tax bases than FUTA's base of $7,000. Each employer's rate is dependent on the account's experience—that is, the amount of benefits charged against the account. The state taxes are collected by the state UI office, and maintained in the unemployment trust fund of the Department of the Treasury. State laws, like FUTA, may provide specific exclusions. In addition, in all but three states— Alabama, Massachusetts, and New York—employers that are excluded from coverage by state law may be given approval by the state agency to voluntarily cover their employees.

In describing the beginning of the UI system in Chapter 1, we said that employers in states that adopt an approved state UI system were originally allowed to deduct up to 90 percent of their state contribution from their federal contribution. Currently, covered employers are allowed to deduct up to 5.4 percent of the 6.2 percent FUTA tax rate because of payment of their state contribution. This is called a *tax offset credit.* If a state law fails to cover services that are covered by FUTA, the tax credit of all employers in that state may be at risk. As a result, state definitions of covered employment often mirror the FUTA definitions in that the language of the state law exactly follows that of FUTA.

At the minimum, state definitions must comply with FUTA definitions in three major employment categories: regular, or nonagricultural, employment; agricultural employment; and domestic employment. Below, we'll look at both FUTA and state definitions of employer liabilitiy in each of these three categories, as well as federal and state laws regarding coverage of other types of employment.

Nonagricultural Employment

Unless there are stated exclusions, nonagricultural employers are subject to FUTA if their quarterly payroll totaled $1,500 or more in the current or preceding calendar year, or if they employed at least one worker on at least one day in each of twenty weeks during the current or preceding calendar year. As we said, state laws must be in compliance with FUTA, but may go *beyond* the federal law by requiring coverage of employers with fewer employees and smaller payrolls. Thirty-three states have adopted the FUTA definition for covered nonagricultural work. For simplicity, rather than listing all thirty-three states here, we will list only those that have adopted definitions that go beyond that of FUTA. If you do not find your state among them, you'll know that it is one of the thirty-three.

Ten states—Alaska, Colorado, the District of Columbia, Hawaii, Maryland, Pennsylvania, Puerto Rico, Rhode Island, the Virgin Islands, and Washington—require coverage of nonagricultural employers who have any employees. The remaining states require less than twenty weeks of service or a $1,500 payroll per quarter for any number of employees. These states and their requirements are as follows: Arkansas requires coverage for only ten days of employment; California, for a quarterly payroll of over $100; Massachusetts, for thirteen weeks of employment; Montana, for a yearly payroll of over $1,000; Nevada, for a quarterly payroll of $225; New Jersey, for a yearly payroll of $1,000; New York, for a quarterly payroll of $300; Oregon, for eighteen weeks of employment; Utah, for a quarterly payroll of $140; and Wyoming, for a yearly payroll of over $500.

Agricultural Employment

Employers of agricultural workers are subject to FUTA if cash wages of $20,000 or more were paid for agricultural labor in any calendar quarter of the current or preceding year, or if ten or more workers were employed on at least one day in each of twenty different weeks during the current or preceding calendar year. The term *cash wages* refers to actual salary payments, as distinguished from the value of room and board or other goods and services given in exchange for labor. It does not mean that payments must be made in hard currency.

Forty-five states have adopted the FUTA definition for covered agricultural work. Eight states have adopted definitions that go beyond that of the federal government. The District of Columbia, Puerto Rico, Rhode Island, and the Virgin Islands require coverage if one or more workers are employed at any time; California, if one worker is employed at any time with a quarterly payroll in excess of $100; Florida, if five workers are employed in twenty weeks, or there is a quarterly payroll of $10,000; Minnesota, if four workers are employed in twenty weeks, or there is a quarterly payroll of $20,000; and Texas, if three workers are employed in twenty weeks, or there is a quarterly payroll of $6,250. In California, Maine, Virginia, and Washington State, the amount of the payroll includes payments other than cash remuneration—payments specifically excluded in the federal definition.

Domestic Employment

Domestic employment includes workers who are employed in people's homes or in other residences such as boarding houses, fraternities, and sororities. Some examples are housekeepers, maids, cooks, butlers, nannies, baby sitters, companions, personal chauffeurs, and gardeners. This employment is subject to FUTA if the employer paid cash wages of $1,000 or more during any calendar quarter of the current or preceding calendar year. Again, cash wages are actual salary payments, rather than goods or services.

All but six states have adopted the FUTA definition of domestic employment. The District of Columbia, New York, and the Virgin Islands require coverage for a quarterly payroll of $500; Hawaii, for a quarterly payroll of $225 for one employee; and Ohio, for a quarterly payment of $1,000 for one employee, or a quarterly payroll of $1,500 for two or more employees. New Hampshire permits coverage on an elective basis. In Arkansas, Maine, Minnesota, and Washington, the amount of the payroll includes payments other than cash remuneration.

Nonprofit Employment

FUTA definitions do not include nonprofit employers, as such employers are exempt from any type of federal taxation. However, federal law does require coverage by state UI laws if the organization employs four or more workers in twenty weeks.

Twenty-one states go beyond the federal definition by requiring coverage if the nonprofit organization employs one or more workers. These states include Arkansas, California, Connecticut, the District of Columbia, Hawaii, Idaho, Iowa, Maryland, Massachusetts, Michigan, Minnesota, Montana, New Hampshire, New Jersey, New Mexico, Oregon, Pennsylvania, Puerto Rico, Rhode Island, the Virgin Islands, and Washington. Services of part-time employees who earn less than $50 per calendar quarter are excluded from coverage in all of the states except Delaware, Idaho, Iowa, Missouri, Montana, Nevada, New Jersey, New Mexico, New York, Oklahoma, Oregon, Puerto Rico, Tennessee, Texas, the Virgin Islands, Washington, West Virginia, and Wyoming. In Alaska, services of part-time employees are excluded if the workers earn less than $250 per quarter. In Maine, the exclusion applies to the services of employees who earn less than $150 per quarter.

Excluded from FUTA requirements for state coverage of non-profit organizations are services performed for churches, and services performed for religious organizations operated mainly for religious purposes and operated and controlled primarily by a church. Excluded, too, are the services of ordained ministers in the exercise of their ministries, and the services of members of a religious order in the exercise of the duties of that order. However, while all states exclude these services from state coverage requirements, most states do allow voluntary coverage.

Local Government Employment

Employment for local government entities—that is, state, county, and municipal governments—is not subject to FUTA. However, since 1978, FUTA has required coverage of this employment under state UI laws. FUTA allows states to exclude from coverage the services of elected officials; members of a legislative body or the judiciary; members of the State National Guard; employees working on a temporary basis due to various types of emergencies; people employed in policy-making or advisory positions; participants in sheltered workshops, such as Good Will or rehabilitative work programs; trainees in unemployment or work-training programs assisted or financed by the federal government, the state government, or any political subdivision; and inmates of custodial or penal institutions.

In the case of some of the services just discussed, some states do require coverage despite the FUTA-allowed exclusions. The District of Columbia and Hawaii cover the services of elected officials. The District of Columbia, Hawaii, Montana, and Washington cover the services of members of legislative bodies and the judiciary. The District of Columbia, Florida, Hawaii, and Montana cover the services of the State National Guard and the Air National Guard. The District of Columbia, Georgia, Hawaii, Montana, and Washington cover the services of temporary emergency employees. And the District of Columbia, Hawaii, and Montana cover services performed in policy-making and advisory positions.

Civil Employment for the United States Government

Civilian employment for the federal government is not covered under FUTA, but is covered under U.S. Code 5. In Chapter 2, we explained that when a former government employee files an initial claim, state UI offices contact the federal employing agency to obtain a report of the claimant's wage and separation information. Determinations regarding eligibility and the amount of the entitlement are then made in accordance with the laws, regulations, and procedures of the state to which the wages are assignable, following Department of Labor regulations that govern the use of federal wages for UI purposes. Although we briefly discussed the assignment of wages in Chapter 2, because this concept is so important, we'll now take a more detailed look at federal wage assignment.

Every federal government employee has an official *duty station,* which is designated by the employing agency. The duty station—which is shown on position descriptions and Standard Form documents—is usually the state in which the work was performed, although it is sometimes the state from which the work was directed. If an individual worked at duty stations in two or more states or for two or more agencies, all Unemployment Compensation for Federal Employees (UCFE) wages are usually assigned to the state of the very last duty station before the filing of the initial claim. There are two exceptions to this general rule regarding wage assignments. One exception applies to the claimant who had covered employment in his or her state of residence subsequent to the federal employment, but before the filing of the initial claim. In this case, all UCFE wages are assigned to the state of residence at the time of the initial filing. The other exception states that wages from federal civilian services performed at duty stations outside the United States—including the District of Columbia, Puerto Rico, and the Virgin Islands—are assigned to the claimant's state of residence at the time the initial claim is filed. Once UCFE wages are assigned, they are "frozen" in that state, although any lag or unused wages may be transferred for use in a subsequent claim.

Please note that UCFE coverage is extended to most employees of agencies of the U.S. Government. However, individuals who contract with the government to perform certain services or tasks are considered contractors. Therefore, neither they nor their employees are covered under this code. Of course, since they are regular, nonagricultural workers, they should be covered under FUTA and state laws. Political appointees, cabinet heads, and ambassadors are also not covered under U.S. Code 5. Elected officials are not covered because they are not employees.

To determine if your civilian employment was covered under U.S. Code 5, find out if your employment was in accordance with procedures controlled by the Office of Personnel Management

(OPM). If the position was posted through the OPM, and if, when you were hired or when any actions such as salary increase occurred, you were issued an OPM Personnel Action notice (Standard Form 50, or an equivalent document), it is likely that your services were covered. If you were not hired by a federal personnel office, or if your payment for services was in the form of a voucher, stipend, or grant, it is not likely that those services were covered.

Service With the United States Armed Forces

Unemployment Compensation for Ex-Servicemembers (UCX) has been in effect, with modifications, since 1958. Like UCFE claims, UCX claims are administered by each state by agreement with the U.S. Department of Labor.

Unlike other UI claims, UCX claims are not based on wages paid. Instead, they are based on the claimant's rank at the time of discharge. Every year, the Department of Labor issues a Schedule of Remuneration, which equates the salary of each service rank with civilian wages. The unemployment offices use this schedule as the basis of the monetary computation of benefits according to each state's formula. The state usually does not have to contact the service branch to gain information needed to process a UCX claim, as most of the information needed is found on the DD-214, the official discharge document issued to servicemembers.

At the time the claim is filed, all UCX wages are assigned to the state of filing, after which they remain "frozen" in that state. Please note that the state of filing is literally the state in which the claim is filed. It does not have to be the claimant's state of residence, nor does it have to be the state in which the claimant was stationed. In fact, ex-servicemembers can file in *any* state. Like lag UI and UCFE wages, lag UCX wages can be transferred for use in subsequent claims.

Certain qualifications must be met in order for service to be covered for UCX benefits. The claimant must have been discharged honorably or under honorable conditions. (Different branches of the service state this in different ways.) If the claimant was an officer, he or she must not have resigned for "the good of the service"—a Department of Defense term meaning that the officer was asked to resign his or her commission. If an enlisted member, the claimant must have completed the first full term of service agreed upon at enlistment, or, if separated before that time, must have been discharged for specific reasons stated in UCX regulations. Since these reasons are technical, we will state them as they are cited in the regulations. They include discharge for the convenience of the government under an early release program; medical disqualification, pregnancy, parenthood, or service-incurred injury or disability; and hardship, personality disorder, or inaptitude. The reasons for discharge—as stated on the DD-214—are not subject to interpretation and adjudication by state UI staff, as are separation statements made by private-industry and federal civilian employers. If an enlisted member's discharge is honorable and he or she has completed the first full term of service, the reason for separation is irrelevant.

Other Means of Determining Coverage

We have discussed coverage of various categories of employment as stated in FUTA and in other bodies of law. You should be aware, however, that states sometimes decide coverage according to considerations other than the amount of the employer's payroll or the number of employees working during a specified period of time. For instance, states also consider the contractual relationship between the employer and the worker—that is, whether or not, and to what degree, the employer maintained control and direction of both the worker and the work product. If the person performing the service controlled the hours of work and the place where the work was performed, and worked without the supervision of the person receiving the service, it is unlikely that an employer-employee relationship can be established. Because it has been concluded that there is no way of determining the number of weeks that a self-employed person is employed, FUTA and all state laws exclude self-employment from coverage. The State of California, however, sometimes allows self-coverage on a voluntary basis.

Another means of determining coverage has to do with work location. To provide coverage of employment for a single employer in more than one jurisdiction and to prevent duplicate taxation, states have adopted a uniform definition for work localization that provides coverage in the state where the work is wholly or mainly performed, or—if routinely performed in various states—coverage in the state where the employer has his or her base of operations. Some employers who have work localized in more than one jurisdiction choose to cover employees separately in each jurisdiction.

WHO IS EXCLUDED FROM COVERAGE?

Sometimes, UI coverage is defined by stating exclusions from coverage. That is, by describing what is excluded, we define what is covered. We already mentioned some of the exclusions when we reviewed coverage. For instance, we noted that federal elected officials are not covered because they are not employees. Now, let us review some other exclusions. Once again, we caution you to check with your state unemployment office to determine if your employment was covered. Don't let assumptions prevent you from filing an unemployment claim.

Student and Work-Study Employment

Employment performed as part of a course of study, or to provide financial assistance to students or their families, is usually not covered, as the employment is already considered a benefit. And since the student is performing services in exchange for academic credits, tuition, or other benefits, there is no clear employer-employee relationship between the school and the student worker. Students who are employed by hospitals, clinics, and medical or dental laboratories operated by a federal agency, and whose employment would normally be covered under the UCFE program, are excluded from coverage, as well. And all states exclude part-time work performed by a full-time student for a college or university in which the student is regularly enrolled and attending classes.

All but eighteen states exclude coverage of spouses of college and university students if the spouse is employed as part of a program to provide financial assistance to the student. The eighteen states that do not make this exclusion are Alaska, Arkansas, Delaware, the District of Columbia, Florida, Hawaii, Idaho, Kansas, Louisiana, Maine, Minnesota, New Mexico, Ohio, Puerto Rico, Rhode Island, Texas, the Virgin Islands, and Virginia. In a case such as this, the employer must have informed the spouse that he or she was hired under a financial assistance program, and that his or her services would not be covered for unemployment benefits. It would be difficult for the spouse not to be informed of this exclusion, since the student and spouse would normally have to apply for financial assistance to gain this type of employment, and the application would include a statement to this effect. If a spouse was not properly informed, the matter of coverage would be adjudicated by the unemployment staff.

All states but the District of Columbia and Hawaii exclude the

---

TIP: *Even if you think that your employment wasn't covered, be sure to file for UI benefits. Don't act on assumptions!*

services of students enrolled in a public and/or nonprofit educational institution's work-study program. Maine excludes only elementary and secondary students in work-study programs. Some states specify that the exclusion applies to students under twenty-two years of age. Work-study programs established by employers or groups of employers are excepted from this exclusion.

Ten states exclude services performed by full-time students in the employ of an organized camp if the services meet certain criteria. These ten states are California, Maine, Maryland, Missouri, North Carolina, Oregon, Tennessee, Texas, Vermont, and Virginia.

Employer's Relatives

All states except New York exclude from coverage the services of individuals in the employment of a son, daughter, or spouse. All states also exclude from coverage the services of a minor child in the employment of his or her parent.

Newspaper Carriers and
Magazine and Newspaper Distributors

All states except California, Delaware, Iowa, New Jersey, New York, Oregon, Puerto Rico, Rhode Island, Tennessee, Vermont, the Virgin Islands, and West Virginia exclude from coverage the delivery of newspapers and shopping news circulars by individuals under eighteen years of age. This exclusion does not apply to the individual who distributes newspapers to certain points for later delivery, regardless of the distributor's age. Thirteen states also exclude the services of workers who distribute newspapers and magazines to the consumer when the distributor's pay is dependent on the profit over and above the consumer's price. These states include Arizona, Arkansas, California, Colorado, Indiana, Maine, Nebraska, North Carolina, Oregon, Pennsylvania, Utah, Washington, and Wisconsin.

Railroad Employees

All states exclude from coverage services performed in employment for railroads. However, such services may be covered under a separate program called the Railroad Retirement Act.

Hospital-Employed Patients

Hospital-employed patients—usually, long-term "boarder" patients who perform services for the hospital in which they're staying—are excluded from UI coverage in all states but the District of Columbia, Hawaii, Louisiana, Missouri, and New York. Even in those states that require coverage, some services may not be covered. For instance, volunteer services and services rendered as a part of occupational therapy are not considered employment. In addition, hospital patients working in federally operated hospitals are not covered by the UCFE program, which usually covers federal employees.

Inmates of Penal Institutions

Services performed by inmates of penal institutions while confined to those institutions are excluded from coverage.

Insurance and Real Estate Agents Working on Commission Only

All states except California, Iowa, Nevada, New York, Puerto Rico, the Virgin Islands, and Wyoming exclude the services of insurance agents who work solely on commission. All states except the District of Columbia, Indiana, Ohio, South Dakota, the Virgin Islands, and West Virginia exclude the services of real estate agents who work solely on commission.

Casual Labor

Casual labor—that is, services that are not a part of the employer's regular course of business, and are not performed by an individual regularly employed by the employer—is excluded from coverage in all but nineteen states. An example of casual labor might be the raking of leaves or removal of snow from store premises performed by an individual other than a regular store employee. The nineteen states that do not exclude coverage are Delaware, Idaho, Illinois, Iowa, Kansas (in some cases), Maine, Michigan, Missouri, Nevada, New Jersey, New Mexico, New York, Oklahoma, South Dakota, Tennessee, Texas, West Virginia, Wisconsin, and Wyoming.

Commercial Fishing

Sixteen states exclude from coverage the services of individuals who catch fish other than salmon or halibut for commercial sales. These states include Alabama, Alaska, Arkansas, the District of Columbia, Florida, Hawaii, Maine, Maryland, North Carolina, Puerto Rico, South Carolina, Tennessee, Vermont, Virginia, the Virgin Islands, and Wisconsin. This exclusion applies only to fishermen on a vessel of less than ten tons' weight or, in Arkansas and Tennessee, a vessel

with less than ten employees. In Maine, the exclusion applies only if the employees' payment is part of the catch.

Student Nurses and Interns

All but twenty-one states exclude the services of student nurses— that is, nurses attending a training school—in the employment of a hospital or training school. The services of medical interns in the employment of a hospital, when such interns have completed a four-year medical-school course of study, are also excluded from coverage. The twenty-one states that do *not* exclude the services of student nurses and medical interns are Alaska, Colorado, Delaware, Iowa, Kansas, Michigan, Missouri, Montana, Nevada, New Mexico, New York, North Carolina, Puerto Rico, Rhode Island, Tennessee, Utah, Vermont, the Virgin Islands, Washington, West Virginia, and Wyoming.

Officers in Self- or Family-Owned Corporations

Corporate officers are considered employees of the corporation, and their services are covered under FUTA. However, Alaska, California, Delaware, Iowa, Minnesota, and North Dakota allow exemption from state UI taxation in those instances in which the corporation is largely self- or family-owned. In addition, some states limit benefit eligibility of corporate owner-officers whose unemployment is brought about by the sale of the corporation.

If you are a corporate officer, especially in a corporation in which you or your family members own shares, you should check with your state unemployment office regarding specific state coverage or exemption provisions.

Illegal Aliens

The wages earned by aliens before they are lawfully admitted to the United States—or lawfully permitted to work—cannot be used as the basis for monetary eligibility on a UI claim. Be aware that this is not really a coverage issue, because the employment may ordinarily be covered. In this case, federal law prohibits the use of wages from covered employment.

Employment for Foreign Governments and International Organizations

Because foreign governments are not subject to FUTA, the services of employees of foreign governments or of agencies of foreign governments are not covered, even though the work has been performed in the United States. An example of this type of employment would be work performed for an embassy of a foreign nation. Some services for international governmental organizations also may not be covered. For instance, employment for the World Bank, the World Health Organization, the Organization of American States, and the United Nations are not covered by FUTA or respective state laws. However, nonprofit international organizations that are registered in the United States—such as the International Association of Firefighters—may cover their employees under state laws.

In this chapter, we have outlined the terms of UI coverage under both the Federal Unemployment Tax Act and related laws. We have also discussed exemptions and exclusions under FUTA, as well as under various state laws. We hope that if you have any doubts about whether your particular employment is covered, you will contact the central unemployment office in the state in which you worked to discover the laws regarding your particular circumstances.

4. DISQUALIFICATIONS

HOW YOUR ACTIONS MAY POSTPONE, REDUCE, OR CANCEL YOUR UI BENEFITS

Unemployment insurance (UI) benefits are intended for people who are unemployed through no fault of their own—because they have been laid off for lack of work, because they have resigned from their jobs with what is termed "good cause" as defined by that particular state's UI laws, or because they have been fired for reasons other than misconduct. Claimants who quit their jobs without good cause or, in most states, without cause that is work-connected or attributable to the employer; who are fired for misconduct; or who refuse suitable work, are suspended or *disqualified* from benefits. Claimants may also be disqualified or suspended for being actively engaged in labor disputes, or for gross misconduct or fraud.

In this chapter, we are going to discuss the various causes of disqualification. In the course of exploring what circumstances might result in disqualification, we will also learn more about what makes a claimant qualify for UI benefits. And we will look at the various types of penalties that may be imposed—penalties that range from the postponement of benefits to the refusal of benefits.

TYPES OF DISQUALIFICATIONS

Before we look at the causes of disqualification, it would be helpful to learn a little about the types of disqualifications that may be imposed on claimants. Generally, disqualifications fall into one of two categories: term and durational.

With a *term disqualification*, a person must wait a specific period of time before he or she can collect benefits. Sometimes, the maximum potential benefit amount that the claimant would have been eligible to receive based on the monetary determination is reduced by an amount corresponding to the number of weeks of the disqualification multiplied by the weekly benefit entitlement. For example, if benefit payments are suspended for ten weeks, the maximum potential benefit amount will be reduced by ten times the weekly benefit amount. Therefore, a claimant who would have qualified for $5,200, payable at the weekly rate of $200 for twenty-six weeks, would qualify for $3,200—$200 for sixteen weeks—*after* the disqualification period was over. A term disqualification may begin with the week in which the disqualifying event occurred, or with the effective week of the unemployment claim, also called the filing week.

A *durational disqualification* lasts for the duration of the period of unemployment. This type of disqualification makes it necessary for the claimant to return to employment and earn a specified amount of money—and, sometimes, work for a specified period of time—before he or she can collect UI benefits. For example, the requalifying provision might specify that a claimant must return to employment and earn at least ten times the weekly benefit amount in employment of at least ten weeks' duration. So if the claimant's monetary entitlement is to be $200 per week, the claimant must earn at least $2,000 from work that lasts at least ten weeks. The durational disqualification begins with the effective date of the claim. Some states that have durational disqualifications also reduce the potential benefit amount.

Keep in mind that the purpose of the durational disqualification is to return the unemployed person to the work force. Therefore, a claimant cannot simply take new employment and then quit when he or she meets the requirements for requalification. The separation from the new employment must be for reasons that are not disqualifying, and the claimant must present proof of the requalifying work or earnings. Such proof could be a statement from the new employer, check stubs, or other payroll records.

"BACKWARD" DISQUALIFICATIONS

Term and durational disqualifications have to do with the *type* of disqualification, or penalty, that is imposed. A "backward" disqualification—which is imposed only in certain states—has to do with the *particular job separation* that will be considered in determining whether there will be a disqualification in those situations in which the claimant has worked for more than one employer.

Usually, the determination with regard to the separation issue—that is, the circumstances under which the claimant left his or her employment or was fired by his or her employer—is based on the separation from the *last job* that the claimant held before filing for

UI benefits. However, the UI system does recognize that the separation from the last period of employment is not always the cause of the current period of unemployment. Some individuals try to avoid disqualification after a problem separation by gaining temporary employment—employment that they know will end, enabling them to receive UI benefits. Nineteen states have specific laws designed to prevent this type of manipulation. The result is that a worker may be disqualified for leaving or being fired from a job other than his or her last one. Let's look at the specific provisions of the nineteen states that use this type of disqualification, which, for the purpose of our discussion, we are calling a *backward disqualification.*

❑ Alabama considers the previous-to-last separation when the last period of employment is not considered "bona fide" employment. In deciding whether employment is bona fide, Alabama examiners may use one or all of three criteria—the duration of the employment, the intent of the claimant and the employer in the hiring agreement, and the reason for the separation from the previous-to-last employment, as that is the real reason for the state of unemployment. (It should be noted that in states other than Alabama, if employment is to be termed "bona fide," it has to have been covered—or, at least, the state must be able to verify that there truly was an employer-employee relationship. Self-employment, employment for a relative, and employment for someone who was not incorporated, registered, or licensed is questionable.)

❑ Alaska, Florida, Iowa, Maryland, Massachusetts, Missouri, and Ohio consider the previous-to-last separation if the last period of employment was not of sufficient duration or did not produce sufficient earnings to satisfy a potential disqualification on the previous-to-last separation. Essentially, these states attempt to prevent claimants from avoiding disqualification by taking questionable employment. Therefore, the states adjudicate the previous-to-last separation. If this results in a disqualification, the very last period of employment is examined to see if it was of sufficient length and produced sufficient wages to satisfy the disqualification.

This concept is difficult, so let's examine a possible scenario. A worker in retail sales leaves her job after two years' employment because she has an offer of a clerical job that pays a dollar more per hour. After three weeks on the new job, the employer dismisses her because her clerical skills are not adequate. She then files an unemployment claim. Now let's look at the claimant's separation from her job in retail sales. If she had filed for UI benefits after this separation, she would have been disqualified, because her reason for leaving was one of personal choice, and the claimant is filing against a state that requires good cause that is attributable to the employer. (See page 67 for more information about good cause.) Her subsequent employment in the office was only of three weeks' duration, and would not satisfy a potential disqualification of ten weeks. So it is the separation from her preceding job in retail sales that will be considered in determining whether she will receive benefits. Suppose that the claimant had worked twelve weeks in the office setting before being separated through no fault of her own. Since twelve weeks exceed the potential disqualification of ten weeks, the separation from the office job would be the one under consideration.

❑ Maine considers the previous-to-last separation if the last period of employment was not in the claimant's usual trade or was intermittent in nature.

❑ The District of Columbia considers the separation from the last covered employment of thirty days' duration.

❑ Virginia considers the separation from the last employment of thirty working days' duration.

❑ South Dakota and West Virginia consider the separation from the last employment of thirty days' duration, except in the case of an additional claim. (See page 32 for a discussion of additional claims.) In the case of an additional claim, employment may be of less than thirty days' duration.

❑ South Carolina considers the separation from the last employment from which the claimant earned at least eight times the weekly benefit amount of the claim.

❑ Kentucky, Michigan, and Nebraska consider separations from *all* base-period employers.

❑ Tennessee considers the separation from any employment from which the claimant earned at least ten times the weekly benefit amount of the claim.

❑ North Dakota considers the separation from any employment from which the claimant earned at least eight times the weekly benefit amount of the claim.

We have discussed the concept of backward disqualification because we want you to understand the workings of the system and the problems you may face if you file a claim against one of the nineteen states mentioned above. But even if you are not filing against one of these states, we caution you against leaving permanent employment or causing dismissal and then "picking up" employment that is only temporary, with the goal of receiving UI benefits. Temporary work is fine for those who wish to set their own work schedule, and it can be a boon to workers who are unable to find enduring full-time employment. But it simply does not provide the security and benefits associated with jobs of longer duration.

REASONS FOR DISQUALIFICATION

Reasons for disqualification usually fall into one of several categories: quitting without good cause, being fired for misconduct, being fired for gross misconduct, refusing suitable work without good cause, unemployment due to involvement in a labor dispute, and fraud. Although some reasons for quitting or being fired are regarded in the same way in most states, there are many state-to-state variations. Let's look at each of these categories and learn more about what may—or may not—be considered a disqualification for UI benefits.

Quitting Without Good Cause

There are many good reasons for quitting a job that are not accepted as good cause. In UI law, *good cause* is said to be "compelling cause." Claims examiners have several tests they can apply to determine whether a claimant had good cause to quit. The first test is to judge whether the reason for leaving would have caused a prudent person to resign. Another test asks what the potential harm would have been to the claimant if he or she had not left the job. The final test asks what steps were taken to solve the problem—that is, what other options were considered before leaving. Claims examiners do not apply each of these tests to each situation, but use whichever test is appropriate to the facts of the case. Most states also have a provision specifying that the cause for quitting must have been connected with the work or attributable to the employer. In these states, there is no need to apply tests for determining good or compelling cause if a claimant's reason for leaving was *not* connected with the work or attributable to the employer, since the claimant will be disqualified anyway.

Table 4.1 shows reasons for quitting a job that are considered good cause in the laws of some of the fifty-three states and jurisdictions. Included in the table is a list of the states that restrict good cause to that connected with the work or attributable to the employer. (You'll learn more about Table 4.1 a little later in our discussion.)

Many states also have statutory exceptions. A statutory exception is a citation in the state UI law or regulations that allows benefits—or, conversely, requires disqualification—for specific situations or occurrences. Most often, these exceptions allow benefits when the separation occurred because of claimant illness. For instance, in some states that generally require work-connected reasons for leaving, a claimant will not be disqualified for leaving due to illness, even if the illness was not work-related. But because you must be able to work in order to be eligible for UI benefits, leaving your job because of physical restrictions or illness can be a double-edged sword, as it nearly always raises the issue of your current ability to work. To avoid disqualification, you must be prepared to present a statement from the physician who advised you to leave, as well as a statement regarding your current medical status, including any current restrictions. Similarly, statutory exceptions that deal with marital and family obligations also raise issues regarding current availability for work.

Whenever a claimant has voluntarily resigned, the claimant bears the burden of demonstrating that he or she had good cause for leaving because the claimant is seen as the *moving party*—that is, the person who initiated or was in control of the separation. Simply stating a reason that you believe to be good cause will not guarantee a favorable determination, even if your reason is allowable under one of the statutory exceptions. If your reason for leaving was connected with on-the-job events, be prepared to document the occurrences, what the potential or actual harm would have been if you had not left, and what reasonable actions you took to improve the situation before leaving.

Most of the reasons for quitting commonly presented by claimants fall into one of several categories. Let's take a look at some of these reasons and see which would, and which would not, probably be considered good cause. Again, you may wish to refer to Table 4.1, which provides a look at some reasons that may be considered good cause for quitting. Be aware that the following discussion of reasons for leaving employment will extend beyond those shown in the table, as the table includes only those reasons actually cited in various state laws. Other reasons—many of which are quite common—are not included in the table because they are not specifically cited in state laws.

Table 4.1 Reasons for Quitting Considered
Good Cause in State Laws*

Reason for Quitting	States
Sexual or unwelcome harassment.	CA, IL, KS, MA, MN, RI, WI.
Compulsory retirement.	CA, CO, IN, MA, MN, MO, RI, WI.
To accept other work.	AL, CT, FL, IL, IN, KS, ME, MA, MI, MN, MO, NH, ND, OH, SD, TX, WA, WV, WI.
Claimant's illness.	AL, AR, CO, CT, DE, FL, IL, IN, IA, KS, ME, MD, MA, MN, NH (by regulation), NC, ND, SD, TN, TX, VT, WA, WV, WI, WY.
To join the armed forces.	IN, KS, OH, TN.
Reason for quitting must be work-connected.	AL, AZ, AR, CO, CT, DE, DC, FL, GA, ID, IL, IN, IA, KS, KY, LA, ME, MD, MA, MI, MN, MS, MO, MT, NH, NJ, NM, NC, ND, OK, SD, TN, TX, VT, WA, WV, WI, WY.

*Many states place limitations and qualifications on the above reasons, or make certain exceptions or additions. Check with your local unemployment office for details.

Sexual Harassment

Sexual harassment, or unwelcome advances, is specifically cited as good cause for leaving employment in the UI laws of California, Illinois, Kansas, Massachusetts, Minnesota, Rhode Island, and Wisconsin. The fact that sexual harassment is illegal means that it probably is considered good cause for leaving your job in all states. However, be aware that benefits will not be allowed automatically. You should be prepared to prove harassment, and to show not only that you took steps to correct the situation, but that you took the *appropriate* steps. In one case, a woman in a state other than the seven listed above was continually harassed by her supervisor. She went to his boss, complained, and then quit. She was disqualified for benefits because the company personnel manual specifically instructed employees to report all infractions to the personnel officer, not to the offending person's superior.

Because sexual harassment is illegal, it's important that you look beyond the issue of your eligibility for UI benefits. If you are a victim of sexual harassment, be sure to document all instances, including witnesses, if any, and to take all the appropriate steps to correct the situation. Then, if the situation is not corrected, take legal action whether or not you decide to leave your job.

Retirement

If you voluntarily retired because you had achieved the necessary age and years of service to do so, it is very likely that you will be disqualified from receiving benefits. However, it may be considered good cause to leave if your only alternative to retirement would have been termination due to reduction in force, office reorganization, or similar reasons. (Many employers offer early retirement incentives when they are trimming staff.)

If you retired on disability, it is probable that you will not be disqualified. However, the fact that you have a disability will call into question your ability to work at another job.

Most states will not consider a forced retirement to be a voluntary separation, so if you were forced to retire, it is unlikely you will be disqualified from receiving benefits. Eight states—California, Colorado, Indiana, Massachusetts, Minnesota, Missouri, Rhode Island, and Wisconsin—have laws that specifically cite forced retirement as good cause for leaving work.

Resignation in Lieu of Termination

If you left your job because termination was likely, your qualification for UI benefits will depend on the reason for the termination. If you were to be terminated due to a reason that is not disqualifying, you will receive benefits, as most states treat forced resignations as involuntary separations. However, you must be prepared to establish that termination was imminent—that is, that you were told by your employer, or by a representative with the authority to terminate employment, that you would be terminated if you did not resign.

Be aware that a warning that work performance or attendance must improve is not considered notice of imminent dismissal, because termination can be avoided through improved performance or attendance. Also note that it is not advisable to leave employment simply because of negative evaluations or rumored layoffs.

Pro Forma Resignations

A *pro forma resignation*—that is, a resignation "as a matter of form"—is a requested or required resignation that is not voluntary. Perhaps the best way to define this type of situation is to offer examples. Many people serving on the executive staff of corporations or governmental entities serve "at the pleasure" of the executive officer, meaning that they can be dismissed at any time.

Often, such people submit an undated resignation along with the employment agreement. Then, at any time the executive officer no longer wants this person on staff, he or she resigns. Given that the reason for this person's termination is not misconduct on his or her part, the resignation usually does not result in disqualification for UI benefits.

Another example of pro forma resignation involves the adult dependents of service members working on bases and installations outside the United States. The Department of Defense reserves some civilian jobs for such dependents. When the service member is transferred to another base or back to the United States, the dependent is required to leave the base—and his or her employment—within a specified period of time.

Our final example is one in which a worker's employment is contingent on an event or occurrence over which he or she does not have complete control—for instance, passing the bar examination or being made a partner in the firm.

It is unlikely that a claimant would be disqualified for resigning in situations such as those just discussed. However, if you find yourself in this position, it is absolutely essential that you explain *why* you were required to resign. You should never make the assumption that the UI staff knows the particulars of your employment situation or that your former employer will explain it to the staff.

Seeking or Accepting Other Work

If you left your job in order to seek other employment but the second job did not materialize, leaving you unemployed, it probably will not be considered good cause. However, if you requested leave to search for work or to attend job interviews, and your request was denied, you may be able to establish that you had good cause to resign. Unemployment office staff usually consider whether the employment left was secure, whether you had leave rights, and what reason the employer had for denying leave. In other words, the staff should look at the harm that would have occurred had you not left, and at any steps you took to resolve the problem before leaving.

In most states that have work-connected provisions—that is, states that require that the reason for leaving be connected with the work or attributable to the employer—you will not be able to establish good cause if you left employment to accept another job and that job did not materialize. Your reason for leaving must be connected with the employment that you left.

Table 4.1 shows those states whose laws allow benefits for

claimants who leave work to accept other employment. If you are filing against one of these states, be prepared to establish that the offer of other employment was genuine and firm. You may have to submit a written statement to that effect from the prospective employer. At the very least, you should establish that you and the prospective employer had agreed on such essentials as salary, duties, and starting date. If the resignation you submitted was based on anything less concrete, it is probable that you will be disqualified from receiving benefits.

Joining the Armed Forces

Four states—Indiana, Kansas, Ohio, and Tennessee—may consider it good cause to voluntarily leave a job to join the Armed Forces. Presumably, you would have to establish that you had clear and concrete expectations of being inducted into the services before you left your employment. Documentation of why induction into the Armed Forces did not occur might be required.

Career Advancement

If you left your employment because it didn't offer an opportunity for career advancement or because you didn't receive an expected promotion, you will probably be disqualified from receiving benefits. Many workers accept employment at an entry or clerical level while gaining the education, credentials, or experience needed to move up. Once they fulfill this need, they naturally feel that they should be promoted, and that if the promotion doesn't come through, they are justified in leaving to gain employment elsewhere.

Although your resignation may have been justified, your employer was under no obligation to promote you simply because you had become more qualified. The need for career advancement is considered good cause for seeking other employment, but not necessarily good cause for leaving.

Job Dissatisfaction

Like career advancement, general job dissatisfaction—the dislike of superiors, co-workers, or job duties, or a feeling of burnout or boredom—is usually not considered good cause for quitting a job, although it is good cause for looking for another job. The controlling factor—that is, the test that will be applied—is whether there would have been compelling or immediate harm posed to you if you had continued employment until another job could be found.

Illness, Physical Restrictions, and Pregnancy

As we explained on page 68, this is one of the reasons for leaving that is most likely to be cited in statutory provisions as being good cause. If your employment caused or aggravated a medical condition, you may be judged as having had good cause for leaving your job. Even if the condition was not caused by the employment, the reason may be considered good cause if the condition prevented you from performing your job. Of course, you must be prepared to supply medical certification establishing that this was the case.

Of course, provisions vary from state to state regarding this cause for leaving work. For example, although the District of Columbia requires work-connected cause for leaving employment, the regulations state that a claimant will not be disqualified if he or she left employment because of a physical disability—whether or not the disability was caused by the work—if it can be established that the claimant provided the employer with medical certification prior to leaving. The same regulation allows resignation due to a condition that was aggravated by the work, although it cautions that the person's ability to do other work must be established, and, again, that the employer must have been given medical certification before the claimant resigned. The purpose of the stipulation regarding written medical certification is to allow the employer to make any adjustment of job duties that would allow for the medical condition or limitations.

Another provision of D.C.'s regulations provides that pregnancy will be treated like any other voluntary separation due to medical conditions. Prior to 1975, many states automatically held women ineligible for UI benefits if they were pregnant, arguing that they were not able to work. After a U.S. Supreme Court decision ruled that these practices were discriminatory, many states changed their laws to omit specific references to pregnancy. For this reason, cases involving pregnancy are usually adjudicated in the same manner as are those involving any other medical condition.

Table 4.1 shows those states that have provisions which allow benefits when a claimant has left employment due to illness. If you resigned due to illness or pregnancy, speak to a UI representative in the state against which you are filing to learn about the regulations applicable in that state.

Lack of Transportation

Lack of transportation may be considered good cause in rural areas not served by public transportation. It is less likely to be deemed good cause in urban areas where there is adequate public transportation. Consideration may also be given to whether the responsibility for providing transportation was yours or that of the employer, as well as to the cause of the loss of transportation. For example, it would probably be considered good cause to leave if the co-worker who normally provided you with transportation would not or could not continue to do so, especially if the job required commuting and you had exhausted other possibilities. Often, consideration is also given to the commuting patterns in your work jurisdiction.

The Reduction of Salary or Work Hours

If you left your job because of a substantial reduction in salary, it probably will be considered good cause. Consideration will be given to your salary rate before and after the reduction, and to the usual rate of pay in your occupation and labor market. Work-hour reduction may sound like the same issue as salary reduction, but bear in mind that—depending on the salary range and on the state's formula for benefit reduction due to part-time earnings—the claimant with reduced hours may qualify for partial unemployment benefits. (Don't worry! We will discuss this benefit reduction on page 181.) On the other hand, you will probably not qualify for partial benefits if only your salary, and not your hours, has been reduced.

Many states have established guidelines to define what is considered a substantial reduction. For instance, North Carolina will not disqualify you for leaving work due to a permanent reduction in full-time work hours of more than 20 percent, or a reduction in pay of more than 15 percent. In many states, quitting is considered good cause when wages are reduced 10 percent or more. Wisconsin requires a one-third reduction before it considers leaving good cause.

Please note that whether we are speaking of the reduction of hours or the reduction of salary, we are speaking of *involuntary* reductions. It is unlikely that you will be held eligible for UI benefits, even on a partial basis, if you *choose* to work part-time for your own personal reasons.

The issue of salary and work-hour reductions often becomes a "hot" topic during recessions, when many employers are faced with the option of either making reductions or closing. If you must choose between salary reduction and resignation, be sure to carefully examine the alternatives. There may be other benefits associated with your job—health insurance, sick leave, pension equity, and seniority rights, for instance—that you will lose while claiming

UI benefits. Moreover, during a recession it is, of course, difficult to find another position, as other employers are being affected by the same conditions that prompted your employer to make reductions.

Working Conditions and Environmental Concerns

If your working conditions were not suitable or if they posed a threat to your safety and health, this may be considered good cause for leaving employment. However, while it is reasonable to expect your employer to supply you with a safe work place, you will not be held eligible for benefits if you left your job because of working conditions that were totally beyond your employer's control, or if the hazardous conditions were intrinsic to—that is, an essential part of—your occupation, as is the case with fire fighters and police officers.

If conditions changed during the course of your employment, it may be determined that you had good cause to leave. New York State, for instance, has ruled that voluntary resignation is not in itself disqualifying if the circumstances that developed in the course of employment would have given the worker just cause to refuse the job in the first place.

If you left a job because of unsafe working conditions, be prepared to demonstrate what harm would have occurred if you had remained on the job, and what steps were taken to correct the problem. You may have to document the threat with safety reports, police or fire department citations, or other records. If you left employment simply because you did not *like* your work surroundings, then whether or not the problem was caused by changed conditions, you will probably be disqualified from receiving benefits under any state law.

Breach of Employment Agreement

It may be considered good cause for leaving work if your employer broke the original employment agreement. You should be prepared to prove what the original agreement was, and to explain what the potential harm would have been if you had not left his or her employment.

Attending School or Training

Unless your state is not a cause-connected-with-work state, or there is a statutory provision governing the issue, it is probable that you will be disqualified if you left employment to enter school or training. The laws of six states—Colorado, Connecticut, Maryland,

Texas, Washington, and West Virginia—specify disqualification for this. In Washington State, the disqualification applies if the claimant is registered at a school that provides twelve or more hours a week of instruction. In some states, there are statutory exceptions for people who leave work to attend approved training—that is, training arranged by or through the state's Employment Security Agency.

If you are still attending school or training at the time you file your claim, there will be the added issue of your availability for work. Nineteen states—Alaska, California, Connecticut, Idaho, Illinois, Iowa, Kansas, Louisiana, Minnesota, Montana, Nebraska, New Jersey, New Mexico, North Carolina, North Dakota, Ohio, Oklahoma, Utah, and Washington—have provisions that disqualify or hold the claimant ineligible because of unavailability for work during periods when he or she is attending school. In Illinois, Kansas, Louisiana, Minnesota, Montana, New Jersey, North Carolina, and Utah, the disqualification is continued through vacation periods. There are rather broad exceptions to these provisions. For instance, in California, the ineligibility is not required for students who have worked part-time and are available for part-time employment. In Arkansas, it is not applicable to a student who worked thirty hours per week while attending school during previous terms, and whose current academic schedule does not preclude full-time work. This exception is similar to the exceptions of several of the eighteen states. They basically say that the claimant will not necessarily be held ineligible if his or her being a student did not cause the condition of unemployment and will not interfere with his or her availability for work. If you are a student or if you plan on becoming a student in one of the nineteen states just listed, you may wish to consult your state unemployment office for the exact wording of the provisions and exceptions in your state. The subject of availability for work and how it applies to eligibility for benefits will be discussed in Chapter 5.

Discrimination

Discrimination on the basis of race, gender, religion, national origin, or disability that does not interfere with job performance is illegal. If you left employment because of any of these types of discrimination, it will probably be deemed good cause. You must be prepared to establish that discrimination occurred, and that you took the appropriate actions to remedy the situation before you left. Keep in mind that because this discrimination is illegal, legal action should be taken in all such cases.

Marital or Family Responsibilities

Unless your state has a statutory exception governing this issue, or you are filing against a state that allows benefits for causes not connected with work, you will not receive benefits if you left work because you married or divorced, causing a change of residence; if your spouse relocated, causing a change of residence (some states do allow benefits if the spouse relocated due to employment, and the relocating spouse is the major family support); if you left work to care for children or aged parents; or for many other good and compelling reasons related to family responsibilities. Six states will specifically disqualify you if you left work to marry. These states include Colorado, Idaho (an exception is made if the claimant is the main support of the family at the time of the filing), Nevada (an exception is made if the claimant is the main support of the family at the time of the filing), New York, Ohio, and West Virginia. Eight states—Colorado, Idaho, Maryland, Massachusetts, Nevada, Texas, Utah, and Virginia—will disqualify you if you left work to move with your spouse. And six states—Idaho, Mississippi, Nevada, Ohio, Washington, and West Virginia—will disqualify you if you left work to perform marital, domestic, or filial duties.

Even if you are filing against a state that allows benefits for reasons that are not work-connected, you should be prepared to document your reason for leaving. In addition, if you quit because of family responsibilities, you should be prepared to show that you are now available for other work.

Penalties for Quitting Without Good Cause

It may seem to you that we are spending a lot of time discussing voluntary resignations. But the fact of the matter is that this is the most common reason for disqualification, and that it is one of the issues most asked about by UI claimants. The reason for this may be that voluntary separation is the situation over which the worker exercises the most control.

In all but five states—Alaska, Colorado, Maryland, Nebraska, and Wisconsin—the disqualification for voluntarily leaving is durational; to qualify for benefits, the claimant must return to work for a specified period of time and/or earn a specific amount, and then be separated through no fault of his or her own. Eight states—Alabama, Alaska, Colorado, Indiana, Louisiana, Nebraska, North Carolina, and Oregon—also reduce the potential benefit amount of the claim.

Table 4.2 gives a state-by-state breakdown of the disqualifications imposed for voluntarily leaving a job. The first part of the table shows those states that postpone benefits for either a fixed number of weeks or a variable number of weeks. In Alaska, for instance, the disqualification begins with the week in which the claimant left work and lasts for five weeks, and the term of the disqualifiction can be ended if the claimant returns to employment and earns eight times the weekly benefit amount of the claim. In Colorado, the disqualification begins with the week the claim was filed and lasts for ten weeks. In Maryland, the disqualification can last anywhere from five to ten weeks, the length being at the discretion of the claims examiner.

Part 2 of Table 4.2 shows those states with durational disqualifications—states in which the claimant is disqualified for the duration of that period of unemployment, and must find another job and earn a specified amount of money and/or work for a specified period of time before being eligible for UI benefits. The length of durational disqualifications is expressed as a length of employment, usually stated as days or weeks, as well as an amount of earnings, stated as a number multiplied by the weekly benefit amount of the claim. In Delaware and the District of Columbia, for instance, there are both wage and length-of-employment requirements. In Delaware, the claimant must return to work of at least four weeks' duration and earn at least four times the weekly benefit amount of his or her claim. In D.C., employment must be of at least ten weeks' duration, although these weeks need not be consecutive, and earnings must be at least ten times the weekly benefit amount.

Part 3 of Table 4.2 shows the amount by which the maximum potential benefit amount can be reduced in those eight states that make benefit reductions a part of the disqualification. In most states, this amount is expressed as a multiple of the weekly benefit amount. For example, in Alabama, the potential benefit amount can be reduced by an amount that's six to twelve times the weekly benefit amount. In some states, though, the reduction is expressed as a percentage. In Indiana, for instance, the potential benefit amount is reduced by 25 percent; in Louisiana, by 50 percent!

Discharge for Misconduct

Another reason for disqualification is discharge for misconduct. People who are discharged for misconduct have not necessarily done something illegal or immoral. Rather, they have committed *industrial misconduct*—that is, they have willfully and deliberately violated or disregarded standards of behavior that an employer has the right to expect from his or her employees. Other definitions of misconduct mention an intentional or substantial disre-

Table 4.2 Penalties for Voluntarily Leaving Employment

State	1. Benefits Postponed for Specified Number of Weeks
AK	Benefits are postponed for 5 weeks, beginning after week claimant left work. Disqualification is terminated if claimant returns to work and earns at least 8 x weekly benefit amount. Disqualifications are applicable to other than last separation if employment or time period subsequent to separation does not satisfy potential disqualification. (See #3 for additional penalty.)
CO	Benefits are postponed for 10 weeks, beginning after week of filing. (See #3 for additional penalty.)
MD	Benefits are postponed for 5–10 weeks, beginning after week claimant left work. The durational disqualification will be imposed if a valid circumstance does not exist. Satisfaction of type not assessed does not serve to end assessed disqualification. Disqualifications are applicable to other than last separation if employment or time period subsequent to separation does not satisfy potential disqualification. (See #2 for additional penalty.)
NE	Benefits are postponed for 7–10 weeks, beginning after week claimant left work. Reduction or forfeiture of benefits is applicable to separations from any base-period employer. An individual who leaves work to accept a better job will be disqualified for the week of leaving and one additional week. (See #3 for additional penalty.)
WI	Durational disqualification is not applied if claimant left employment because of transfer to work paying less than 2/3 immediately preceding wage rate. However, claimant is ineligible for the week of separation and the next 4 following weeks. (See #2 for additional penalty.)

State	2. Terms of Durational Disqualification
AL	Claimant must earn 10 x weekly benefit amount. Preceding separation may be considered if last employment was not considered bona fide work. (See #3 for additional penalty.)
AZ	Claimant must earn 5 x weekly benefit amount.
AR	Claimant must return to work of 30 days' duration.
CA	Claimant must earn 5 x weekly benefit amount.
CT	Claimant must earn 10 x weekly benefit amount. Voluntary retiree is disqualified for duration of unemployment and until 40 x weekly benefit amount is earned.
DE	Claimant must return to work of 4 weeks' duration and earn 4 x weekly benefit amount.
DC	Claimant must return to work of 10 weeks' duration and earn 10 x weekly benefit amount. Disqualifications are applicable to other than last separation if employment was less than 30 days' duration, unless on an additional claim.
FL	Claimant must earn 17 x weekly benefit amount. Disqualifications are applicable to other than last separation if employment or time period subsequent to separation does not satisfy potential disqualification.

State	2. Terms of Durational Disqualification
GA	Claimant must earn 10 x weekly benefit amount.
HI	Claimant must earn 5 x weekly benefit amount.
ID	Claimant must earn 16 x weekly benefit amount.
IL	Claimant must earn weekly benefit amount in each of 4 weeks.
IN	Claimant must earn weekly benefit amount in each of 8 weeks. (See #3 for additional penalty.)
IA	Claimant must earn 10 x weekly benefit amount. Disqualifications are applicable to other than last separation if employment or time period subsequent to separation does not satisfy potential disqualification.
KS	Claimant must earn 3 x weekly benefit amount.
KY	Claimant must return to covered work of 10 weeks' duration and earn 10 x weekly benefit amount. Reduction or forfeiture of benefits is applicable to separations from any base-period employer.
LA	Claimant must earn 10 x weekly benefit amount. (See #3 for additional penalty.)
ME	Claimant must earn 4 x weekly benefit amount. Disqualifications are applicable to most recent previous separation if last work was not in usual trade or was intermittent. Claimant is disqualified for duration of unemployment if voluntarily retired or retired as a result of recognized employer policy under which he receives pension and until claimant earns 6 x weekly benefit amount.
MD	Claimant must earn 15 x weekly benefit amount. The durational disqualification will be imposed if a valid circumstance does not exist. However, satisfaction of type not assessed does not serve to end assessed disqualification. Disqualifications are applicable to other than last separation if employment or time period subsequent to separation does not satisfy potential disqualification. (See #1 for additional penalty.)
MA	Claimant must return to work of 8 weeks' duration and earn 8 x weekly benefit amount.
MI	Claimant must earn lesser of 7 x weekly benefit amount or 40% of state minimum hourly wage x 7. A separation determination must be made for each base-period employer, starting with the most recent one. Disqualification excludes those wages from computation.
MN	Claimant must return to work of 4 weeks' duration and earn 8 x weekly benefit amount.
MS	Claimant must earn 8 x weekly benefit amount.
MO	Claimant must earn 10 x weekly benefit amount. Disqualifications are applicable to other than last separation if employment or time period subsequent to separation does not satisfy potential disqualification.

State	2. Terms of Durational Disqualification
MT	Claimant must earn 6 x weekly benefit amount. Disqualification ends after claimant attends school for 3 consecutive months and is otherwise eligible.
NV	Claimant must earn 10 x weekly benefit amount. Claimant is disqualified for 4 weeks, beginning week claimant left work, if individual voluntarily left most recent work to enter self-employment. Claimant who left his last or next-to-last work to seek better employment will be disqualified until he secures better employment or earns remuneration in each of 10 weeks. Claimant who during the last or next-to-last work performed services for a private employer while incarcerated in a custodial or penal institution and who leaves the employment because of transfer or release from the institution is ineligible for benefits for the week of leaving and until the individual earns remuneration equal to the weekly benefit amount in each of 10 weeks.
NH	Claimant must return to covered work of 5 weeks' duration and earn 20% more than weekly benefit amount in each week.
NJ	Claimant must return to covered work of 4 weeks' duration and earn 6 x weekly benefit amount.
NM	Claimant must earn 5 x weekly benefit amount in covered work.
NY	Claimant must work 3 days in each of five weeks and earn 5 x weekly benefit amount.
NC	Claimant must return to work of 5 weeks' duration and earn 10 x weekly benefit amount. The commission may reduce permanent disqualification to a time certain but not less than 5 weeks. When permanent disqualification is changed to time certain, benefits shall be reduced by weekly benefit amount x weeks of disqualification. Disqualification is reduced if individual quits due to impending separation to the greater of 4 weeks or the period from the week of filing until the end of the week of separation. (See #3 for additional penalty.)
ND	Claimant must earn 8 x weekly benefit amount. Disqualifications are applicable to other than last separation for any employer with whom the individual earned 8 x weekly benefit amount.
OH	Claimant must return to covered work of 6 weeks' duration and earn 27.5% of the state's average weekly wage. Disqualifications are applicable to other than last separation if employment or time period subsequent to separation does not satisfy potential disqualification.
OK	Claimant must earn 10 x weekly benefit amount.
OR	Claimant must earn 4 x weekly benefit amount. (See #3 for additional penalty.)
PA	Claimant must earn 6 x weekly benefit amount.
PR	Claimant must return to work of 4 weeks' duration and earn 10 x weekly benefit amount.
RI	Claimant must return to work of 4 weeks' duration and earn 20 x minimum hourly wage in each week.

State	2. Terms of Durational Disqualification
SC	Claimant must earn 8 x weekly benefit amount.
SD	Claimant must return to covered work of 6 weeks' duration and earn weekly benefit amount in each week. Disqualifications are applicable to other than last separation if employment was of less than 30 days' duration, unless on an additional claim.
TN	Claimant must earn 10 x weekly benefit amount in covered work. Disqualifications are applicable to other than last separation for any employer with whom the individual earned 10 x weekly benefit amount.
TX	Claimant must return to work of 6 weeks' duration or earn 6 x weekly benefit amount.
UT	Claimant must earn 6 x weekly benefit amount.
VT	Claimant must earn 6 x weekly benefit amount. Claimant is disqualified for 1–6 weeks if health precludes discharge of duties of work left.
VA	Claimant must return to work of 30 days' duration. Disqualifications are applicable to last 30-day employing unit.
VI	Claimant must return to work of 4 weeks' duration and earn 4 x weekly benefit amount.
WA	Claimant must return to work of 5 weeks' duration and earn 5 x weekly benefit amount in each week.
WV	Claimant must return to work of 30 days' duration. Disqualifications are applicable to other than last separation if employment was of less than 30 days' duration, unless on an additional claim.
WI	Claimant must return to work of 4 weeks' duration and earn 4 x weekly benefit amount. (See #1 for additional penalty.)
WY	Claimant must return to work of 12 weeks' duration and earn 12 x weekly benefit amount.

State	3. Amount by Which Potential Benefits Are Reduced
AL	Benefits are reduced by 6–12 x weekly benefit amount. (See #2 for additional penalty.)
AK	Benefits are reduced by 3 x weekly benefit amount. (See #1 for additional penalty.)
CO	Benefits are reduced by 10 x weekly benefit amount. (See #1 for additional penalty.)
IN	Benefits are reduced by 25%. (See #2 for additional penalty.)
LA	Benefits are reduced by 50%. (See #2 for additional penalty.)
NE	Benefits are reduced by number of weeks of disqualification x weekly benefit amount. (See #1 for additional penalty.)

State	3. Amount by Which Potential Benefits Are Reduced
NC	The commission may reduce permanent disqualification to a time certain but not less than 5 weeks. When permanent disqualification is changed to time certain, benefits shall be reduced by weekly benefit amount x weeks of disqualification. Disqualification is reduced if an individual quits due to an impending separation to the greater of 4 weeks or the period from the week of filing until the end of the week of separation. (See #2 for additional penalty.)
OR	Benefits are reduced by 8 x weekly benefit amount. (See #2 for additional penalty.)

gard of the employer's interests or of the employee's duties and obligations, and carelessness and negligence that have been shown to such a degree, or so repeatedly, that they indicate wrongful intent. Most important to remember is that the offense or omission must have been willful—that is, the worker must have known the rule that he or she violated, and the worker's action must have been deliberate.

Following are a number of questions that serve as tests in determining whether a separation was due to misconduct. Of course, not all tests are relevant in each case. Each claims examiner should ask only those questions appropriate to the discharge that's being considered.

❑ Was the broken rule an established one, or was it made up on the spot?

❑ Was the breaking of the rule the actual cause for the discharge?

❑ Was the infraction serious enough to merit discharge?

❑ Were there extenuating circumstances?

❑ Was the act deliberate?

❑ Had a warning previously been given? (This question is not applicable in cases of gross misconduct, which is discussed on page 87.)

It is important to note that not every instance of misconduct is a violation of a written rule. Some standards of behavior are generally expected in our society and our places of work. Moreover, misconduct does not include mere inefficiency, unsatisfactory job performance, failure to perform well because of a physical or mental inability, isolated and ordinary mistakes or negligence, or good-faith errors in judgement or discretion.

Since misconduct is a violation against the employer, and since the employer is the party that makes the decision to sever the employment relationship, the employer also bears the burden of showing that a discharge is due to misconduct. Some states are more lenient than others in the test of this burden. Due to a court ruling, the District of Columbia requires that the employer show not only that the claimant knew or should have known of the violated rule—that is, that the worker had received an employee conduct handbook or a previous warning—but also that the rule was a reasonable one and was consistently and uniformly enforced. In most states, an employer must also show that he or she made some attempt to prevent or change the behavior that led to the discharge, and that the claimant failed to respond to these opportunities.

We have mentioned that misconduct is generally connected to work—that is, to occurrences in the course of work or on the work premises. But not all instances of misconduct have to occur during work hours or on the job premises. For instance, a law enforcement official who commits a crime that's totally unconnected with his or her job may be discharged for misconduct—and, therefore, disqualified for UI benefits—because as a law enforcement officer, he or she has sworn to uphold the law.

Following are some actions that often lead to discharge for misconduct. Please note that the listing, as well as the explanation of each reason, is not meant to be exhaustive, but is designed to show what types of actions may or may not ultimately lead to disqualification.

Attendance Violations

Excessive and repeated tardiness, absence, or failure to follow established procedures for notifying the employer when you are going to be late or absent is generally considered to be misconduct. Consideration may be given to the reasons for the absence or tardiness, the number of times it occurred, and the extent of the infraction. *Absence without leave*—failure to gain the employer's permission to take leave during regular working hours—and *abandonment of position*—walking off the job or failing to come to work without prior notice—are nearly always considered misconduct, as they leave the employer no chance to counsel the worker and no course of action other than dismissal.

Insubordination

Insubordination—failure or refusal to follow the order or instructions of a superior—is considered misconduct. Generally, it must be shown that the order or instructions were reasonable, and that the refusal was deliberate. Of course, it is often difficult to establish that failure to perform was deliberate. If a person was not able to meet performance standards, regarding either quality or speed, that is usually not considered misconduct. However, misconduct can be established whenever there is deliberate negligence or sabotage of a work product.

Rudeness to Clients or Co-Workers

As the nation—indeed, the world—moves toward a service economy, interpersonal relationships with clients and co-workers are becoming increasingly important. As a result, deliberate rudeness or profanity can be cause for dismissal, and may be considered misconduct.

Theft or Misuse of the Employer's Property or Time

Just as it is illegal to take anyone's property, it is considered misconduct to take an employer's property, whether the property is material goods or simply time that's misused by conducting one's personal life on the employer's time clock. "Borrowing" company vehicles without permission, making unauthorized use of equipment such as copy machines, running up long-distance phone bills, using company time for personal visits—all can be considered misconduct. Depending on the value of the item taken or misused, civil or criminal charges can be filed in addition to the discharge.

Fighting

Except in the case of self-defense, fighting on the job—whether or not it is provoked, and whether or not injury results—is generally considered misconduct, and can lead to discharge and disqualification from UI benefits. Indeed, fighting is often considered gross misconduct.

The Use of Controlled Substances

Because it impairs physical and mental abilities, using controlled substances at the work place, or reporting for work under the influence of such substances, is widely regarded as misconduct—or even gross misconduct—depending on the state and the substance. In most states, to establish misconduct, the employer need not show that the substance was consumed on the premises. He or she need show only that the worker's condition indicated use. And because the use of certain substances is illegal, more serious repercussions may result from this charge.

The Falsification of Records

The falsification of applications or personnel records is another circumstance that can be considered misconduct, depending on the occupation and the nature of the record that was falsified or misrepresented. Many occupations that involve the handling of money, securities, or others' records require security clearances or bonding. For instance, employees of banks and investment firms must be cleared of any criminal charges, while insurance brokers may require bonding. Other highly specialized or technical occupations—such as medical doctors, electricians, and plumbers—may require specific training or licenses. If it is established that you falsified or misrepresented records relevant to your job requirements, disqualification from UI benefits is likely.

Penalties for Misconduct

The penalty for being fired for misconduct is usually the same as, or similar to, the penalty for quitting without good cause. However, some states that impose a durational disqualification, or "new work" requirement, for voluntarily quitting merely impose a term disqualification or postponement of benefits for misconduct. These states include Alabama, Alaska, Arkansas, Colorado, the District of Columbia, Maryland, Missouri, Nebraska, New Jersey, North Carolina, South Carolina, Vermont, and West Virginia. Florida imposes both types of disqualification.

Table 4.3 shows the types of disqualifications imposed for misconduct in each state. As you can see, the first part of the table shows the length of the disqualification in those states that postpone benefits for either a set number of weeks or a variable number of weeks. In Alaska, for instance, the disqualification for misconduct begins with the week the disqualifying act occurred and lasts for five weeks. In Alabama, the disqualification begins with the week of occurrence and lasts from three to seven weeks, the length of the disqualification being at the discretion of the claims examiner.

Part 2 of Table 4.3 shows the amount of earnings—usually expressed as a number multiplied by the weekly benefit amount—and/or the length of the employment period needed for the claimant to requalify after a durational disqualification. In Delaware, for instance, the claimant must return to employment of at least four weeks' duration and earn at least four times the weekly benefit amount.

Part 3 of the table shows those states that reduce the maximum potential entitlement along with the term or durational disqualification. For instance, Alabama—which has a variable-term disqualification of three to seven weeks—also reduces the potential claim entitlement by an amount arrived at by multiplying the weekly benefit amount by a number equal to the length of the disqualification. So if a claimant is disqualified for five weeks, the claim will be reduced by five times the weekly benefit amount. Indiana reduces the maximum potential benefit amount by 25 percent; Louisiana, by 50 percent.

States listed in Part 4 cite specific disqualification provisions for disciplinary suspensions in their state laws. Alabama, for example, disqualifies the worker for one to three weeks, beginning with the week in which the action that caused the suspension occurred. Florida disqualifies for the duration of the suspension. And Georgia imposes the same penalty as that imposed for *discharge* for misconduct. Other states may also impose a penalty when a person who is suspended for disciplinary reasons files a claim. These states specify the disqualification in their laws.

Discharge for Gross Misconduct

Thirty-one states define certain actions as *gross misconduct*—usually defined as a crime committed in connection with work—and impose stringent penalties for these actions. Examples of gross misconduct are theft, fighting on the job, assault, intoxication including use of illegal substances, arson, sabotage, and willful disregard of safety regulations. Those states that recognize gross misconduct are Alabama, Arkansas, Colorado, the District of Columbia, Florida, Georgia, Illinois, Indiana, Iowa, Kansas, Kentucky, Louisiana, Maine, Maryland, Michigan, Minnesota, Missouri, Montana, Nebraska, Nevada, New Hampshire, New Jersey, New York, North Dakota, Ohio, Oregon, South Carolina, Utah, Vermont, Washington, and West Virginia. In a few of these states, the disqualification lasts for one year. In other states, it lasts for the duration of the claimant's unemployment. In most states, there is a reduction of the maximum potential benefit amount or cancelation, in whole or in part, of the wage credits. This means that prior earnings cannot be used to compute monetary eligibility. When complete cancelation occurs, the claim is no longer valid, and all benefit rights are canceled.

Table 4.3 Penalties for Discharge for Misconduct

State	1. Benefits Postponed for Specified Number of Weeks
AL	Benefits are postponed for 3–7 weeks, beginning after week disqualifying act occurred. Disqualification is applicable to preceding separation if last employment is not considered bona fide work. (See #3 and #4 for additional penalties.)
AK	Benefits are postponed for 5 weeks, beginning after week disqualifying act occurred. Disqualification is terminated if claimant returns to work and earns 8 x weekly benefit amount. Disqualification is applicable to other than last separation if employment or time period subsequent to separation does not satisfy potential disqualification. If claimant is discharged for commission of felony or theft in connection with work, claimant is disqualified for 1–51 weeks, or until claimant earns 20 x weekly benefit amount. (See #3 and #4 for additional penalties.)
AR	Benefits are postponed for 7 weeks, beginning after week disqualifying act occurred. (See #4 for additional penalty.)
CO	Benefits are postponed for 10 weeks, beginning after week of filing. Claimant will be eligible for benefits if separated due to use of alcohol or controlled substance on or off the job if claimant admits to addiction and substantiates addiction with a licensed physician's statement, and if claimant commences participation in an approved program of corrective action to deal with addiction. (See #3 for additional penalty.)
DC	Benefits are postponed for 7 weeks, beginning after week of filing. Disqualification is applicable to last 30-day employing unit on new claims and to most recent employer on additional claims. (See #3 for additional penalty.)
FL	Benefits are postponed for 1–52 weeks, beginning after week disqualifying act occurred. Both term and duration-of-unemployment disqualifications are imposed. Disqualification is applicable to other than last separation if employment or time period subsequent to the separation does not satisfy a potential disqualification. (See #2 and #4 for additional penalties.)
MD	Benefits are postponed for 5–10 weeks, beginning after week disqualifying act occurred. Disqualification is applicable to other than last separation if employment or time period subsequent to the separation does not satisfy a potential disqualification. (See #4 for additional penalty.)
MO	Benefits are postponed for 4–16 weeks, beginning after week of filing. Disqualification is terminated if claimant returns to work and earns 8 x weekly benefit amount. Disqualification is applicable to other than last separation if employment or time period subsequent to the separation does not satisfy a potential disqualification. Weeks of disqualification must be otherwise compensable weeks.(See #4 for additional penalty.)
NE	Benefits are postponed for 7–10 weeks, beginning after week disqualifying act occurred. Reduction or forfeiture of benefits is applicable to separations from any base-period employer. (See #3 for additional penalty.)
NJ	Benefits are postponed for 5 weeks, beginning after week disqualifying act occurred.

State	1. Benefits Postponed for Specified Number of Weeks
NC	Commission may reduce permanent disqualification to a time certain but not less than 5 weeks. When permanent disqualification is changed to time certain, benefits shall be reduced by an amount determined by multiplying number of weeks of disqualification by weekly benefit amount. The state disqualifies claimant for substantial fault that is connected with work but not rising to level of misconduct. Disqualification varies from 4–13 weeks, depending on circumstances. (See #2, #3, and #4 for additional penalties.)
SC	Benefits are postponed for 5–26 weeks, beginning after week of filing. (See #3 for additional penalty.)
VT	Benefits are postponed for 6–12 weeks, beginning after week following filing of claim.
WV	Benefits are postponed for 6 weeks, beginning after week disqualifying act occurred. Disqualification is applicable to last 30-day employing unit on new claims, and to most recent employer on additional claims. (See #3 for additional penalty.)

State	2. Terms of Durational Disqualification
AZ	Claimant must earn 5 x weekly benefit amount.
CA	Claimant must earn 5 x weekly benefit amount.
CT	Claimant must earn 10 x weekly benefit amount.
DE	Claimant must return to work of 4 weeks' duration and earn 4 x weekly benefit amount.
FL	Claimant must earn 17 x weekly benefit amount. Both term and duration-of-unemployment disqualifications are imposed. Disqualification is applicable to other than last separation if employment or time period subsequent to the separation does not satisfy a potential disqualification. (See #1 and #4 for additional penalties.)
GA	Claimant must earn 10 x weekly benefit amount. Claimant shall be disqualified if separated from training approved by commission due to claimant's failure to abide by rules of training facility. (See #3 and #4 for additional penalties.)
HI	Claimant must earn 5 x weekly benefit amount.
ID	Claimant must earn 16 x weekly benefit amount. Disqualification is applicable to other than last separation if employment or time period subsequent to the separation does not satisfy a potential disqualification.
IL	Claimant must earn weekly benefit amount in each of 4 weeks.
IN	Claimant must earn weekly benefit amount in each of 8 weeks. (See #3 for additional penalty.)
IA	Claimant must earn 10 x weekly benefit amount. (See #4 for additional penalty.)

State	2. Terms of Durational Disqualification
KS	Claimant must earn 3 x weekly benefit amount. Claimant will be disqualified for use of, possession of, or impairment caused by nonprescribed controlled substance or alcoholic or malt beverage if evidence shows such abuse.
KY	Claimant must return to covered work of 10 weeks' duration and earn 10 x weekly benefit amount. Reduction or forfeiture of benefits is applicable to separations from any base-period employer.
LA	Claimant must earn 10 x weekly benefit amount. Claimant shall be disqualified for use of illegal drugs on or off the job. (See #3 for additional penalty.)
ME	Claimant must earn 4 x weekly benefit amount.
MA	Claimant must return to work of 8 weeks' duration and earn 8 x weekly benefit amount. Disqualification is applicable to other than last separation if employment or time period subsequent to the separation does not satisfy a potential disqualification.
MI	Claimant must earn lesser of 7 x weekly benefit amount or 40 x state minimum hourly wage x 7. Claimant may be eligible for benefits based on wage credits earned subsequent to disqualification.
MN	Claimant must return to work of 4 weeks' duration and earn 8 x weekly benefit amount. (See #4 for additional penalty.)
MS	Claimant must earn 8 x weekly benefit amount.
MT	Claimant must earn 8 x weekly benefit amount.
NV	Claimant must earn weekly benefit amount in each of 15 weeks.
NH	Claimant must return to work of 5 weeks' duration and earn 20% more than weekly benefit amount in each week. (See #4 for additional penalty.)
NM	Claimant must earn 5 x weekly benefit amount in covered work.
NY	Claimant must work 3 days in each of five weeks and earn 5 x weekly benefit amount.
NC	Claimant must return to work of 5 weeks' duration and earn 10 x weekly benefit amount. (See #1, #3, and #4 for additional penalties.)
ND	Claimant must earn 10 x weekly benefit amount. Disqualification is applicable to any employer with whom the claimant earned 8 x weekly benefit amount. (See #4 for additional penalty.)
OH	Claimant must return to covered work of 6 weeks' duration and earn 27.5% of state's average weekly wage in each week. Disqualification is applicable to other than last separation if employment or time period subsequent to the separation does not satisfy a potential disqualification. (See #4 for additional penalty.)
OK	Claimant must earn 10 x weekly benefit amount. Claimant shall be disqualified for refusing to undergo drug or alcohol testing or for testing positive for drugs or alcohol.

State	2. Terms of Durational Disqualification
OR	Claimant must earn 4 x weekly benefit amount. (See #3 and #4 for additional penalties.)
PA	Claimant must earn 6 x weekly benefit amount. (See #4 for additional penalty.)
PR	Claimant must return to work of 4 weeks' duration and earn 10 x weekly benefit amount. (See #4 for additional penalty.)
RI	Claimant must earn 20 x minimum hourly wage in each of 4 weeks.
SD	Claimant must return to covered work of 6 weeks' duration and earn weekly benefit amount in each week. Disqualification is applicable to last 30-day employing unit on new claims, and to most recent employer on additional claims. (See #4 for additional penalty.)
TN	Claimant must earn 10 x weekly benefit amount. Disqualification is applicable to any employer with whom the claimant earned 10 x weekly benefit amount.
TX	Claimant must return to work of 6 weeks' duration or earn 6 x weekly benefit amount.
UT	Claimant must earn 6 x weekly benefit amount in covered work.
VA	Claimant must return to work of 30 days' duration. Disqualification is applicable to last 30-day employing unit.
VI	Claimant must return to work of 4 weeks' duration and earn 4 x weekly benefit amount. (See #4 for additional penalty.)
WA	Claimant must return to work of 5 weeks' duration and earn weekly benefit amount in each week. (See #4 for additional penalty.)
WI	Claimant must return to work of 7 weeks' duration and earn 14 x weekly benefit amount. (See #3 for additional penalty.)
WY	Claimant must return to work of 12 weeks' duration and earn 12 x weekly benefit amount.

State	3. Amount by Which Potential Benefits Are Reduced
AL	Benefits are reduced by number of weeks of disqualification x weekly benefit amount. (See #1 and #4 for additional penalties.)
AK	Benefits are reduced by 3 x weekly benefit amount. (See #1 and #4 for additional penalties.)
CO	Benefits are reduced by 10 x weekly benefit amount. Reduction due to a single act shall not reduce potential benefits to less that one week. (See #1 for additional penalty.)
DC	Benefits are reduced by 8 x weekly benefit amount. (See #1 for additional penalty.)
GA	Benefits are reduced by 10 x weekly benefit amount. (See #2 and #4 for additional penalties.)

State	3. Amount by Which Potential Benefits Are Reduced
IN	Benefits are reduced by 25%. (See #2 for additional penalty.)
LA	Benefits are reduced by 50%. (See #2 for additional penalty.)
NE	Benefits are reduced by number of weeks of disqualification x weekly benefit amount. Reduction or forfeiture of benefits is applicable to separations from any base-period employer. (See #1 for additional penalty.)
NC	Commission may reduce permanent disqualification to a time certain but not less than 5 weeks. When permanent disqualification is changed to time certain, benefits shall be reduced by weekly benefit amount x weeks of disqualification. (See #1, #2, and #4 for additional penalties.)
OR	Benefits are reduced by 8 x weekly benefit amount. (See #2 and #4 for additional penalties.)
SC	Benefits are reduced by number of weeks of disqualification x weekly benefit amount. (See #1 for additional penalty.)
WV	Benefits are reduced by 6 x weekly benefit amount. Deduction is recredited if claimant returns to covered work for 30 days during benefit year. (See #1 for additional penalty.)
WI	Benefit rights based on any work involved are canceled. Claimant may be eligible for benefits based on wage credits earned subsequent to disqualification. (See #2 for additional penalty.)

State	4. Benefits Postponed for Disciplinary Suspension
AL	Benefits are postponed for 1–3 weeks, beginning after week disqualifying act occurred.
AK	Penalty is same as that for discharge for misconduct.
AR	Benefits are postponed for lesser of 8 weeks or duration of suspension.
CT	Penalty is same as that for discharge for misconduct.
FL	Disqualification is for duration of suspension.
GA	Penalty is same as that for discharge for misconduct.
IA	Penalty is same as that for discharge for misconduct.
MD	Disqualification is for duration of suspension or until claimant earns 20 x weekly benefit amount.
MN	Disqualification is for duration of suspension.
MO	Penalty is same as that for discharge for misconduct.
NH	Disqualification is for duration of suspension.
NC	Claimant is disqualified if claim is filed at time of disciplinary suspension.
ND	Disqualification is for duration of suspension.

State	4. Benefits Postponed for Disciplinary Suspension
OH	Disqualification is for duration of suspension.
OR	Penalty is same as that for discharge for misconduct.
PA	Penalty is same as that for discharge for misconduct.
PR	Penalty is same as that for discharge for misconduct.
SD	Penalty is same as that for discharge for misconduct.
VI	Penalty is same as that for discharge for misconduct.
WA	Penalty is same as that for discharge for misconduct.
WI	Claimant is disqualified until 3 weeks have elapsed since end of week of suspension or until suspension is terminated, whichever occurs first.

Penalties for Gross Misconduct

Table 4.4 shows the types of disqualifications imposed by those states that define gross misconduct. The first part of the table shows those states that postpone benefits for a fixed or variable number of weeks. Colorado, for instance, postpones benefits for twenty-six weeks in cases of gross misconduct, and Missouri disqualifies for four to sixteen weeks, beginning after the week the claim is filed.

Part 2 of Table 4.4 shows durational disqualifications, along with the amount of wages and/or period of employment needed to requalify. For instance, in Alabama, the claimant must return to employment and earn at least ten times the weekly benefit amount of his or her claim. In Arkansas, the claimant must return to work of at least ten weeks' duration and earn the weekly benefit amount in each of those weeks.

In Part 3, you'll see those states that reduce benefits or cancel wage credits. Alabama, for instance, cancels wage credits earned during the employment in which the gross conduct was committed. And many states cancel all prior wage credits for gross misconduct.

Refusing Suitable Work

Another reason for disqualification is the refusal of suitable work. Usually, when we think of a suitable job, we think of long-term, more or less permanent employment. However, most states will disqualify you for refusing even a short-term job that they consider suitable. For instance, employers have been known to tell the unemployment office that they have just one day's work waiting for the workers they just laid off. A claimant who refuses to take that one day's work may be disqualified from receiving benefits. And, naturally, the em-

Table 4.4 Penalties for Discharge for Gross Misconduct

State	1. Benefits Postponed for Specified Number of Weeks
CO	Benefits are postponed for 26 weeks. (See #3 for additional penalty.)
FL	Benefits are postponed for up to 52 weeks. (See #2 for additional penalty.)
MO	Benefits are postponed for 4–16 weeks, beginning after week of filing. Disqualification is applicable to other than last separation within 1 year preceding claim. It is agency's option to cancel all or part of wages, depending on seriousness of misconduct. Only wage credits based on work involved in misconduct are canceled.
MT	Benefits are postponed for 12 months. (See #3 for additional penalty.)
NH	Benefits are postponed for 4–26 weeks, beginning after week of discharge. If claimant is discharged for intoxication or use of drugs that interfere with work, disqualification is 4–26 weeks. If discharged for arson, sabotage, felony, or dishonesty, all prior wage credits are canceled. (See #3 for additional penalty.)
NY	Benefits are postponed for 12 months. No days of unemployment deemed to occur for following 12 months if claimant is convicted or signs statement admitting act that constitutes a felony in connection with employment.
ND	Benefits are postponed for 12 months.
SC	Benefits are postponed for 5–26 weeks, beginning after week of filing. (See #3 for additional penalty.)
UT	Benefits are postponed for 51 weeks, beginning after week of discharge. (See #2 and #3 for additional penalties.)
State	**2. Terms of Durational Disqualification**
AL	Claimant must earn 10 x weekly benefit amount. Disqualification is applicable to other than last separation from bona fide work only if employer files timely notice alleging disqualifying act. (See #3 for additional penalty.)
AR	Claimant must return to work of 10 weeks' duration and earn weekly benefit amount in each week.
DC	Claimant must return to work of 10 weeks' duration and earn 10 x weekly benefit amount.
FL	Claimant must earn 17 x weekly benefit amount. (See #1 for additional penalty.)
GA	If claimant is discharged for assault or for theft of $100 or less, claimant must earn 12 x weekly benefit amount. If claimant is discharged for property loss or damages of up to $2,000, theft of over $100, sabotage, or embezzlement, claimant must earn 16 x weekly benefit amount.
KS	Claimant must earn 8 x weekly benefit amount. (See #3 for additional penalty.)
KY	Unspecified durational disqualification is imposed.

State	2. Terms of Durational Disqualification
LA	Claimant must earn 10 x weekly benefit amount. Disqualification is applicable to other than last separation from beginning of base period if claimant is unemployed because of dishonesty in connection with employment. (See #3 for additional penalty.)
ME	Claimant must earn greater of $600 or 8 x weekly benefit amount.
MD	Claimant must earn 20 x weekly benefit amount. Claimant can also be disqualified for aggravated misconduct.
MI	Claimant must earn lesser of 7 x weekly benefit amount or 40 x state minimum hourly wage x 7. Claimant may be eligible for benefits based on wage credits earned subsequent to disqualification. (See #3 for additional penalty.)
MN	At discretion of commissioner, claimant is disqualified until he or she returns to insured work of 4 weeks' duration and earns 4 x weekly benefit amount, or for remainder of benefit year. (See #3 for additional penalty.)
NJ	Claimant must return to covered work of 4 weeks' duration and earn 6 x weekly benefit amount. (See #3 for additional penalty.)
UT	Claimant must earn 6 x weekly benefit amount. (See #1 and #3 for additional penalties.)
VT	Claimant must earn in excess of 6 x weekly benefit amount.
WV	Claimant must return to covered work of 30 days' duration.

State	3. Benefits Are Reduced or Canceled
AL	Wages earned from involved employer are canceled. (See #2 for additional penalty.)
CO	Benefits are reduced by 26 x weekly benefit amount. (See #1 for additional penalty.)
IL	Wages earned from any employer are canceled.
IN	All prior wage credits are canceled.
IA	All prior wage credits are canceled.
KS	All prior wage credits are canceled. (See #2 for additional penalty.)
LA	Wages earned from involved employer are canceled. Disqualification is applicable to other than last separation from beginning of base period if claimant is unemployed because of dishonesty in connection with employment. (See #2 for additional penalty.)
MI	Benefits are reduced by lesser of 7 x weekly benefit amount or 40 x state minimum hourly wage x 7 in current or succeeding benefit year. (See #2 for additional penalty.)
MN	Wages earned from involved employer are canceled. (See #2 for additional penalty.)

State	3. Benefits Are Reduced or Canceled
MO	It is agency's option to cancel all or part of wages, depending on seriousness of misconduct. Only wage credits based on work involved in misconduct are canceled. (See #1 for additional penalty.)
MT	Benefits are reduced by 52 x weekly benefit amount. (See #1 for additional penalty.)
NE	All prior wage credits are canceled.
NV	Benefit rights based on any work involved are canceled. If claimant is discharged for assault, arson, sabotage, grand larceny, embezzlement, or wanton destruction of property in connection with work, claimant shall be denied benefits based on wages earned from that employer if misconduct is admitted in writing, under oath, or in hearing of record, or if misconduct has resulted in conviction.
NH	All prior wage credits are canceled. (See #1 for additional penalty.)
NJ	Wages earned from involved employer are canceled. (See #2 for additional penalty.)
OH	Benefit rights based on any work involved are canceled. Disqualification is applicable to other than last separation from beginning of base period if claimant is unemployed because of dishonesty in connection with employment.
OR	All prior wage credits are canceled.
SC	It is agency's option to reduce benefits by number of weeks of disqualification x weekly benefit amount. (See #1 for additional penalty.)
UT	All prior wage credits are canceled. (See #1 and #2 for additional penalties.)
WA	If claimant is discharged for work-connected felony or gross misdemeanor of which claimant is convicted or which claimant has admitted committing to a competent authority, all base-period credits earned in any work prior to discharge are canceled.

ployer's tax rate will not be raised by any unemployment benefits that the disqualified claimant does not receive.

When the refused work was of short duration, the UI office usually considers whether this type of employment is customarily of short duration, and whether the claimant's work history shows that he or she usually works at short-term employment. While it may be considered reasonable for a worker who is accustomed to working at long-term career employment to refuse work of short duration, it is less reasonable for a person whose entire work history consists of short-term or temporary positions to decline this type of work.

Naturally, the definition of suitability varies somewhat from state to state. While some states let a claimant refuse a job that pays less than the union wage, other states disqualify a claimant for doing this. It is doubtful that any state will allow benefits to a claimant who refuses below-union-wage employment if the claimant is not or was not a member of the union at the time he or she became unemployed. However, federal law does prohibit the disqualification of any claimant who refuses suitable work if accepting the employment would require the worker to join or resign from a union.

Because the U.S. Department of Labor defines principles for determining whether a person will be disqualified for refusing work, these principles should be fairly uniform in all states and jurisdictions. To determine the suitability of work, the claims examiner should first discover if the employer made a bona fide job offer. To accomplish this, the claims examiner should find out if an opening actually existed at the time of the alleged offer, when the job was to start, what the salary was, what the working hours were, and how and when the offer was made. The mere mention of a job opening or the sending of a job announcement does not constitute a job offer. It must have been clear to the worker that he or she was being offered the job.

The second test asks whether the work was suitable for the claimant. To determine this, the unemployment staff may look at the claimant's prior employment history, salary rate, or educational attainments, or inquire about the claimant's physical capabilities as they apply to the position. Consideration may also be given to the length of the claimant's period of unemployment, as a few states whose laws include definitions of suitable work also permit a change of that definition as the period of unemployment continues.

The third test asks whether the claimant had good cause to decline the work. Just as with good cause for leaving available work, the word *good* means *compelling.* There is often great similarity between reasons for leaving work and reasons for refusing work when unemployed, and the likelihood of benefits being allowed for these reasons is also parallel. And just as reasons for leaving available work often raise questions about the claimant's present ability to or availability for work, declining work while unemployed may also raise these questions.

As is true in cases of discharge for misconduct, the employer bears the burden of establishing that a work offer was bona fide, as it is the employer who was the moving party in making the work offer and, usually, in raising the issue. The worker, on the other hand, bears the burden of establishing good cause for declining a job.

If you are offered employment, even tentatively, or given a job referral by your state's employment service office immediately upon separation or while filing for UI benefits, you should be aware of the tests discussed above. Regardless of who raises the issue of work refusal and who bears the burden of establishing a key point, you may be required to defend your actions. We certainly do not recommend that you decline employment simply to get or continue getting UI benefits. But you should be aware that you have the right to decline employment that is not suitable to your particular qualifications, abilities, and experience. Before making a decision, be sure to weigh the advantages of the offered position—the salary and health insurance benefits, for instance—against the temporary nature of UI benefits. If you are faced with a situation in which you believe you are being offered a job but the offer is not concrete, don't hesitate to ask for the specifics of the position, such as salary, job responsibilities, and starting date. Or simply ask if you are, in fact, being offered employment.

Penalties for Refusing Suitable Work

In the majority of the states, penalties for refusing suitable work are durational. That is, to requalify for UI benefits, the claimant must gain new work, work for a specified period of time and/or earn a specified amount, and then be separated without fault. Six states have provisions that call for fixed-term disqualifications, while eight states impose variable-term disqualifications. Thirteen states reduce the benefit entitlement.

Table 4.5 shows the types of disqualifications imposed by the different states and jurisdictions. The first part of the table shows those states that postpone benefits for a fixed or variable number of weeks. Alaska, for instance, postpones benefits until five weeks after the week of the refusal, while Alabama postpones benefits for one to ten weeks after the week of the refusal.

Part 2 of Table 4.5 shows those states with durational disqualifications. For example, Arizona requires that the claimant return to work and earn at least eight times the weekly benefit amount to requalify. You may notice that Florida imposes both a term and durational disqualification for refusal of suitable work, while in North Carolina, a durational disqualification may be reduced to a term disqualification of not less than five weeks.

The states shown in Part 3 impose benefit reductions. Alaska, for instance, reduces benefits by a sum equal to three times the weekly benefit amount.

Looking at Part 4, you'll note that three states have alternative-earnings provisions through which the claimant can requalify even when other requirements have not been met. For instance, Alaska disqualifies a claimant for five weeks after the job refusal. But if the claimant gains new employment at which he or she earns a sum equal to eight times the weekly benefit amount, the claimant can requalify for benefits even if the five-week disqualification period has not expired.

Involvement in a Labor Dispute

The U.S. Department of Labor recommends that claimants involved in a labor dispute or strike be denied UI benefits. The Department of Labor states that such unemployment is caused by the claimant's own action, and that UI benefits are not meant to cover self-caused unemployment. (New York State *does* grant benefits if the strike lasts more than eight weeks.)

Of more importance, perhaps, is the fact that a strike can cause *others* to be denied UI benefits. For instance, a union carpenter may be out of work because the operating engineers are on strike—engineers who must be present in order for the carpenter to work. Eight states—Alabama, California, Delaware, Kentucky, New York, North Carolina, Ohio, and Utah—deny benefits to claimants who are not working due to a strike, even if neither they nor any other worker of the same grade or class is participating in the dispute, financing the strike, or directly interested in the strike.

Penalties for Unemployment Due to a Labor Dispute

Nearly all states disqualify workers who are unemployed due to a labor dispute. However, there are some exceptions when the labor dispute is due to actions of the employer. All states except Alaska, Arizona, Maine, Minnesota, New Hampshire, Oregon, and West Virginia disqualify claimants from receiving benefits if they are not working because of a strike caused by the employer's failure to conform to a contract. All states except Alaska, Arizona, Maine, Minnesota, Montana, New Hampshire, and Utah disqualify claimants who are not working due to the employer's failure to conform to the labor law.

Twenty-eight states grant UI benefits during lockouts—labor disputes in which the employer closes down the place of employment as a means of leverage in negotiations. These states are Arkansas, California, Colorado, Connecticut, Delaware, the District of Columbia, Florida, Georgia, Illinois, Kentucky, Maryland, Massachusetts, Michigan, Minnesota, Mississippi, Ohio, Oklahoma, Oregon, Pennsylvania, Rhode Island, South Dakota, Tennessee, Texas, Utah, Vermont, the Virgin Islands, West Virginia,

Table 4.5 Penalties for Refusing Suitable Work

State	1. Benefits Postponed for Specified Number of Weeks
AL	Benefits are postponed for 1–10 weeks, beginning after week of refusal.
AK	Benefits are postponed for 5 weeks, beginning after week of refusal. (See #3 and #4 for additional penalties.)
AR	Benefits are postponed for 7 weeks, beginning after week of refusal. Weeks of disqualification must be weeks in which claimant is otherwise eligible for benefits or earns weekly benefit amount.
CA	Benefits are postponed for 1–9 weeks, beginning after week of refusal. Weeks of disqualification must be weeks in which claimant meets reporting and registration requirements. Agency may add 1–8 weeks more for successive disqualifications.
CO	Benefits are postponed for 20 weeks, beginning after week of refusal. (See #3 for additional disqualification.)
FL	Benefits are postponed for 1–5 weeks, beginning after week of refusal, and claimant must earn 17 x weekly benefit amount. Aliens who refused resettlement or relocation employment are disqualified for 1–7 weeks, or a reduction of benefits is made by not more than 5 weeks. (See #2 and #3 for additional penalties.)
MD	Benefits are postponed for 5–10 weeks, beginning after week of refusal. Either of the two possible penalties may be imposed at discretion of agency. However, satisfaction of type not assessed does not serve to end assessed disqualification. (See #4 for alternative penalty.)
MA	Benefits are postponed for 7 weeks, beginning after week of refusal. (See #3 for additional penalty.)
MI	Benefits are postponed for 6 weeks, beginning after week of refusal. Weeks of disqualification must be weeks in which claimant earns at least $25.01 or otherwise meets eligibility requirements. (See #3 for additional penalty.)
MS	Benefits are postponed for 1–12 weeks, beginning after week of refusal.
NE	Benefits are postponed for 7–10 weeks, beginning after week of refusal. (See #3 for additional penalty.)
NJ	Benefits are postponed for 3 weeks, beginning after week of refusal.
NC	Commission may reduce permanent disqualification to a time certain but not less than 5 weeks. When permanent disqualification is changed to time certain, benefits shall be reduced by number of weeks of disqualification x weekly benefit amount. (See #2 for alternative penalty.)
WV	Benefits are postponed for 4 weeks, beginning after week of refusal. Additional weeks are added as job offer remains open. (See #3 for additional penalty.)
State	**2. Terms of Durational Disqualification**
AZ	Claimant must earn 8 x weekly benefit amount.

State	2. Terms of Durational Disqualification
CT	Claimant must earn 6 x weekly benefit amount.
DE	Claimant must return to work of 4 weeks' duration and earn 4 x weekly benefit amount.
DC	Claimant must return to work of 10 weeks' duration and earn 10 x weekly benefit amount.
FL	Claimant must earn 17 x weekly benefit amount. Both term and duration-of-unemployment disqualifications are imposed. (See #1 and #3 for additional penalties.)
GA	Claimant must earn 8 x weekly benefit amount.
HI	Claimant must earn 5 x weekly benefit amount.
ID	Claimant must earn 16 x weekly benefit amount.
IL	Claimant must earn weekly benefit amount in each of 4 weeks.
IN	Claimant must earn weekly benefit amount in each of 8 weeks. (See #3 for additional penalty.)
IA	Claimant must earn 10 x weekly benefit amount.
KS	Claimant must earn 3 x weekly benefit amount.
KY	Claimant must return to covered work of 10 weeks' duration and earn 10 x weekly benefit amount.
LA	Claimant must earn 10 x weekly benefit amount.
ME	Claimant must earn 8 x weekly benefit amount. If claimant has refused work for necessitous and compelling reason, disqualification terminates when claimant is again able to and available for work.
MN	Claimant must return to work of 4 weeks' duration and earn 8 x weekly benefit amount.
MO	Claimant must earn 10 x weekly benefit amount.
MT	Claimant must earn 6 x weekly benefit amount. (See #3 for additional penalty.)
NV	Claimant must earn weekly benefit amount in each of 15 weeks.
NH	Claimant must return to covered work of 5 weeks' duration and earn 20% more than weekly benefit amount in each week.
NM	Claimant must earn 5 x weekly benefit amount. (See #3 for additional penalty.)
NY	Claimant must return to 3 days' work in each of 5 weeks and earn 5 x weekly benefit amount.
NC	Claimant must earn 10 x weekly benefit amount in at least 5 weeks. (See #1 for alternative penalty.)
ND	Claimant must earn 10 x weekly benefit amount.

State	2. Terms of Durational Disqualification
OH	Claimant must return to covered work of 6 weeks' duration and earn 27.5% of state average weekly wage in each week.
OK	Claimant must earn 10 x weekly benefit amount. Claimant who refuses offer of work due to illness, death of family member, or other circumstance beyond claimant's control is disqualified for week of refusal.
OR	Unspecified durational disqualification is imposed. (See #3 and #4 for additional penalties.)
PA	Unspecified durational disqualification is imposed.
PR	Claimant must return to work of 4 weeks' duration and earn 10 x weekly benefit amount.
RI	Claimant must earn 20 x minimum hourly wage in each of 4 weeks.
SC	Claimant must earn 8 x weekly benefit amount.
SD	Claimant must return to covered work of 6 weeks' duration and earn weekly benefit amount in each week.
TN	Claimant must earn 10 x weekly benefit amount in covered work.
TX	Claimant must return to work of 6 weeks' duration or earn 6 x weekly benefit amount. Disqualification is applicable to refusals during other than current period of unemployment within current benefit year.
UT	Claimant must earn 6 x weekly benefit amount. Claimant is not disqualified if reasons for refusal were of such a nature that disqualification would be contrary to equity and good conscience.
VT	Claimant must earn in excess of 6 x weekly benefit amount.
VA	Claimant must return to work of 30 days' duration.
VI	Claimant must return to work of 4 weeks' duration and earn 4 x weekly benefit amount.
WA	Claimant must earn weekly benefit amount in each of 5 weeks.
WI	Claimant must earn 4 x weekly benefit amount and 4 weeks must have elapsed. Claimant is not disqualified if claimant accepts work that he or she could have refused with good cause and then terminates employment with good cause within 10 weeks after starting work.
WY	Claimant must return to work of 12 weeks' duration and earn 12 x weekly benefit amount.

State	3. Amount by Which Potential Benefits Are Reduced
AK	Benefits are reduced by 3 x weekly benefit amount. (See #1 and #4 for additional penalties.)

State	3. Amount by Which Potential Benefits Are Reduced
CO	Benefits are reduced by 20 x weekly benefit amount. (See #1 for additional penalty.)
FL	Reduction of benefits is optional. (See #1 and #2 for additional penalties.)
IN	Benefits are reduced by 25%. (See #2 for additional penalty.)
MA	Benefits may be reduced for as many weeks as director shall determine from circumstances of each case, not to exceed 8 weeks. (See #1 for additional penalty.)
MI	Benefits are reduced by 6 x weekly benefit amount in current or succeeding benefit year. Claimant may be eligible for benefits based on wage credits earned subsequent to refusal. (See #1 for additional penalty.)
MT	Benefits are reduced by 6 x weekly benefit amount. (See #2 for additional penalty.)
NE	Benefits are reduced by number of weeks of disqualification x weekly benefit amount. (See #1 for additional penalty.)
NM	Benefits are reduced by 5 x weekly benefit amount. (See #2 for additional penalty.)
NC	Commission may reduce permanent disqualification to a time certain but not less than 5 weeks. When permanent disqualification is changed to time certain, benefits shall be reduced by number of weeks of disqualification x weekly benefit amount. (See #2 for alternative penalty.)
OR	Benefits are reduced by 8 x weekly benefit amount. (See #2 and #4 for additional penalties.)
WV	Benefits are reduced by number of weeks of disqualification x weekly benefit amount. (See #1 for additional penalty.)
State	**4. Alternative-Earnings Requirement**
AK	Claimant must earn 8 x weekly benefit amount to avoid term disqualification.
MD	Claimant must earn 10 x weekly benefit amount to avoid term disqualification. Either disqualification may be imposed at agency's discretion. However, satisfaction of type not assessed does not serve to end assessed disqualification.
OR	Claimant must earn 4 x weekly benefit amount to avoid term disqualification.

and Wisconsin. In Colorado, the claimant is not disqualified unless the lockout results from the demands of the employees, as opposed to the employer's attempt to deprive employees of some advantage they already possess. In Michigan, claimants are eligible for UI benefits during lockouts only if their place of work is "functionally integrated" with the establishment in which the lockout occurred, meaning that the work product is connected with or dependent on the second establishment. Other states may make other exceptions.

If this discussion of labor disputes seems very technical and complicated, it is because the labor dispute issue itself is so complex. And just as labor disputes often lead to court proceedings, determinations involving labor disputes often lead to appeals. Some states have special arbitrators or examiners who deal with the issue of labor disputes on a group basis so that whatever determination is made can be applied to each claimant in that union or each claimant involved in that dispute. Except in New York, disqualifications due to labor disputes last as long as there is work stoppage due to the dispute, or for the duration of the dispute, or as long as the condition of unemployment is due to the labor dispute. In New York, benefits may be allowed after the eighth consecutive week of the labor dispute. In cases of disqualifications due to labor disputes, there is no reduction of the maximum potential benefit amount as there is with other disqualifications. Determinations regarding separations that occur after or outside the dispute are based on the circumstances of the separation.

If you are a union worker and are engaged in or about to become engaged in a labor dispute, be sure to remain in touch with your union officials for information regarding UI filing procedures. Like mass layoffs, these are situations in which the initial claim filing is commonly done through a group filing at a specified time and place. In fact, union officials and state UI officials often coordinate these activities even before the dispute occurs.

Fraudulent Misrepresentation

The harshest disqualifications are reserved for claimants who, in order to obtain or increase benefits, willfully misrepresent facts that are material to UI eligibility. The penalty for this action may include disqualification for benefits for up to one year after the end of the fifty-two-week benefit year of the claim on which the misrepresentation occurred. Some or all of the remaining entitlement may be reduced, and some or all of the wages used to compute monetary eligibility may be canceled. In addition, because fraud is a criminal offense, all state laws have provisions specifying fine and/or imprisonment upon prosecution and conviction for fraud.

In order to establish willful misrepresentation, it must be shown that the claimant deliberately and purposely concealed information or gave false information on the UI claim, and that this was done in the belief that it would enable the claimant to obtain benefits greater than those to which he or she would have been entitled had the misrepresentation not occurred. Please note that it is not necessary for the claimant to have *received* the benefits. Since intent is a deciding factor, the mere attempt to obtain benefits fraudulently is sufficient to result in disqualification.

Fraud or willful misrepresentation can be committed on the claim application or accompanying documentation, on continued claim forms, in testimony or evidence offered at fact-finding interviews and appeals hearings—indeed, at any point at which the claimant supplies information that could affect eligibility. Perhaps the most common form of fraudulent misrepresentation is the claiming of benefits while working without reporting the fact of employment or earnings.

Penalties for Fraudulent Misrepresentation

Table 4.6 shows the penalties imposed by the different states in cases of fraudulent misrepresentation. You'll note that the second column of Table 4.6 shows the duration of the disqualification for each state, while the third column shows the reduction or cancellation of benefits. For example, in Arkansas, the disqualification lasts for thirteen weeks, measured from the first compensable week after delivery of the determination, plus three weeks for each week in which fraud occurred. Any benefits remaining in the claim balance are then reduced by 50 percent.

Since so much of the UI system is based on the weighing of facts and the truthfulness of the parties involved, the commission of fraud is viewed very harshly. In addition to disqualification from benefits and possible imposition of fines or imprisonment, all states have programs for recovering any money paid in error, whether through cash repayment or through the deduction of benefits from future entitlements. While there is sometimes a waiver of overpayments that occur through no fault of the claimant, overpayments due to fraud cannot be waived as, by definition, fraud is the fault of the claimant.

Even claimants who worked in covered employment are sometimes disqualified from receiving UI benefits because of the circumstances in which they left work or for other reasons. Still, as you've learned in this chapter, it is often possible to receive reduced or postponed payments even in cases of disqualification. In the next chapter, you'll learn about other actions and circumstances that may prevent you from receiving full benefit payments as we explore ineligibility.

Table 4.6 Penalties for Fraudulent Misrepresentation

State (1)	Benefits Postponed for Specified Amount of Time (2)	Amount by Which Benefits Are Reduced (3)
AL	—	Benefits are reduced by 4 x weekly benefit amount to maximum benefit amount payable in benefit year. Provision is applicable at discretion of agency.
AK	Benefits are postponed for 6–52 weeks beginning after week in which fraud was committed.	Before disqualification period ends, wage credits may have expired in whole or in part, depending on disqualification imposed and/or end of benefit year.
AZ	Benefits are postponed for 1–52 weeks. Period of disqualification is measured from date of claim or registration for work. Provision is applicable only if claim is filed within 2 years after offense.	Before disqualification period ends, wage credits may have expired in whole or in part, depending on disqualification imposed and/or end of benefit year.
AR	Benefits are postponed for 13 weeks plus 3 weeks for each week of fraud, beginning first compensable week after determination is mailed or delivered.	Benefits are reduced by 50% of remaining entitlement.
CA	If claimant is convicted, benefits are postponed for 52 weeks. Period of disqualification is measured from week determination is mailed or served, or any subsequent week for which claimant is first otherwise eligible for benefits; or, if claimant is convicted, from week in which criminal complaint is filed. Provision is applicable only if claim is filed within 3 years following date determination was mailed or served. Disqualification may be served concurrently with disqualification imposed for any of 3 major causes if individual registers for work for such week as required under latter disqualifications.	Before disqualification period ends, wage credits may have expired in whole or in part, depending on disqualification imposed and/or end of benefit year.
CO	Benefits are postponed for 4 weeks for each week that benefits were fraudulently claimed and/or received. Any overpayment may have to be repaid at amount equal to 1½–3 x benefit amount fraudulently received.	—

State (1)	Benefits Postponed for Specified Amount of Time (2)	Amount by Which Benefits Are Reduced (3)
CT	Benefits are postponed for 2–39 weeks for which claimant is otherwise eligible for benefits. Period of disqualification is measured from waiting or compensable week after discovery of fraud. Provision is applicable only if claim is filed within 6 years after benefit year during which offense occurred.	Benefits are reduced by number of weeks of disqualification x weekly benefit amount. Reduction is mandatory.
DE	Benefits are postponed for 51 weeks. Period of disqualification begins after week in which fraud was committed.	Before disqualification period ends, wage credits will have expired in whole or in part, depending on end of benefit year.
DC	Benefits are postponed for all or part of remainder of benefit year, and for 1 year commencing with the end of such benefit year. Provision is applicable at discretion of agency.	Before disqualification period ends, wage credits will have expired in whole or in part, depending on end of benefit year.
FL	Benefits are postponed for 1–52 weeks. Period of disqualification is measured from waiting or compensable week after discovery of fraud.	Before disqualification period ends, wage credits may have expired in whole or in part, depending on disqualification imposed and/or end of benefit year.
GA	Benefits are postponed for remainder of current quarter and next 4 quarters. Provision is applicable only if determination of fraud is made within 4 years after offense. If false representation or failure to disclose material fact is made more than once in a benefit year, or if benefits received exceed $4,000, the individual shall upon conviction be guilty of a felony and be punished by imprisonment of 1–5 years. These penalties also apply to fictitious employers who receive benefits to which they are not entitled.	Provision is applicable only if determination of fraud is made within 4 years after offense. Reduction is mandatory.
HI	Benefits are postponed for 24 months. Period of disqualification is measured from week fraud is detected. Provision is applicable only if claim is filed within 2 years after offense.	Before disqualification period ends, wage credits will have expired in whole or in part, depending on end of benefit year.
ID	Benefits are postponed for 52 weeks. Period of disqualification is measured from date of determination of fraud. Amounts fraudulently received must be repaid or deducted from future benefits. Provision is applicable only within 8 years from final determination establishing liability to repay.	Before disqualification period ends, wage credits will have expired in whole or in part, depending on end of benefit year.

State (1)	Benefits Postponed for Specified Amount of Time (2)	Amount by Which Benefits Are Reduced (3)
IL	Benefits are postponed for 6 weeks plus 2 additional weeks for each subsequent offense. Period of disqualification begins after week of determination of fraud.	Before disqualification periods ends, wage credits may have expired in whole or in part, depending on disqualification imposed and/or end of benefit year.
IN	Benefits are postponed up to current benefit year. Cancelation of all wage credits means that period of disqualification will extend into second benefit year, depending on amount of wage credits for such a year accumulated before fraudulent claim.	All wage credits prior to commission of fraud are canceled.
IA	Benefits are postponed up to current benefit year. Period of disqualification is measured from date of determination of fraud.	Benefits are reduced by number of weeks of disqualification x weekly benefit amount. Reduction is mandatory.
KS	Benefits are postponed for 1 year after fraud is committed or first day following last week for which benefits were paid, whichever is later.	Before disqualification period ends, wage credits will have expired in whole or in part, depending on end of benefit year.
KY	Benefits are postponed for up to 52 weeks. If fraudulent benefits were received, benefits are postponed until such amounts are repaid or for 10 years. Period of disqualification is measured from date of discovery of fraud.	Before disqualification period ends, wage credits may have expired in whole or in part, depending on disqualification imposed and/or end of benefit year.
LA	Benefits are postponed for 52 weeks. Period of disqualification is measured from date of determination of fraud. If fraudulent benefits were received, benefits are postponed until such amounts are repaid.	Before disqualification period ends, wage credits will have expired in whole or in part, depending on end of benefit year.
ME	Benefits are postponed for 6 months–1 year. Period of disqualification is measured from mailing date of determination.	—
MD	Benefits are postponed for 1 year, and until benefits are repaid. Period of disqualification is measured from date of determination of fraud. Provision is applicable only if determination of fraud is made within 3 years after offense.	Before disqualification period ends, wage credits will have expired in whole or in part, depending on end of benefit year.

State (1)	Benefits Postponed for Specified Amount of Time (2)	Amount by Which Benefits Are Reduced (3)
MA	Benefits are postponed for 1–10 weeks for which claimant is otherwise eligible for benefits. Period of disqualification is measured from waiting or compensable week after discovery of fraud. Provision is applicable at discretion of agency.	—
MI	Benefits are postponed for current benefit year and until benefits are repaid or withheld. Period of disqualification is measured from date of discovery of fraud. Provision is applicable only if claim is filed within 6 years after benefit year during which offense occurred.	All uncharged credit weeks are canceled.
MN	Benefits are postponed for up to 52 weeks. Period of disqualification is measured from date of determination of fraud.	Before disqualification period ends, wage credits may have expired in whole or in part, depending on disqualification imposed and/or end of benefit year.
MS	Benefits are postponed for up to 52 weeks. Period of disqualification is measured from date determined by agency.	—
MO	Benefits are postponed up to current benefit year. Cancelation of all wage credits means that period of disqualification will extend into second benefit year, depending on amount of wage credits for such a year accumulated before fraudulent claim.	All or part of wage credits prior to act are canceled.
MT	Benefits are postponed for 1–52 weeks and until benefits are repaid. Period of disqualification is measured from date of determination of fraud.	—
NE	Benefits are postponed up to current benefit year. Cancelation of all wage credits means that period of disqualification will extend into second benefit year, depending on amount of wage credits for such a year accumulated before fraudulent claim.	All or part of wage credits prior to act are canceled.
NV	Benefits are postponed for 1–52 weeks. Period of disqualification begins after week in which fraud was committed.	Before disqualification period ends, wage credits will have expired in whole or in part, depending on end of benefit year.

State (1)	Benefits Postponed for Specified Amount of Time (2)	Amount by Which Benefits Are Reduced (3)
NH	Benefits are postponed for 4–52 weeks. If claimant is convicted, benefits are postponed for 1 year after conviction. Also, benefits must be repaid or withheld. Period of disqualification is measured from date of determination of fraud. Provision is applicable at discretion of agency.	Benefits are reduced by number of weeks of disqualification x weekly benefit amount. Reduction is mandatory.
NJ	Benefits are postponed for 1 year. Period of disqualification is measured from date of discovery of fraud.	Before disqualification period ends, wage credits may have expired in whole or in part, depending on disqualification imposed and/or end of benefit year.
NM	Benefits are postponed for not more than 52 weeks. Period of disqualification is measured from date of determination of fraud.	Before disqualification period ends, wage credits will have expired in whole or in part, depending on end of benefit year.
NY	Benefits are postponed for 4–80 days for which claimant is otherwise eligible for benefits. Period of disqualification is measured from waiting or compensable week after discovery of fraud. Provision is applicable only if claim is filed within 2 years after offense.	Benefits are reduced by number of weeks of disqualification x weekly benefit amount. Reduction is mandatory.
NC	Benefits are postponed for 52 weeks. Period of disqualification begins week after mailing date of determination.	Before disqualification period ends, wage credits will have expired in whole or in part, depending on end of benefit year.
ND	Benefits are postponed for 51 weeks. Period of disqualification is measured from week in which fraud occurs.	Before disqualification period ends, wage credits will have expired in whole or in part, depending on end of benefit year.
OH	Benefits are postponed for duration of unemployment plus 6 weeks in covered work. Claimant must earn 3 x average weekly wage or $360, whichever is less. In addition, claims shall be rejected within 4 years and benefits denied for 2 weeks for each weekly claim canceled.	—
OK	Benefits are postponed for 51 weeks. Period of disqualification is measured from date of determination of fraud. Provision is applicable only if claim is filed within 2 years after offense. A new base period and benefit year may not be established during period of disqualification.	—

State (1)	Benefits Postponed for Specified Amount of Time (2)	Amount by Which Benefits Are Reduced (3)
OR	Benefits are postponed for up to 26 weeks. Period of disqualification is measured from date determined by agency. If claimant is convicted, benefits are postponed until benefits are repaid or withheld. Provision is applicable for 3 years after date of decision.	If claimant is convicted, all wage credits prior to conviction are canceled. Cancelation of all wage credits means that period of disqualification will extend into second benefit year, depending on amount of wage credits for such a year accumulated before fraudulent claim.
PA	Benefits are postponed for 2 weeks plus 1 week for each week of fraud or, if claimant is convicted of illegal receipt of benefits, for 1 year after conviction. Provision is applicable at discretion of agency. Also, if finding of fault on part of claimant has been made, benefits must be withheld or repaid. Provision is applicable only if claim is filed within 2 years following determination of fraud.	Before disqualification period ends, wage credits will have expired in whole or in part, depending on end of benefit year.
PR	Benefits are postponed for 51 weeks. Period of disqualification begins after week of determination of fraud. Provision is applicable only if claim is filed within 2 years after offense.	—
RI	If claimant is convicted, benefits are postponed for 1 year after conviction.	Before disqualification period ends, wage credits will have expired in whole or in part, depending on end of benefit year.
SC	Benefits are postponed for 10–52 weeks. Period of disqualification begins after week of determination of fraud.	Before disqualification period ends, wage credits may have expired in whole or in part, depending on disqualification imposed and/or end of benefit year.
SD	Benefits are postponed for 1–52 weeks. Period of disqualification begins after week of discovery of fraud.	Before disqualification period ends, wage credits may have expired in whole or in part, depending on disqualification imposed and/or end of benefit year.

State (1)	Benefits Postponed for Specified Amount of Time (2)	Amount by Which Benefits Are Reduced (3)
TN	Benefits are postponed for 4–52 weeks. Period of disqualification begins after week of discovery of fraud.	Before disqualification period ends, wage credits may have expired in whole or in part, depending on disqualification imposed and/or end of benefit year.
TX	Benefits are postponed for current benefit year.	Benefits or remainder of benefit year is canceled.
UT	Benefits are postponed for 13–49 weeks, and until benefits received fraudulently are repaid. Benefits are postponed for 13 weeks for first week of fraud, and 6 weeks for each additional week. No benefits are paid until overpayment is repaid as well as a civil penalty equal to the benefits fraudulently received.	Before disqualification period ends, wage credits will have expired in whole or in part, depending on end of benefit year.
VT	If claimant is not prosecuted, benefits are postponed until amount of fraudulent benefits are repaid and benefits are withheld for 1–26 weeks. Period of disqualification is measured from date of determination of fraud. Provision is applicable for 3 years after date of decision.	Before disqualification period ends, wage credits may have expired in whole or in part, depending on disqualification imposed and/or end of benefit year.
VA	Benefits are postponed for 52 weeks and until benefits are repaid. Period of disqualification begins after week of determination of fraud. If claimant is convicted, benefits are postponed for 1 year after conviction. Provision is applicable only if determination of fraud is made within 3 years after offense.	Before disqualification period ends, wage credits may have expired in whole or in part, depending on disqualification imposed and/or end of benefit year.
VI	Benefits are postponed for 51 weeks. Period of disqualification begins after week determination is mailed or delivered. Provision is applicable only if claim is filed within 2 years after offense.	Before disqualification period ends, wage credits may have expired in whole or in part, depending on disqualification imposed and/or end of benefit year.
WA	Benefits are postponed for week of fraudulent act plus 26 weeks following filing of first claim after determination of fraud. Provision is applicable within 2 years following determination of fraud.	Before disqualification period ends, wage credits will have expired in whole or in part, depending on end of benefit year.
WV	Benefits are postponed for 52 weeks. Period of disqualification is measured from date of determination of fraud.	—

State (1)	Benefits Postponed for Specified Amount of Time (2)	Amount by Which Benefits Are Reduced (3)
WI	Benefits are postponed for each week of fraud.	Benefits are canceled or reduced by 1–4 x weekly benefit amount. Provision is applicable at discretion of agency.
WY	If claimant is convicted, benefits are postponed for 2 years after conviction.	Before disqualification period ends, wage credits may have expired in whole or in part, depending on disqualification imposed and/or end of benefit year.

5. INELIGIBILITIES

FAILING TO MEET UI REQUIREMENTS

In previous chapters, you learned that to receive unemployment insurance (UI) benefits, you must have worked in covered employment and you must have avoided disqualifying actions, such as quitting without good cause. In addition to this, you must meet specific eligibility requirements. If not, you may be deemed *ineligible*, and may either receive no UI benefits or receive reduced benefits. It should be noted that since ineligibility is based on a condition that is not being met, an ineligibility, unlike a disqualification, is usually not regarded as a penalty. Understandably, though, it may be thought of as such by the claimant who receives a notice of ineligibility instead of a benefit check.

As discussed earlier in the book, all states have two basic eligibility requirements: the claimant must be able to work, and the claimant must be available for work. In this chapter, we will take another look at these two requirements, and will also learn about three other factors that may affect your eligibility: the reasonable assurance of resuming work, citizenship status, and deductible income.

ABILITY TO WORK

To be eligible for UI benefits, you must be physically able to work. This does not mean that you must be physically able to do the type of work you've been doing, or that you must be able to perform all types of work. Rather, you must be able to work *without undue*

TIP: *Even if physical restrictions limit the work you can perform, be sure to file for UI benefits. You may be eligible for benefits or for other types of assistance.*

---

restrictions. The determination of your eligibility should take into account not only your abilities and restrictions, but also the types of work that are available in your job market. If the type of work you can perform is restricted, you will probably have to provide medical certification regarding your limits. This will be especially important if you left a job because of a physical inability to perform certain tasks.

Should you avoid filing a claim because of physical restrictions? Certainly not! In some states, the disability compensation office and the UI office are divisions of the same agency or department. In other cases, state laws contain provisions that deal with disability, and the state UI staff will be able to assist you in determining which benefits other than UI might be appropriate. And, as you will recall from earlier discussions, the office that houses unemployment compensation often also houses the public employment service. Through employment counseling, you may be able to find jobs that will accommodate your restrictions.

Many determinations of eligibility are based on temporary disability—that is, illness or injury from which a person is expected to recover in a specified period of time. If you are unemployed because of a temporary condition and do not plan to change your employment or to seek other work that can accommodate your condition, you will probably be held ineligible to receive UI benefits. For instance, if your doctor has restricted you from working due to pregnancy, or if you have left or declined work because of pregnancy, you will probably be held ineligible due to that restriction.

Some state laws and regulations specify that an individual must be *mentally* as well as physically able to work. These two types of eligibility are treated the same way as far as their effect on UI benefits. In both cases, it is the claimant's responsibility to show that he or she is able to work, and to provide the necessary medical certification to establish that ability.

AVAILABILITY FOR WORK

All states require that claimants be available for work. One indication of availability is registration with the public employment service. Most states, in fact, require registration before benefit payment is made. In other states, registration with the employment service may be delayed or even waived in special circumstances such as a general layoff of known duration or a mass layoff of an entire labor market's principal employer.

The laws of Alabama, Alaska, Arkansas, California, Colorado, Florida, Maine, Maryland, Minnesota, Missouri, New Jersey, and

---

TIP: *Make it a point to keep notes on your work search. You may be asked to document the places where you sought work.*

New York specify that an unemployed individual who is otherwise eligible for benefits but is serving jury duty will not be held ineligible solely because of jury duty. Many other states make allowances for jury service by interpretation or regulation because such service is regarded as a civic responsibility, and because the timing of such service is beyond the control of the claimant.

Generally, availability for work means being willing and ready to work, and usually must be demonstrated by an active in-person work search. Nearly all states require you to document the places where you sought work, if not every time you file a continued claim, then at least periodically during eligibility reviews. As with ability-to-work issues, the question of availability often arises as a result of a voluntary separation or refusal of work. Depending on the nature of the restriction, you may be required to document the fact that you have removed the restriction. For example, you may be required to provide the name and phone number of a care taker for children who are not of school age, or you may be required to submit course schedules showing that you have changed school attendance hours to those that will not conflict with the work hours customary in your classification. If you have placed restrictions on the types of work you can or will perform, you must be available to accept the prevailing wage at a job you can and will accept, regardless of whether this was the type of work you most recently performed.

In some states, you will be given an opportunity to change or alter any restrictions *before* the determination of eligibility is made, and you may be paid benefits for any weeks claimed before the issue came to light. In other states, you will be held ineligible until the condition is altered.

REASONABLE ASSURANCE OF RESUMING WORK

For many years, a good number of state, county, and municipal workers were not covered for UI benefits. But in 1976, the federal unemployment law was amended to require coverage of these workers. At the same time, it was recognized that many workers had employment that was seasonal by nature, and that the payment of benefits during season breaks would impose a burden on public funds. So Public Law 94-566 amended the federal law to deny benefits to school personnel and to employees of educational service agencies between successive academic years or during regularly scheduled vacations or holiday periods, provided that the employees have a contract or other reasonable assurance that they will resume employment when school again begins. More recent amendments allow benefits to nonacademic employees such as cafeteria workers, bus drivers, and school nurses.

In brief, this law denies benefits based on wages earned during the regular school term. Some individuals who have had other covered employment may qualify based on other wages, provided they are also unemployed from that work.

The same law requires the states to make retroactive payments to any such employees—other than those performing services in instructional, research, or administrative capacities—who were denied benefits but not rehired when the season or school term resumed. Claimants are required to file timely continued claims during the denial period and to meet other state eligibility requirements in order to receive retroactive benefits if and when they are not rehired.

Public Law 94-566 also requires states to deny benefits to professional athletes between two successive sports seasons if the athletes have contracts or other reasonable assurance that they will resume similar services when the next season begins.

If you are a nontenured employee of a school or educational service organization—that is, if you do not have a continuing contract—and you are not certain if you will be rehired when school resumes, we recommend that you file an initial claim application and continued claims during the break. Benefits may be allowed if it is determined that you do not have a reasonable assurance of re-employment. Even if you are not determined eligible during the break, you will be paid retroactive benefits for the period claimed if you are not rehired when school resumes. Professional athletes should file for unemployment benefits at the time they are cut from the team. Remember, though, that *you will not be paid retroactively if you do not file the claim application and the continued claims.*

CITIZENSHIP STATUS

Public Law 94-566 also affects the eligibility of some aliens. It requires state laws to deny UI benefits based on services performed by aliens unless the aliens were lawfully admitted for permanent residence status at the time the services were performed, were lawfully present in the United States to perform the services, or were permanently residing in the United States "under color of law." The employment in question must be covered employment. A simpler way of stating this requirement is that wages cannot be used to establish UI eligibility unless the alien was lawfully admitted to this country and had a work permit.

DEDUCTIBLE INCOME

As you know, UI benefits are paid to workers on the basis of their being unemployed or employed to a lesser degree than they were previously. The program is almost totally financed by employers. Because of these two factors, certain types of income are deductible from UI benefits. The purpose of making such deductions is clearly to prevent duplicate compensation for the same period of time. Whether the deduction causes total or only partial ineligibility is dependent on the nature of the income, and also on the amount of the UI entitlement and the amount of the other source of income. In some states, receipt of certain types of benefits causes total ineligibility regardless of the amount of the income, because the state's laws, rules and regulations, or court decisions specify that these sources of income or benefits preclude the payment of UI benefits. Let's look at several types of deductible income.

Partial Unemployment

All states provide for partial benefit payments when individuals are otherwise eligible for unemployment insurance but are employed "less than full-time" or have incidental or temporary employment, whether from their regular employer or from another employer. Usually, the phrase "less than full-time" is defined as employment of less than forty hours per week and/or employment that provides earnings less than the weekly benefit amount of the claim. Note that these partial benefits are available only to workers who previously had *full-time* employment, and to part-time workers whose work hours have been substantially reduced.

Most states disregard a portion of any part-time earnings before making the deduction that determines the adjusted partial benefit amount. In some states, the portion to be disregarded is stated as a dollar amount; in others, it is a percentage of the gross wages or

---

TIP: *Remember that it is gross wages—before-tax wages— that are considered when computing benefit payments based on partial unemployment.*

of the weekly benefit amount of the claim. The purpose of allowing partial benefits and for disregarding a portion of the part-time earnings is to avoid discouraging workers from accepting part-time employment simply because they fear a loss of benefits.

When we discussed the continued claims process in Chapter Two, we stated how important it is to report total gross earnings each time you file a continued claim form. It is the responsibility of the UI staff to compute the appropriate deduction and determine the amount of the adjusted benefit check. Some states issue a formal written notice each time an adjustment is made; others issue a notice only when the earnings are great enough to cause total ineligibility. Even if your filing state does not issue formal determinations in every instance, at any time you disagree with the adjustment, you should request a written determination so that you can exercise your right of appeal. This should be done as soon as possible. Of course, if your filing state does issue formal notices whenever an adjustment is made, the appeals period will be stated on your notice of determination. (See page 25 for more about the notice of determination, and page 37 for more about the appeals process.)

If your full-time job is reduced to part-time, if you gain part-time employment after having worked full-time, or if you retain a part-time job after having worked at two jobs and lost one, it would probably be to your advantage to file a claim and let the UI staff make the determination about your eligibility for partial benefits. Certainly, it is to your benefit to retain or accept this part-time employment. In addition to possibly being eligible for partial UI benefits, you will be maintaining contact with an employer—a circumstance that could lead to full-time employment or serve as a reference when you apply for full-time work. And if the part-time employment is covered, you will also be accumulating wage credits that could be used to obtain further UI benefits when your current claim expires. Especially in periods of recession, it is best to maximize all possibilities. (To learn how benefits are computed during weeks of partial unemployment, see page 181.)

Pensions

Pensions are regular—usually monthly—retirement payments based on years of service and made by an employer or by a pension fund contributed to by an employer. The pension programs we're concerned with in this discussion may also include disability pensions. However, they do not usually include public or private pension funds contributed to solely by the worker and withdrawn when employment ends, nor do they include payments for armed service-incurred disabilities.

Three states—the District of Columbia, Vermont, and the Virgin Islands—deduct all pensions. Arkansas deducts all pensions except military retirement pensions based on service that occurred before the claimant's base period. The other forty-nine states and jurisdictions deduct only those pensions that were contributed to wholly or partially by the base-period employers of the claim. Federal law requires deduction from UI for any regular retirement payment based on previous work and maintained or contributed to by a base-period employer or by an employer who is liable for charges on the claim. Usually, the deduction of pension payments is made on a dollar-for-dollar basis once the monthly pension entitlement has been divided into weekly amounts.

The receipt of a pension sometimes raises the issue of the claimant's availability for work. However, many people who retire from one career do go on to another, and are no less available for work simply because they receive a pension. Receipt of a disability pension does, of course, raise a question about the claimant's ability to work. But, as we discussed on page 115, physical restrictions do not necessarily result in ineligibility for unemployment compensation as long as the claimant is able to perform some type of work.

Worker's Compensation

Worker's compensation is monetary compensation made for injury or disability incurred on the job. Like UI, it is financed by the employer, usually through payments made to a private insurance carrier. Very often, worker's compensation is administered through the same state agency, although not the same work unit, as is UI.

About half of the state laws actually list worker's compensation as "disqualifying income," meaning that it causes total ineligibility for UI benefits. Whether or not your state law specifically cites worker's compensation as such, it may be deducted from your UI benefits, and you will probably not be eligible for UI benefits if you are unable to work due to injury. However, if you receive compensation as a result of a long-term or permanent diminishment of some capacity, but are still able to work, you may be eligible for UI in those states that do not deduct worker's compensation. Column two of Table 5.1 shows those states that disqualify claimants for receiving worker's compensation, and those that reduce UI benefits by deducting worker's compensation payments.

Severance Pay

Severance pay, dismissal pay or *dismissal allowance, wages in lieu of notice,* and *separation pay* or *separation allowance* are all terms describing the same thing—payment made by an employer when employment ends before the worker, and sometimes the employer, expects it to end. Such payments are made as a result of formal employer policies or an employment or union contract, or simply through arbitration or negotiation. Large-scale employers with highly structured employment policies are more likely to have formulas for computing payments when employment ends unexpectedly. Such payments are made on involuntary separations for reasons other than misconduct, although they may be part of a negotiated mutual-agreement separation.

Generally, severance pay and similar payments cause ineligibility for the weeks *when* they are paid, or for the weeks *for which* they are paid—in other words, the weeks for which they are attributable. In Table 5.1, columns three and four show those states that disqualify for severance pay by paying no UI benefits for a week when a severance payment is made or a week to which a severance payment is attributable, and those states that reduce the UI benefit entitlement by the weekly prorated amount of the income.

Procedures vary from state to state regarding how and when this type of income is deducted. For instance, in some states, payments are deductible for the period of time for which they are paid, so that a separated worker who is receiving or is going to receive dismissal or severance pay that is equivalent to, say, twenty weeks' salary is ineligible for UI benefits for the twenty weeks following separation. In another state, the deduction resulting in ineligibility may be applicable only to the week in which payment of the separation or severance pay is actually made. When separation payments are made in lump sums, some states require proration to a weekly basis, while others do not.

If you become separated from your job and are entitled to dismissal pay, it may be worthwhile to check with the staff of your local unemployment office to find out if, how, and when the payments will be deducted from your UI benefits. Certainly, neither potential nor actual ineligibility for such payments should prevent you from filing a claim. Even if you are held ineligible, the ineligibility will pertain only to those weeks during which or for which you receive the income. And, of course, you may find out that you are eligible for UI benefits.

Holiday or Vacation Pay

If you are not working due to a holiday or vacation, you are not eligible for UI benefits because you are not unemployed. However, if you accumulated vacation time during your employment and were then laid off, this may have an impact on your eligibility for UI benefits.

Generally, accrued vacation or annual leave that is paid after a separation is not deductible from UI benefits. Column five of Table 5.1 shows those states that do make some deductions or deny benefits for weeks of holiday pay. Column seven shows the same for vacation pay. Again, different states handle the deduction of this type of income in different ways. If your filing state is one showing an entry in these categories, it may be helpful to ask a UI representative about your specific situation.

Back Pay Awards

Back pay awards are payments made by the employer after the worker is separated from employment, either for specific weeks during the employment period or for weeks immediately following the separation. Such payments may be made because of a dispute over wages during the employment period, or as part of a settlement of a dispute over the separation.

Since back pay awards are made after the separation, they are often paid after the worker has filed and been paid UI benefits for the same weeks. When this occurs, the back payments may cause ineligibility. Seven states—Colorado, the District of Columbia, Indiana, Mississippi, Missouri, North Carolina, and Washington—require the employer to deduct any unemployment benefits paid to the worker from the award in order to reimburse the state UI fund. Other states permit the claimant to authorize the employer to make this deduction, and some require the claimant to repay the UI fund directly. Column six of Table 5.1 shows those states that reduce benefits based on back pay and those states that deny benefits.

If you are reinstated to your job with back pay, you will, without doubt, be ineligible for UI benefits, as you will no longer be unemployed. Reinstatement with back pay usually results from the appeal and arbitration of wrongful separations, and simply means that an arbitrator or civil court has ordered the employer to return the worker to his or her job with back payment for the period between the separation and the issuance of the order. If you are appealing your separation or you expect back payment from your

Table 5.1 Effect of Disqualifying Income on Weekly Benefit Amount

State (1)	Worker's Compensation (2)	Wages In Lieu of Notice (3)	Dismissal Payments (4)
AL	Benefit is reduced.	No benefit is paid.	No benefit is paid.
AK	—	Benefit is reduced.	Benefit is reduced.
AZ	—	—	—
AR	—	No benefit is paid. Not applicable to severance payments or accrued leave pay based on service for Armed Forces.	No benefit is paid. Not applicable to severance payments or accrued leave pay based on service for Armed Forces.
CA	Benefit is reduced.	Benefit is reduced (by interpretation).	—
CO	Benefit is reduced.	Benefit is reduced.	Benefit is reduced.
CT	No benefit is paid. If worker's compensation benefits are received subsequent to receipt of UI benefits, claimant is liable to repay UI benefits in excess of worker's compensation benefits.	No benefit is paid.	No benefit is paid. Not applicable to severance payments or accrued leave pay based on service for Armed Forces.
DE	Benefit is reduced.	—	Benefit is reduced.
DC	—	—	Benefit is reduced.
FL	Benefit is reduced.	Benefit is reduced.	—
GA	No benefit is paid.	No benefit is paid.	No benefit is paid.
HI	—	—	—
ID	—	—	—
IL	Benefit is reduced.	Benefit is reduced (by regulation).	—

Holiday Pay (5)	Back Pay (6)	Vacation Pay (7)
—	No benefit is paid.	—
Benefit is reduced.	—	Benefit is reduced.
—	—	—
—	Benefit is reduced.	Claimant will be paid amount equal to weekly benefit amount less that part of vacation pay payable for week that is in excess of 40% of weekly benefit amount.
—	Benefit is reduced.	—
—	Benefit is reduced. If receiving benefits at time of award, employer shall withhold from award the amount of benefits paid and remit to division of employment.	No benefit is paid.
—	—	—
—	Benefit is reduced.	—
—	Benefit is reduced. If receiving benefits at time of award, employer shall withhold from award the amount of benefits paid and remit to unemployment office.	—
—	—	—
—	—	No benefit is paid.
—	—	—
—	—	—
Benefit is reduced.	—	Benefit is reduced.

State (1)	Worker's Compensation (2)	Wages In Lieu of Notice (3)	Dismissal Payments (4)
IN	—	Benefit is reduced. Excludes greater of first $3 or $\frac{1}{5}$ weekly benefit amount from other than base-period employer.	Benefit is reduced. Excludes greater of first $3 or $\frac{1}{5}$ weekly benefit amount from other than base-period employer.
IA	Benefit is reduced.	Benefit is reduced.	Benefit is reduced.
KS	No benefit is paid.	—	—
KY	—	Benefit is reduced.	—
LA	Benefit is reduced.	Benefit is reduced.	Benefit is reduced. Duration is reduced, but not less than 1 week, for each week base-period employer provided severance pay which equaled or exceeded weekly benefit amount.
ME	—	Benefit is reduced.	Benefit is reduced.
MD	—	Benefit is reduced. Not applicable if claimant's unemployment was caused by abolition of job.	Benefit is reduced. Not applicable if claimant's unemployment was caused by abolition of job.

Holiday Pay (5)	Back Pay (6)	Vacation Pay (7)
Benefit is reduced. Excludes greater of first $3 or ⅕ weekly benefit amount from other than base-period employer.	Benefit is reduced. Excludes greater of first $3 or ⅕ weekly benefit amount from other than base-period employer. If receiving benefits at time of award, employer shall withhold from award the amount of benefits paid and remit to division of employment.	Benefit is reduced. Excludes greater of first $3 or ⅕ weekly benefit amount from other than base-period employer.
—	—	Deductibility of vacation pay is limited to 1 week if claimant is separated from employment and scheduled to receive vacation pay during period of unemployment attributable to employer, and employer does not designate vacation period to which payments will be allocated. However, if employer designates more than 1 week as vacation period, such payments are deductible.
—	No benefit is paid.	—
—	Benefit is reduced.	—
—	—	Benefit is reduced.
Benefit is reduced.	—	Benefit is reduced.
No benefit is paid. Not applicable to holiday pay attributable to any period outside terms of an employment agreement that specifies scheduled vacation or holiday periods.	—	No benefit is paid. Not applicable to holiday pay attributable to any period outside terms of an employment agreement that specifies scheduled vacation or holiday periods.

State (1)	Worker's Compensation (2)	Wages in Lieu of Notice (3)	Dismissal Payments (4)
MA	No benefit is paid.	No benefit is paid.	—
MI	—	No benefit is paid.	—
MN	Benefit is reduced.	Benefit is reduced.	Benefit is reduced.
MS	—	—	—
MO	Benefit is reduced.	—	—
MT	No benefit is paid.	—	—
NE	Benefit is reduced.	Benefit is reduced.	Benefit is reduced.
NV	—	No benefit is paid.	No benefit is paid.
NH	Benefit is reduced.	Benefit is reduced.	Benefit is reduced.
NJ	—	No benefit is paid.	—
NY	—	—	—
NM	—	Benefit is reduced (by regulation).	Benefit is reduced (by regulation).
NC	—	No benefit is paid.	No benefit is paid.
ND	—	—	—
OH	Benefit is reduced.	Benefit is reduced.	Benefit is reduced. Not applicable to severance payments or accrued leave pay based on services for the Armed Forces.
OK	—	—	—

Holiday Pay (5)	Back Pay (6)	Vacation Pay (7)
No benefit is paid.	—	—
No benefit is paid.	No benefit is paid.	No benefit is paid.
—	Benefit is reduced.	Benefit is reduced.
—	No benefit is paid. If receiving benefits at time of award, employer shall withhold from award the amount of benefits paid and remit to division of employment.	—
—	Benefit is reduced. If receiving benefits at time of award, employer shall withhold from award the amount of benefits paid and remit to division of employment.	—
—	—	—
—	—	—
—	—	No benefit is paid.
—	—	—
—	—	—
No benefit is paid.	—	No benefit is paid.
—	Benefit is reduced (by regulation).	—
—	No benefit is paid. If receiving benefits at time of award, employer shall withhold from award the amount of benefits paid and remit to division of employment.	No benefit is paid.
—	—	—
—	—	Benefit is reduced.
—	—	—

State (1)	Worker's Compensation (2)	Wages in Lieu of Notice (3)	Dismissal Payments (4)
OR	—	—	—
PA	—	—	—
PR	—	—	—
RI	Benefit is reduced.	—	—
SC	—	—	—
SD	Benefit is reduced.	Benefit is reduced.	Benefit is reduced.
TN	No benefit is paid.	No benefit is paid.	—
TX	No benefit is paid.	No benefit is paid.	—
UT	—	Benefit is reduced.	Benefit is reduced.
VT	Benefit is reduced.	Benefit is reduced.	—
VI	—	—	—
VA	—	Benefit is reduced.	Benefit is reduced.
WA	—	—	—
WV	No benefit is paid.	No benefit is paid.	—
WI	Benefit is reduced.	—	Benefit is reduced. Reduction as wages for a given week only when definitely allocated by close of such week and payable to claimant for that week at full applicable wage rate, and claimant has had due notice of such allocation.
WY	—	Benefit is reduced.	Benefit is reduced.

Holiday Pay (5)	Back Pay (6)	Vacation Pay (7)
Holiday and vacation pay may or may not be deductible, depending on circumstances under which claimant receives them.	—	Holiday and vacation pay may or may not be deductible, depending on circumstances under which claimant receives them.
—	—	No benefit is paid.
—	—	Benefit is reduced.
—	—	Benefit is reduced.
—	—	—
Benefit is reduced.	—	—
—	—	—
—	—	—
—	—	Benefit is reduced.
Benefit is reduced.	Benefit is reduced.	Benefit is reduced.
—	—	—
—	—	Benefit is reduced.
—	If receiving benefits at time of award, employer shall withhold from award the amount of benefits paid and remit to division of employment.	—
—	—	No benefit is paid.
—	—	—
—	—	—

employer because of a salary dispute, it is advisable to ask what effect this may have on your future eligibility for UI benefits.

In this chapter, we've shown how the failure to meet certain requirements can result in complete ineligibility for UI benefits, as well as how certain types of income can result in partial or total ineligibility. Hopefully, we've also shown that if you become separated from your employment, it makes sense to file a claim—even if you strongly suspect that you are ineligible for benefits. In some circumstances, you may discover that you qualify for other types of assistance. And, of course, you may find that you are in fact eligible for full or partial UI payments.

6. UNDERSTANDING HOW BENEFITS ARE COMPUTED

Understandably, most unemployment insurance (UI) claimants are quite interested in the amount of unemployment insurance that can be paid to them based on their earnings from covered employment. In this chapter, we will explain the base periods and wage requirements for basic eligibility in each of the fifty states, the District of Columbia, Puerto Rico, and the Virgin Islands, enabling you to make comparisons that will allow you to maximize your benefits. We will expand on earlier explanations of combined wage and interstate claims. We will explain how benefit entitlement is computed, and will see how the weekly benefit check can be affected by dependents' allowance and part-time employment. Finally, we will see how you can qualify for a second, or subsequent, claim.

When looking at monetary eligibility, be aware that the various factors that affect your benefit amount—the base period, the benefit year, qualifying wages, etc.—are very much interrelated. In fact, these factors are so interwoven that it is nearly impossible to explain one factor without citing another.

Always keep in mind that your unemployment office will make all the necessary computations on your claim. You most certainly won't have to determine your own base-period wages or make any other calculations! Still, it will be helpful if you understand the basis of the unemployment office's computations, as this may enable you to maximize your eligibility and detect any problems with your claim. Be aware that nowadays, computation is largely computerized, and that whatever the computer does is based on its program—a program that was devised by human beings and can use only data entered by human beings. Sometimes the source of that data is the claimant, sometimes it is the employer, and sometimes it is the unemployment office staff. At any point, necessary information can be omitted, incorrectly recorded, or misunderstood. If you have some grasp of the computation process, you will be more likely to spot any errors and take the appropriate action to correct them.

If you do decide to learn as much as you can about the computation of monetary eligibility, you may find it helpful to contact your local unemployment office and request the "claimant's handbook" or other written information for clarification of the regulations in your state. If any questions arise on your part, you should, of course, directly contact a UI representative for help. Before you seek clarification, though, try to formulate questions that are as concrete and specific as possible. This chapter should give you a better working knowledge of the UI process and help you to pinpoint those areas that you might need help in understanding.

UNDERSTANDING THE BASE PERIOD

UI benefits are based on past earnings from covered employment paid in a fifty-two-week period called the *base period*. Each state's base period is defined by state law and is determined by the initial filing date of the claim. All states use a fifty-two-week period, but they do not all use the *same* fifty-two-week period. Several states have provisions that allow the extension of the base period beyond the fifty-two weeks that would normally constitute it when the claimant has been disabled from working and/or has been filing for worker's compensation during what would have been the state's usual base period. This flexibility allows greater eligibility by eliminating periods of unemployment and including employment that would not have been in the usual base period. A few states allow adjustment of the base period when there are successive claims, and a few allow alternative base periods when a claimant does not qualify monetarily in the usual one. Below, we will explain and illustate the five regular—that is, unadjusted—types of base periods. Table 6.1 will show you which base period applies in your state.

Base Period One

The first type of base period, used in Michigan and New York, includes the fifty-two-week period that occurs immediately before the establishment of a valid claim. (Massachusetts used to use this base period, too, but as of October 1993, it adopted base period five.) In Michigan, claims are effective the Sunday of the week in which the application is filed. So if you submit your claim applica-

Table 6.1 The Five Base Periods

Base Period	States
Base Period One. Includes the 52-week period completed immediately before the establishment of a valid claim.	Michigan and New York.
Base Period Two. Includes the 4 calendar quarters completed before the establishment of a valid claim.	Nebraska.
Base Period Three. Includes the first 4 of the last 5 calendar quarters completed at filing, but does not change until one additional month has passed.	California.
Base Period Four. Extends from January through December of the calendar year preceding the claim filing. Uniform for all claims filed through June 30, with the base period changing on July 1 of each year.	New Hampshire.
Base Period Five. Includes the first 4 of the last 5 calendar quarters completed before the establishment of a valid claim.	All states except Michigan, New York, Nebraska, California, and New Hampshire.

tion on a Monday, the included wages will be those that were paid to you during the fifty-two-week period that ended the previous Saturday. In New York, claims are effective the Monday following the week in which a valid application is filed. In this case, if you submit your claim on Monday, the base period would end on the previous Sunday.

This base period has the advantage of using the claimant's most recent wages, which are often the highest wages, as well. This base period is also the most beneficial to the recently employed, who may have had employment only in the last few months as opposed to the last few years. However, since there is little or no lag period between the end of the base period and the effective date of the claim, there are no lag wages on which a subsequent claim can be based. A *lag period* is that time between the end of the base period and the effective date of the claim, and *lag wages* are wages paid during that period and beyond—wages not used for claim computation because they were not paid during the base period. Not surprisingly, the states that use this first base period are also wage request states, meaning that the employer must be contacted for a wage report only when a claim is filed. Clearly, with the base period having ended only a week before the claim was filed, employers did not have time to report wages to the state, nor would the employers have known which wages to report, as the base period changes each week.

Base Period Two

The second type of base period is used only by the State of Nebraska. Claims are based on wages paid during the four calendar quarters completed before the initial claim was established. Figure 6.1 will help you visualize this base period. In each row, the base period has been shaded, and the current or filing quarter is shown to the right of the line of base period quarters. As time progresses and each new quarter arrives, the base period drops the oldest quarter and picks up the newest completed quarter. Thus, for a claim established in January, February, or March of 1994, the base period is January 1, 1993 through December 31, 1993.

This type of base period, like the base period previously discussed, has the advantage of using very recent wages, which are often higher than earlier wages. Also, like the first type of base period, it is usually most beneficial to those whose employment record is very recent. Unlike base period one, however, this base period may provide some lag wages—anywhere from one week of

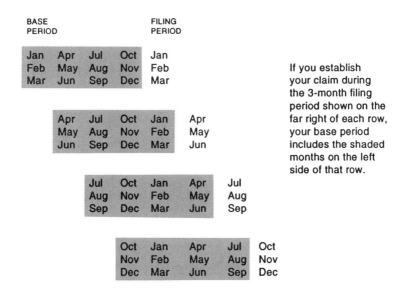

Figure 6.1. Base Period Two

wages, if the claim was filed in the first week of the current quarter, to thirteen weeks of wages, if the claim was filed in the last week of the current quarter. However, it is doubtful that a subsequent claim could be established *solely* on these lag wages as there would not be a sufficient distribution of the wages over the new base period. (We will discuss basic eligibility requirements and requirements for subsequent claims later in this chapter.)

Base Period Three

California's base period includes the first four of the last five calendar quarters completed at filing. However, the base period does not change for one additional month, so that the lag period may be as much as four to seven months in length. Figure 6.2 gives you a visual representation of this base period. As in the previous figure, the filing period—which is three months in each case, but not a standard calendar quarter—appears at the far right of each row. The base-period quarters are shaded a dark gray, and appear to the far left of each row. The lag period, which is shaded a light gray, is shown to the immediate right of the base period. Thus, for a claim filed in November or December 1993 or January 1994, the base period would be July 1, 1992 through June 30, 1993.

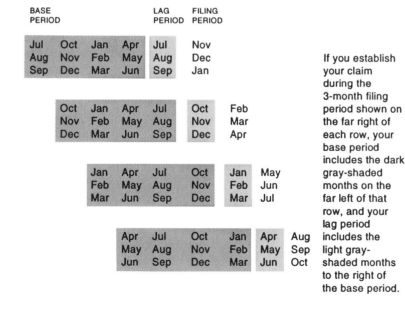

Figure 6.2. Base Period Three

As you can see, this base period has one whole lag quarter and one month before the base period changes, plus whatever time elapses in the current or filing quarter, all of which is the lag period. Because this type of base period does not make use of the most recent earnings, it is less beneficial than other base periods for claimants who became employed relatively recently, and for claimants who recently experienced a great increase in covered wages. However, the longer lag period and possibility of greater lag wages are potentially beneficial in that they may be used to help establish a subsequent claim.

Base Period Four

Only the State of New Hampshire uses the fourth type of base period. This base period is uniform in that for all claims filed from July 1 of one year through June 30 of the following year, the base period includes the full calendar year completed before July 1 of the first year. This base period changes only once a year, on July 1. The following table clarifies base period four.

If you file a claim between:	*Your base period is*:
July 1, 1992–June 30, 1993	January 1, 1991–December 31, 1991
July 1, 1993–June 30, 1994	January 1, 1992–December 31, 1992
July 1, 1994–June 30, 1995	January 1, 1992–December 31, 1993

This base period has a widely varying lag period—anywhere from six months, if you file your claim during the month of July right after the new base period is in effect, to eighteen months, if you file your claim the next June. This could be very beneficial for long-term workers, but has great disadvantages for the recently employed.

Base Period Five

The fifth type of base period, and by far the most common, includes wages paid during the first four of the last five calendar quarters completed at the time of the initial filing. In all, forty-eight states currently use this base period. (See Table 6.1.)

Figure 6.3 should help you visualize this base period. Again, the current quarter, or filing quarter, is shown to the far right of the row of base-period quarters, which are shaded a dark gray. In addition to the current quarter, there is a lag quarter, found to the immediate right of the base period and shaded a light gray. So, for example, for a claim filed in January through March 1994, the base period would extend from October 1992 to September 1993, and the lag quarter would extend from October to December 1993.

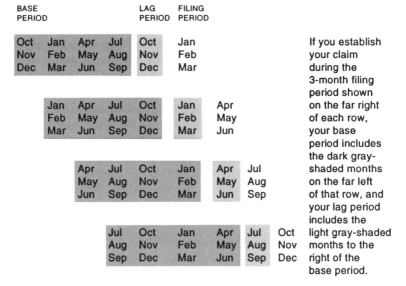

Figure 6.3. Base Period Five

This type of base period has the same advantages and disadvantages of the third type. Like base period three, it does not make use of the most recent wages. However, because of the relatively long lag period—one complete lag quarter, plus whatever has passed of the filing quarter—the claimant may have a great deal of unused wages that could be helpful in establishing a subsequent claim.

Two points should be highlighted regarding base periods that are defined by calendar quarters. First, it is important to note that some states consider a new quarter as starting the first day of the first month of a new quarter—that is, on January 1, April 1, July 1, and October 1. Each of these dates, then, brings about a change in the base period. In other states, the quarter starts with the first full week of the quarter. For example, January 1, 1993 occurred on a Friday. In states where the quarter begins on the first full week of the month, the change of base period did not occur until January 3, the Sunday of the first full week of that quarter. You may wish to ask your unemployment office when the base period changes in your state.

The other point we wish to highlight is that when making a monetary eligibility computation, states generally consider earnings only on a *when paid* basis. So even if you earned wages before the base period ended, they would not be included in the computation unless they were paid to you before the end of the base period.

COMPARING BASE PERIODS

If you have worked in covered employment in only one state, the explanation of base periods might seem like an academic exercise, as you can file your claim only against the state in which you worked, and you are bound by the base period of that state. Even in this situation, however, it is beneficial to understand how the base period is determined. And in other circumstances, of course, a knowledge of the base period is vital to maximizing UI benefits. In the following sections, we will look at a number of different employment situations in which comparisons of base periods might yield larger benefit checks.

Covered Employment in One State

As just discussed, even if you have held employment in one state only, you may benefit from an understanding of the base period in your state. Suppose you were employed for well over a year in the same state for the same employer, but only recently received a substantial salary increase. You may wish to delay filing until the quarter in which you received the salary increase becomes part of the base period. Of course, because your claim cannot be back-dated, it would be advisable to delay filing only if you could manage financially during the delay. In other words, you must weigh the financial advantage of waiting—a higher weekly benefit amount—against the disadvantage of waiting—the postponement of benefit checks. And, of course, it would not be wise to delay if your salary before the increase was sufficient to qualify you for a maximum claim, unless you were laid off just before a new calendar year or at a time when you know that the state maximum weekly benefit amount is about to be increased. In many states, the weekly benefit amount is subject to annual review, and projected increases are published. If you were laid off the week before such an increase, you may wish to wait until the week of the increase to file your initial claim.

Before you decide to delay filing to increase your benefit amount, we suggest that you verify your strategy by checking with knowledge-able UI staff. You will need to double-check actual base-period change dates, benefit-amount change dates, and other pertinent facts. Don't rely on information given to you at reception desks or in newspaper reports. Either of these sources could be wrong.

Covered Employment in More Than One State

Workers who have covered employment in more than one state

stand to gain the most from comparing base periods. Depending on their situation, these workers can enjoy the advantage of filing a *combined wage claim* under the Interstate Arrangment for Combining Wages and Employment, commonly called the Combined Wage Agreement; a straight *interstate claim*; or, in rare instances, an *interstate combined wage claim*. Let's look at each of these three types of claims, and see how they may be able to help you qualify for and maximize your UI benefits.

Combined Wage Claims

As we stated in Chapter 2, the basic requirement for a combined wage claim is the earning of covered wages in two states during the filing state's base period. The amount of earned wages in each of the states doesn't really matter, as long as the overall amount and distribution are sufficient to meet the filing state's monetary requirements. Be aware that you do not have to have wages in the filing state itself—just in its base period. But you do usually have to file your application in the state that you're filing against. It is this state—the filing state—that is the *liable* state. In other words, once wages are transferred to that state, all determinations with regard to monetary entitlement are made by that state.

The purpose of the Interstate Arrangement for Combining Wages and Employment is to provide UI benefits for those individuals who have worked in two or more states, and who need to combine these wages to qualify for a basic claim or to qualify for a better claim. Obviously, this arrangement was not designed so that claimants could "shop around"—that is, arbitrarily choose and file against whatever state has the highest benefit rates, even though they may have never worked or lived in that state. Nevertheless, it is possible to visit a state in person simply to file a claim. Just remember that you must be available for and seeking work in the labor market in which your claim has been filed.

Let us say that you have worked for the last two years in the States of Virginia and Maryland, where the maximum weekly benefit amount is less than $250. Chances are that if you worked in both of these states, you live in the District of Columbia's metropolitan area. Therefore, if your salary rate is sufficient to qualify you for the maximum weekly benefit amount, you should file against the District of Columbia, where the maximum weekly benefit amount is $335. Note, however, that in order to file a claim against D.C., you have to file the claim *in* D.C. Before you decide to travel to another state simply to file an unemployment claim, be sure to find out if there are any requirements with regard to having a local address and attachment to the labor market. Keep in mind that you must check the regulations of the state that you plan to file against, because that is the state that will make the determinations on your claim.

Two other rules regarding combined wage claims merit discussion. First, be aware that if you combine wages from any two states, you must combine wages from all states in which you had covered employment during the base period. You cannot arbitrarily choose to omit one state because you do not wish that employer or state to be charged for your claim or to discover that you are filing a claim. Second, be aware that it is unlawful to cancel a combined wage claim in one state and then try to establish a combined wage claim in another state using the same wages or periods of employment. Obviously, it is best to look into your options before you file your initial claim.

Interstate Claims

It often happens that an individual who qualifies for a claim in each of the states in which he or she worked chooses to file a "straight" interstate claim against whichever state has the highest weekly benefit amount. In other words, the claim is filed against one state from another state in which the claimant had performed services in covered employment. In this case, the state in which the claim is filed acts as an agent by accepting the claim for the paying state or liable state—the state where the claimant had covered employment. The claim is based only on wages earned in the paying state, and the paying state makes all determinations regarding entitlement and eligibility.

Of course, sometimes claimants don't realize that a straight interstate claim might provide them with the greatest benefits. Fortunately, if you file a combined wage claim and later discover that you would have qualified for greater weekly benefits on an interstate claim, most states will allow you to cancel the combined wage claim in favor of a backdated interstate claim. If you have already received benefit checks from the combined wage claim, you will have to either agree to repay the resulting overpayment when the interstate claim is established, or authorize the liable state to deduct the appropriate amount from your new benefits. While this will not result in a loss of money for you, it may result in a delay of benefit payments as well as a considerable amount of paperwork.

According to the terms of the Combined Wage Agreement, the wages transferred from another state as the result of a combined wage claim should be used only if they are needed to qualify the claimant for benefits, or if they will increase the weekly or maximum benefit amount. So if you file a combined wage claim and the filing state realizes that you would have qualified for greater benefits had you filed against one of the transferring states, you should be so notified and given the option of either continuing the combined wage claim or canceling it in favor of the interstate claim. And if you would qualify for a maximum entitlement against your filing state without the transferred wages, the filing state will be obliged to return the transferred wages without using them. Generally, your filing state will give you notice that the wages from the other state were returned because they would not have increased your benefit entitlement.

Interstate Combined Wage Claims

Because states have different base periods and different wage qualification requirements, it is possible for a claimant to have earned wages in two or more states, and yet not qualify for a combined wage claim in the state where he or she is submitting the claim application. Since forty-eight of the fifty-three jurisdictions share a common base period, this is a rare occurrence. However, when it does occur, the claimant may still get UI benefits through an interstate combined wage claim—a claim in which wages are transferred from two or more states and filed against a state other than the one in which the claim application was submitted.

How does the interstate combined wage claim work? When a claimant does not monetarily qualify for a combined wage claim against the state in which he or she filed, the first option is to allow him or her to file an interstate combined wage claim against the state in which he or she last worked. If this does not result in monetary eligibility, he or she may file against another state in which he or she worked. Only in the unlikely event that the claimant does not qualify in the filing state or in any of the states in which he or she worked can the claimant file an interstate combined wage claim against *any* state.

Consecutive Claims

Our discussion of interstate and combined wage claims would not be complete without a word about consecutive claims. If you earned sufficient wages in each of the two states in which you worked to qualify for claims in either state, it may actually be best to file a claim against one state and then, after that claim has been exhausted, to file against the second state and exhaust those benefits. (Be aware that you may file only one UI claim at a time.) Why would you choose to file two separate claims rather than one larger combined wage claim? Some very good reasons come to mind. For instance, it may be that the employment in your industry is becoming obsolete, and you fear that finding a new job may take a long time. Or you may reside in an area that is experiencing economic decline, with no recovery expected in the near future. Whatever the reason, you might want to consider maximizing the *length* of the eligibility rather than opting for short-term higher weekly benefit amounts. And, of course, it could be that your salaries will qualify you for the maximum weekly benefit amount in both states.

If you do decide to file in first one state and then the other, be aware that if the two states have a common base period, it would be preferable to file first against the state in which you have the earlier work history. This will increase the likelihood that after the first state's benefits have been exhausted, the wages paid in the second state will still be usable. If the two states have different base periods, your decision may require a considerable amount of research.

THE BENEFIT YEAR

The *benefit year*—the life span of a claim—usually is the fifty-two-week period during which the claimant may draw those benefits to which he or she is entitled. If the claimant returns to work, stops claiming benefits, and then becomes unemployed again within that benefit year, the claimant can file an *additional claim,* which will enable him or her to receive the balance remaining on the existing claim. Since the benefit year entitlement will have already been established in a case such as this, further monetary computation will not be necessry. And in those states that have waiting periods, the claimant will not have to serve a new waiting period. However, if there is a separation issue on the additional claim, it will have to be resolved before benefits can be paid. At the end of the benefit year, the claimant usually loses further benefit rights on that claim whether or not the entitlement has been exhausted.

Forty-nine of the fifty-three jurisdictions—all the states except Massachusetts, New York, Arkansas, and New Hampshire—begin their benefit years on the week of the initial filing. In Massachusetts, the benefit year begins on the Sunday preceding the filing of the claim. In New York, the benefit year begins on the Monday after the filing of the claim. In Arkansas, the benefit year begins with the quarter in which the claim is filed, and because the quarter may have begun weeks before the filing, the benefit year can last anywhere from forty to fifty-two weeks. In New Hampshire, the benefit year begins with a uniform date, the first of April. There are also uniform dates stipulated in Florida's state laws for that state's cigar-industry workers, and in Puerto Rico's state laws for that state's agricultural workers. (For all other workers in Florida and Puerto Rico, the benefit year begins on the week of the initial filing.) In instances in which there is a uniform benefit year, the worker ordinarily qualifies for a new benefit year immediately upon the expiration of the current one as long as his or her entitlement has not yet been exhausted.

Table 6.2 shows when each of the fifty-three jurisdictions begins its benefit year. A *Yes* in the second column indicates that the state begins the benefit year with the week of filing. The third column shows those states that begin the benefit year at a different time either for all workers or for certain workers. (The last two columns of Table 6.2 will be discussed later in this chapter.)

In a few states, the benefit year begins with the week of the initial filing only if the claimant meets one or more nonmonetary eligibility requirements. If not—if, for instance, the claimant is found to be employed or unavailable for work at the time of filing—the benefit year is canceled. In New York, for example, the benefit year begins on the Monday after the filing of the claim only if the claimant is not disqualified. If the claimant is disqualified or suspended, the benefit year begins when the disqualification is over.

Once the claimant has exhausted the potential monetary entitlement in one state, he or she must wait until that benefit year has expired before filing another claim against the same state. Other requirements that must be met when filing successive claims against the same state will be discussed later in this chapter.

THE WAITING PERIOD

The waiting period is a week of unemployment for which the claimant receives no compensation, but during which he or she must be otherwise eligible for UI benefits. Generally, the waiting period is the first week of the claim. All but eleven states have a one-week waiting period that must be served before benefits can be paid for total unemployment. Ten of the eleven exceptions—Connecticut, Delaware, Georgia, Iowa, Kentucky, Maryland, Michigan, Nevada, New Hampshire, and Wisconsin—have no waiting period at all for partial or total unemployment. Alabama requires no waiting period on claims for total unemployment, but does for partial unemployment.

Usually, a week of partial unemployment can be counted as

Table 6.2 Benefit Years and Waiting Periods

State (1)	Benefit Year Begins on Filing Week (2)	Benefit Year Begins at Other Time (3)	Waiting Period for Total Unemployment (4)	Waiting Period for Partial Unemployment (5)
AL	Yes	—	No	Yes
AK	Yes	—	Yes	Yes
AZ	Yes	—	Yes	Yes
AR	No	Begins with the filing quarter.	Yes	Yes
CA	Yes	—	Yes	Yes
CO	Yes	—	Yes	Yes
CT	Yes	—	No	No
DE	Yes	—	No	No
DC	Yes	—	Yes	Yes
FL	Yes	Uniform date for cigar industry workers.	Yes	Yes
GA	Yes	—	No, by interpretation.	No, by interpretation.
HI	Yes	—	Yes	Yes
ID	Yes	—	Yes	Yes
IL	Yes	—	Yes	Yes
IN	Yes	—	Yes	Yes
IA	Yes	—	No	No
KS	Yes	—	Yes	Yes
KY	Yes	—	No	No
LA	Yes	—	Yes	Yes
ME	Yes	—	Yes	Yes
MD	Yes	—	No	No
MA	No	Begins the Sunday before filing.	Yes	Yes
MI	Yes	—	No	No
MN	Yes	—	Yes	Yes
MS	Yes	—	Yes	Yes
MO	Yes	—	Yes	Yes
MT	Yes	—	Yes	No
NE	Yes	—	Yes	Yes
NV	Yes	—	No	No
NH	No	Begins April 1.	No	No
NJ	Yes	—	Yes	Yes
NM	Yes	—	Yes	Yes

State (1)	Benefit Year Begins on Filing Week (2)	Benefit Year Begins at Other Time (3)	Waiting Period for Total Unemployment (4)	Waiting Period for Partial Unemployment (5)
NY	No	Begins the Monday after filing.	Yes	Yes
NC	Yes	—	Yes	Yes
ND	Yes	—	Yes	Yes
OH	Yes	—	Yes	Yes
OK	Yes	—	Yes	Yes
OR	Yes	—	Yes	Yes
PA	Yes	—	Yes	Yes
PR	Yes	Uniform date for agricultural workers.	Yes	Yes
RI	Yes	—	Yes	Yes
SC	Yes	—	Yes	Yes
SD	Yes	—	Yes	Yes
TN	Yes	—	Yes	Yes
TX	Yes	—	Yes	Yes
UT	Yes	—	Yes	Yes
VT	Yes	—	Yes	Yes
VA	Yes	—	Yes	Yes
VI	Yes	—	Yes	Yes
WA	Yes	—	Yes	Yes
WV	Yes	—	Yes	Yes
WI	Yes	—	No	No
WY	Yes	—	Yes	Yes

the waiting period if the claimant would have qualified for partial benefits that week. For instance, if you were laid off on a Monday and filed your claim that very week, you would be able to count that week as your waiting period as long as your earnings for that week did not exceed the definition of partial unemployment in your state. Of the forty-two states that require a one-week waiting period for total unemployment, only Montana does not require a waiting period on claims for partial benefits. Even in the case of the states that require a one-week waiting period, exceptions are sometimes made. For instance, in California, the governor may suspend the waiting period requirement in an emergency situation. In New York, the waiting period does not have to be the first week of the claim; instead, it can be "accumulated" by counting four days of unemployment within four weeks.

Four states allow UI benefit payments for the waiting period under certain conditions. In Missouri, the waiting period is paid after nine consecutive weeks of compensable unemployment after the waiting period. (The term *compensable* refers to a period of time when the claimant is eligible for benefits and files claims.) In New Jersey, the waiting period is paid after three such weeks. In Texas, the waiting period is paid after receipt of benefits that are equal to three times the weekly benefit amount of the claim. And in Minnesota, the waiting period is paid if the claimant gains full-time employment after four weeks of receiving benefits.

Columns four and five of Table 6.2 provide a state-by-state look at waiting periods. Those states that impose a waiting period for total unemployment are marked with a *Yes* in the fourth column. Those states that impose a waiting period for partial unemployment are marked with a *Yes* in the fifth column.

MONETARY QUALIFICATION REQUIREMENTS
or, how much money do you need to make and/or how long do you have to work before you can get UI?

Throughout this chapter, we have made reference to monetary qualification and distribution requirements. Now it is time to explain what these terms mean. Before we begin our discussion, though, be aware that if you have worked steadily at full-time employment throughout your state's base period, you need not worry about minimal earnings or distribution requirements. Your employment will be sufficient to qualify you for the maximum claim weeks. The discussion of minimum earning and distribution requirements is necessary only for claimants who have been sporadically employed during the base period.

All states require claimants to have worked a minimum length of time *or* to have earned a minimum amount of wages in order to qualify for UI benefits in that state. Florida, for instance, requires twenty weeks of employment; Oregon, eighteen weeks; and Washington State, 680 hours. Often, states with length-of-employment requirements also specify a minimum amount of money that must have been earned during the required number of weeks. Sometimes this is stated as a minimum average, like the $20 per week required by Florida. In other states, it is stated as an amount that is defined by the wage laws or earning averages of the state, such as the requirement of twenty times the minimum hourly wage that is the case in Michigan, or the minimum of 20 percent of the statewide average weekly wage that is the case in New Jersey.

Other states require a minimum amount of earnings in the base period overall, as well as in the highest quarter of the base period. (The term *high quarter* refers to the quarter in which the claimant earned the highest amount of wages. This may be any one of the four quarters in the base period.) Usually, the total base-period amount has to be equal to or greater than one and one-half times the high-quarter earnings. Most states require wages in at least two quarters of the base period for qualification, whether this is specifically stated in the state's laws or simply required by the mathematics of the qualification formula.

Still other states that require an amount of wages express the requirement as a multiple of the weekly benefit amount of the claim. For instance, Arkansas requires base-period earnings equal to twenty-seven times the weekly benefit amount, and several states require earnings equal to forty times the weekly benefit amount. A claimant with a minimal or sporadic work history might have to actually file a claim to determine whether this type of qualification requirement has been met.

UI staff members are often asked how long a person has to work to be eligible for UI benefits. In states that have the two-quarter requirement, a five-month period of employment is the general rule. But this is really just shorthand for the more complicated requirement that a claimant must have wages in two quarters of the base period, and that wages must be distributed so that the total base-period wages are at least one and one-half times the wages earned in the highest quarter. In states that do not specify a number of weeks of work, one could conceivably earn $10,000 in one week of one base-period quarter and $6,000 in another week of a second base-period quarter, and still qualify for benefits. But whether the requirement is stated as a length of employment or an amount of wages, qualification usually requires employment in more than one quarter, with one quarter being thirteen weeks in length.

Table 6.3 summarizes each state's basic requirements for benefits and the actual wage amounts that are required for the minimum claim. The second column of Table 6.3 shows those states that have a length-of-employment requirement—a requirement normally expressed as weeks or hours. As you'll see, some of these states define a week of work in terms of a minimum amount of money that must have been earned in that week. For instance, as mentioned earlier, Florida requires twenty weeks of employment, and this is defined in Florida law as earnings of twenty times an average weekly wage of $20.

The third column shows those states that require amounts of base-period wages that are at least one and one-half or one and one-fourth times the wages earned in the highest quarter; those states that require base-period wages that are a specific multiple of the weekly benefit amount; and those states that have a "flat amount" requirement, meaning that the state law declares a definite amount of wages that must be earned to qualify for benefits.

The fourth column of Table 6.3 shows the required distribution of base-period wages. As we noted, most states require wages in at least two base-period quarters. Other states, however, have more complex requirements. For instance, Illinois specifies that there must be at least $440 in earnings outside the highest quarter. Kentucky specifies that there must be earnings of at least eight times the weekly benefit amount of the claim in the last two quarters of the base period, *and* that there must be $750 in earnings outside the highest quarter.

The fifth column of Table 6.3 shows the actual dollar amounts needed in the base period for the minimum claim in each state. Finally, the sixth column shows the actual dollar amount needed in the high quarter for those states with high-quarter requirements.

It's worth emphasizing once more that those claimants who have worked without interruption at full-time jobs need not worry about meeting the qualification requirements discussed here. It's also worth pointing out that the table just discussed does not tell the whole story. For instance, you may remember from an earlier discussion that some states have alternative base periods when a person does not qualify monetarily under that state's usual base period. So even if your own calculations have shown you to be ineligible for benefits, you should most certainly file your claim application. You may be pleasantly surprised!

THE WEEKLY BENEFIT AMOUNT

If you have read this chapter to this point, you should have a pretty good idea of whether you qualify for minimum UI benefits in your state, based on your employment record. If you do qualify, you're certainly interested in finding out how much compensation you'll be receiving each week. For this reason, it's now time to learn about the *weekly benefit amount*—the amount payable for one week of total unemployment without an addition of any dependents' allowance or a deduction for any type of income earned. (Later in the chapter, we'll learn about both the dependents' allowance and deductions for partial unemployment.)

The weekly benefit amount may be computed in four different ways, which will be discussed shortly. Regardless of the method of computation used, the weekly benefit amount is nearly always based on gross earnings—that is, wages earned before any deductions for income tax, health insurance, Social Security, or union dues, as well as other possible deductions. The weekly benefit amount also always falls within a range set by the state. This range is defined by minimum and maximum weekly benefit amounts, which are often computed annually or semiannually, based on the average weekly wage in covered employment in that state.

Table 6.4, which shows how weekly benefit amounts are computed for each state, groups the states into four categories according to the basis each state uses for its computations. As you can see, in thirty-one states—referred to in the table as "High-Quarter-Formula States"—the weekly benefit amount is based on wages paid during the highest quarter of the base period. As shown in column 2, to arrive at the weekly benefit amount, these wages are multiplied by a specified fraction or percentage. You will note that some states have variable rates. For instance, in California, the rates vary from 1/23 to 1/33. According to at least one source, in some states, this variable rate is meant to give a greater proportion of benefits to lower-paid workers, and in other states, it is meant to give a greater amount to claimants with dependents. The third column of the table indicates whether the state rounds cents to the next higher dollar or the next lower dollar, as benefits are always paid in whole-dollar amounts. The minimum weekly benefit amount for each state is shown in column 4, and the maximum weekly benefit amount is shown in column 5.

Eleven states—referred to in the table as "Multi-Quarter-Formula States"—base the weekly benefit amount on the wages paid in more than just the highest quarter. Usually, the two highest quarters are used, but some states use other quarters or portions of other quarters. Again, to reach the benefit amount, the specified wages are multiplied by a specified fraction.

In six states—referred to in the table as "Annual-Wage-Formula States"—the weekly benefit amount is computed as a percentage of the total wages earned in the base period. Again, some states have variable rates.

In the five remaining states—referred to as the "Average-Weekly-Wage-Formula States"—the weekly benefit amount is based on the average weekly wage earned during the base period or during part of the base period. As shown in column 2, the weekly benefit amount is a specified percentage of these wages. For instance, the weekly benefit amount in Florida is 50 percent of the claimant's
(Copy continues on page 160.)

Table 6.3. Wage and Employment Requirements for Benefits

State (1)	Minimum Length-of-Employment Requirement (2)	Minimum Base-Period Wage Requirement (3)
AL	—	1½ x high-quarter wages.
AK	—	Flat amount specified by state.
AZ	—	1½ x high-quarter wages. For alternative flat-amount requirement, claimant must have earned wages in 2 quarters of base period, wages in 1 quarter sufficient to qualify for maximum weekly benefit amount, and total base-period wages equal to or greater than taxable wage base ($7,000).
AR	—	27 x weekly benefit amount.
CA	—	1¼ x high-quarter wages. Claimant must have earned either $1,300 in high quarter or $900 in high quarter with base-period wages equal to 1.25 x high-quarter wages.
CO	—	40 x weekly benefit amount.
CT	—	40 x weekly benefit amount.
DE	—	36 x weekly benefit amount. If claimant fails to meet qualifying requirement for weekly benefit amount computed on high-quarter wages but does meet qualifying requirement for next lower bracket, claimant is eligible for lower weekly benefit amount. State provides stepdown of 5 brackets.
DC	—	1½ x high-quarter wages.
FL	20 weeks, expressed as 20 x average weekly wage of at least $20 in base period, is equivalent to 20 weeks' employment with wages averaging at least $20.	20 x average weekly wage of at least $20 in base period, equivalent to 20 weeks' employment with wages averaging at least $20.
GA	—	1½ x high-quarter wages. For alternative flat-amount requirement, claimant must have earned wages in 2 quarters of base period and total base-period wages of 40 x weekly benefit amount.
HI	—	26 x weekly benefit amount.
ID	—	1¼ x high-quarter wages.

Minimum Wage Distribution Requirement (4)	Minimum Total Base-Period Wage Requirement (5)	Minimum High-Quarter Wage Requirement (6)
Wages in 2 quarters.	$1,032.00	$516.01
Wages in 2 quarters.	$1,000.00	—
Wages in 2 quarters.	$1,500.00	$1,000.00
Wages in 2 quarters.	$1,215.00	$607.50
—	$1,125.00. Claimant needs either $1,300 in high quarter, or $900 in high quarter with base-period wages equal to 1.25 x high-quarter wages.	$900.00
—	$1,000.00	—
Wages in 2 quarters.	$600.00	—
—	—	$965.99
Wages in 2 quarters.	$1,950.00	$1,300.00
Wages in 2 quarters.	$400.00	—
Wages in 2 quarters.	$1,350.00	$900.00
Wages in 2 quarters.	$130.00	—
Wages in 2 quarters.	$1,430.01	$1,144.01

State (1)	Minimum Length-of-Employment Requirement (2)	Minimum Base-Period Wage Requirement (3)
IL	—	Flat amount specified by state.
IN	—	1¼ x high-quarter wages.
IA	—	1¼ x high-quarter wages. Claimant must also have 1½ x high-quarter amount computed at 3.5% of the statewide average weekly wage.
KS	—	30 x weekly benefit amount.
KY	—	1½ x high-quarter wages.
LA	—	1½ x high-quarter wages.
ME	—	Flat amount specified by state.
MD	—	1½ x high-quarter wages. The multiple (1½) is not applied to claimant's high-quarter wages; but the qualifying amount, shown in a schedule, is computed at upper limit of each wage bracket. If claimant fails to meet qualifying requirement for weekly benefit amount computed on high-quarter wages but does meet qualifying requirement for next lower bracket, claimant is eligible for lower weekly benefit amount. State provides stepdown of 6 brackets.
MA	—	30 x weekly benefit amount.
MI	20 weeks' in which claimant earned 20 x state minimum hourly wage ($67). For alternative flat-amount requirement, claimant must have had 14 weeks' employment and base-period wages equal to 20 x state average weekly wage.	20 x state minimum hourly wage ($67).
MN	15 weeks, with no specified weekly amount.	1¼ x high-quarter wages.

Minimum Wage Distribution Requirement (4)	Minimum Total Base-Period Wage Requirement (5)	Minimum High-Quarter Wage Requirement (6)
$440 in quarter outside high quarter.	$1,600.00	—
$1,500.00 in last 2 quarters.	$2,500.00	$750.00
Wages in 2 quarters.	$1,090.00	$730.00
Wages in 2 quarters.	$1,860.00	—
8 x weekly benefit amount in last 2 quarters, and $750 outside high quarter.	$1,500.00	$750.00
Wages in 2 quarters.	$1,200.00	$800.00
2 x annual average weekly wage in each of 2 quarters. Additional requirement for claimants at maximum weekly benefit amount is 6 x average weekly wages in base period.	$2,286.90	—
Wages in 2 quarters.	$900.00	$576.01
—	$2,400.00	—
Wages in 2 quarters.	$1,340.00	—
Wages in 2 quarters.	$1,250.00	$1,000.00

State (1)	Minimum Length-of-Employment Requirement (2)	Minimum Base-Period Wage Requirement (3)
MS	—	40 x weekly benefit amount.
MO	—	1½ x high-quarter wages. For alternative flat-amount requirement, claimant must have earned wages in 2 quarters of base period of 1½ x maximum Missouri taxable wage base for that year.
MT	—	1½ x high-quarter wages.
NE	—	Flat amount specified by state.
NV	—	1½ x high-quarter wages. Claimant needs either base-period wages of 1½ x high-quarter wages, or wages in 3 of 4 quarters of base period.
NH	—	Flat amount specified by state.
NJ	20 weeks, defined as 20% of statewide average weekly wage (currently $123). For alternative flat-amount requirement, claimant must have earned 12 x average weekly wage in base period, or worked 770 hours in production and harvesting of agricultural crops.	20% of statewide average weekly wage (currently $123).
NM	—	1¼ x high-quarter wages.
NY	20 weeks, with minimum average weekly wage the greater of 21 x minimum wage in effect, or $80. If claimant does not meet regular qualifying requirement, claimant can qualify if he or she has 15 weeks' employment in 52-week period, and total of 40 weeks' employment in 104-week period preceding benefit year.	20 weeks, with minimum average weekly wage the greater of 21 x minimum wage in effect, or $80.

Minimum Wage Distribution Requirement (4)	Minimum Total Base-Period Wage Requirement (5)	Minimum High-Quarter Wage Requirement (6)
Wages in 2 quarters.	$1,200.00	$780.00. High-quarter wages must not be less than 26 x minimum weekly benefit amount, which is computed annually.
Wages in 2 quarters.	$1,500.00	$1,000.00
Wages in 2 quarters.	$5,400.00	—
$400 in each of 2 quarters.	$1,200.00	$400.00
Wages in 2 quarters.	$600.00	$400.00
$1,200.00 in each of 2 quarters.	$2,800.00	—
Wages in 2 quarters.	$2,460.00	—
Wages in 2 quarters.	$1,284.72	$1,027.78
Wages in 2 quarters.	$1,600.00	—

State (1)	Minimum Length-of-Employment Requirement (2)	Minimum Base-Period Wage Requirement (3)
NC	—	1½ x high-quarter wages. Wages in at least 2 quarters is automatic requirement for all claimants. Additional requirement for claimants at maximum weekly benefit amount is 6 x state average weekly wage, and high-quarter wages of at least 1½ x state average weekly wage.
ND	—	1½ x high-quarter wages.
OH	20 weeks' employment, with wages of 27% of state average weekly wage.	20 x 27.5% of state average weekly wage.
OK	—	Flat-amount requirement of $10,400 in base period. Claimant needs 40% of taxable wages and 1½ x high-quarter wages.
OR	18 weeks' employment, with no weekly amount specified.	—
PA	16 weeks at weekly minimum earnings of $50.	37–40 x weekly benefit amount. If claimant fails to meet qualifying requirement for weekly benefit amount computed on high-quarter wages but does meet qualifying requirement for next lower bracket, claimant is eligible for lower weekly benefit amount. State provides stepdown of 3 brackets.
PR	—	40 x weekly benefit amount. If claimant fails to meet qualifying requirement for weekly benefit amount computed on high-quarter wages but does meet qualifying requirement for next lower bracket, claimant is eligible for lower weekly benefit amount. State has unlimited stepdown provision.
RI	—	1½ x high-quarter wages. For alternative flat-amount requirement, claimant must earn 3 x total minimum (400 x the minimum hourly wage) in the base period.
SC	—	1½ x high-quarter wages.
SD	—	—

Minimum Wage Distribution Requirement (4)	Minimum Total Base-Period Wage Requirement (5)	Minimum High-Quarter Wage Requirement (6)
Wages in at least 2 quarters is automatic requirement for all claimants. Additional requirement for claimants at maximum weekly benefit amount is 6 x state average weekly wage, and high-quarter wages of at least 1½ x state average weekly wage.	$2,323.98	$581.00
Wages in 2 quarters.	$2,795.00	$1,118.00
Wages in 2 quarters.	$1,702.00	—
Wages in 2 quarters.	$4,160.00	$2,693.33
Wages in 2 quarters.	$1,000.00	—
⅕ of wages outside high quarter.	$1,320.00	$800.00
Wages in 2 quarters. Agricultural workers may qualify on basis of earnings in single calendar quarter.	$280.00	$75.00. Agricultural workers may qualify on basis of earnings in single calendar quarter.
Wages in 2 quarters. Claimant needs 200 x minimum hourly wage in 1 quarter and base-period wages of 1½ x high quarter. However, base-period wages must be at least 400 x minimum hourly wage.	$1,780.00	$890.00
Wages in 2 quarters.	$900.00	$540.00
20 x weekly benefit amount outside high quarter.	$1,288.00	$728.00

State (1)	Minimum Length-of-Employment Requirement (2)	Minimum Base-Period Wage Requirement (3)
TN	—	40 x weekly benefit amount.
TX	—	37 x weekly benefit amount.
UT	—	1½ x high-quarter wages. Requires 1½ x high quarter or 20 weeks' insured work, with 5% of monetary base-period wage requirement (8% of state average fiscal year wages in base period, rounded to higher $100) in each week.
VT	—	$1,163 in a quarter, and base-period wages of at least 40% of total high-quarter wages. High-quarter wages are adjusted by percentage increase equal to percentage increase in state minimum wage for prior year.
VA	—	50 x weekly benefit amount.
VI	—	1½ x high-quarter wages. For alternative flat-amount requirement, claimant must earn $858 in high quarter and 39 x weekly benefit amount in base period.
WA	680 hours.	—
WV	—	Flat amount specified by state.
WI	—	30 x weekly benefit amount. Weeks of employment include all weeks in which individual receives or is entitled to receive holiday and vacation pay, termination pay, sick pay, and back pay.
WY	—	1.4 x high-quarter wages.

average weekly wage during the base period, up to the maximum amount allowable in Florida, currently $250. Footnote 15 advises us that the weekly benefit amount in Michigan is 70 percent of the after-tax (net) earnings, making Michigan the only state that does not base its weekly benefit amount on gross earnings.

What about the remaining four columns of Table 6.4? Columns 6 and 7 show the minimum wage amounts needed in the high quarter and the overall base period to qualify the claimant for the minimum claim. Columns 8 and 9 show the minimum wage amounts needed in the high quarter and the overall base period

Minimum Wage Distribution Requirement (4)	Minimum Total Base-Period Wage Requirement (5)	Minimum High-Quarter Wage Requirement (6)
6 x weekly benefit amount or $900 outside high quarter.	$1,560.02	$780.01
Wages in 2 quarters.	$1,480.00	—
Wages in 2 quarters.	$1,900.00	$1,266.67
—	$1,628.20	$1,163.00
Wages in 2 quarters.	$3,250.00	$1,625.00
Wages in 2 quarters.	$1,287.00	$858.00
—	—	—
Wages in 2 quarters.	$2,200.00	—
8 x weekly benefit amount outside high quarter.	$1,350.00	$1,150.00
Wages in 2 quarters.	$1,650.00. Requirement is defined in law as 8% of state average annual wage in base period, rounded to lower $50.	$1,000.00. Requirement is defined in law as 8% of state average annual wage in base period, rounded to lower $50.

to qualify for a claim with a maximum weekly benefit amount and maximum duration. Keep in mind that a few states—Kentucky, for instance—don't have high-quarter requirements, leaving some blanks in the "High Quarter" columns.

When using the data provided in column 2 to compute your weekly benefit amount, keep in mind that you must check the resulting figure against the maximum weekly benefit amount listed in column 5. Even if your base-period earnings were quite high, your weekly benefit amount can exceed the maximum allowable amount *only* if a dependents' allowance is added in those few states

Table 6.4 Weekly Benefits for Total Unemployment

State (1)	Method of Computing Weekly Benefit Amount[1] (2)	Amount Is Rounded to Higher, Lower, or Nearest $ (3)	Minimum Weekly Benefit Amount[2] (4)
High-Quarter-Formula States[3]			
AZ	$\frac{1}{25}$ x high-quarter wages	Nearest $	$40.00
AR	$\frac{1}{26}$ x high-quarter wages	Lower $	$45.00[6]
CA	$\frac{1}{23}$–$\frac{1}{33}$ x high-quarter wages[18]	Higher $	$40.00
CO	$\frac{1}{26}$ x high-quarter wages[4]	Lower $	$25.00
CT	$\frac{1}{26}$ x high-quarter wages + dependents' allowance	Lower $	$15.00–$22.00
DC	$\frac{1}{26}$ x high-quarter wages + dependents' allowance	Lower $	$50.00
HI	$\frac{1}{21}$ x high-quarter wages	Higher $	$5.00
ID	$\frac{1}{26}$ x high-quarter wages	Lower $	$44.00
IN	1, 10	Lower $	$50.00[2]
IA	$\frac{1}{19}$–$\frac{1}{23}$ x high-quarter wages	Lower $	$31.00–$38.00
KS	4.25% x high-quarter wages	Lower $	$62.00[6]
ME[13]	$\frac{1}{22}$ x high-quarter wages + dependents' allowance	Lower $	$35.00–$52.00
MD	$\frac{1}{24}$ x high-quarter wages + dependents' allowance	Higher $	$25.00–$33.00
MA	$\frac{1}{21}$–$\frac{1}{26}$ x high-quarter wages + dependents' allowance[3]	Lower $	$14.00–$21.00

Maximum Weekly Benefit Amount[2] (5)	High-Quarter Wages Required for Minimum Claim (6)	Base-Period Wages Required for Minimum Claim (7)	High-Quarter Wages Required for Maximum Claim (8)	Base-Period Wages Required for Maximum Claim (9)
$185.00	$1,000.00	$1,500.00	$4,612.50	$14,428.51
$254.00	$607.50	$1,215.00	$6,604.00	$19,812.00
$230.00	$900.00	$1,125.00	$7,633.34	$11,958.01
$261.00	$520.13	$1,000.00	$6,786.00[7]	$27,144.00[7]
$317.00– $367.00	$150.00	$600.00	$8,242.00	$12,680.00
$335.00[2]	$1,300.00	$1,950.00	$8,710.00	$17,420.00
$337.00	$32.50	$130.00	$7,056.01	$8,762.00
$235.00	$1,144.01	$1,430.01	$6,110.00	$19,857.50
$170.00– $192.00[2]	$750.00	$2,500.00	$4,550.00[2]	$15,785.71[2]
$211.00– $259.00	$730.00	$1,090.00	$4,853.00	$16,458.00
$250.00	[6]	$1,860.00	$5,882.36	$19,500.00
$198.00– $297.00	$762.30	$2,286.90	$4,356.00	$15,444.00
$223.00	$576.01	$900.00	$5,328.01	$8,028.00
$325.00– $487.00	$300.00	$2,400.00	$8,450.00	$27,083.33

State (1)	Method of Computing Weekly Benefit Amount[1] (2)	Amount Is Rounded to Higher, Lower, or Nearest $ (3)	Minimum Weekly Benefit Amount[2] (4)
High-Quarter-Formula States[3]			
MN	$\frac{1}{26}$ x high-quarter wages	Lower $	$38.00
MS	$\frac{1}{26}$ x high-quarter wages	Lower $	$30.00
MO	4.5% x high-quarter wages	Lower $	$45.00
NE	$\frac{1}{20}$–$\frac{1}{24}$ x high-quarter wages	Lower $	$20.00
NV	$\frac{1}{25}$ x high-quarter wages	Lower $	$16.00
NM	$\frac{1}{26}$ x high-quarter wages	Lower $	$39.00[6]
OK	$\frac{1}{25}$ x high-quarter wages	Lower $	$16.00
PA	$\frac{1}{23}$–$\frac{1}{25}$ x high-quarter wages[9]	Lower $	$35.00–$40.00
PR[5]	$\frac{1}{11}$–$\frac{1}{26}$ x high-quarter wages	Lower $	$7.00
RI	4.62% x high-quarter wages	Lower $	$41.00–$51.00[6]
SC	$\frac{1}{26}$ x high-quarter wages[4]	Lower $	$20.00
SD	$\frac{1}{26}$ x high-quarter wages	Lower $	$28.00
TX	$\frac{1}{25}$ x high-quarter wages	Higher $	$41.00
UT	$\frac{1}{26}$ x high-quarter wages	Lower $	$17.00
VI	$\frac{1}{26}$ x high-quarter wages	Lower $	$32.00
WI	4.0% x high-quarter wages	Nearest $	$46.00
WY	4.0% x high-quarter wages	Lower $	$40.00

Maximum Weekly Benefit Amount[2] (5)	High-Quarter Wages Required for Minimum Claim (6)	Base-Period Wages Required for Minimum Claim (7)	High-Quarter Wages Required for Maximum Claim (8)	Base-Period Wages Required for Maximum Claim (9)
$305.00	$1,000.00	$1,250.00	$7,930.00	$23,790.00
$165.00	$780.00	$1,200.00	$4,290.00	$12,870.00
$175.00	$1,000.00	$1,500.00	$3,888.89	$13,650.00
$154.00	$400.00	$1,200.00	$4,250.00	$12,009.00
$230.00	$400.00	$600.00	$5,750.00	$17,940.00
$197.00	$1,027.78	$1,284.72	$5,122.00	$8,536.67
$237.00	$2,693.33	$4,160.00	$5,925.00	$15,405.00
$329.00–$337.00[13]	$800.00	$1,320.00	$8,163.00	$13,080.00
$133.00	$75.00	$280.00	$3,432.00	$5,320.00
$310.00–$387.00	$890.00	$1,780.00	$6,709.95	$22,388.88
$203.00	$540.00	$900.00	$5,278.00	$15,834.00
$168.00	$728.00	$1,288.00	$4,368.00	$13,104.00
$245.00	$975.25	$1,480.00	$6,100.25	$23,588.89
$248.00	$1,266.67	$1,900.00	$6,448.00	$23,881.48
$211.00	$858.00	$1,287.00	$5,486.00	$16,458.00
$243.00	$1,150.00	$1,380.00	$6,075.00	$15,795.00
$220.00	$1,000.00	$1,650.00	$5,500.00	$18,333.34

State (1)	Method of Computing Weekly Benefit Amount[1] (2)	Amount Is Rounded to Higher, Lower, or Nearest $ (3)	Minimum Weekly Benefit Amount[2] (4)
Multi-Quarter-Formula States[12]			
AL	$\frac{1}{24}$ x specified wages[1,12]	Higher $	$22.00
DE	[11]	Lower $	$20.00
GA	$\frac{1}{50}$ x specified wages[10]	Lower $	$37.00
IL	[11, 4]	Nearest $	$51.00[2]
LA	$\frac{1}{25}$ x specified wages[11]	Lower $	$10.00
NC	$\frac{1}{52}$ x specified wages	Lower $	$22.00
ND	[11]	Lower $	$43.00
TN[17]	$\frac{1}{26}$–$\frac{1}{32}$ x specified wages	Lower $	$30.00
VT	[10]	Nearest $	$36.00
VA	$\frac{1}{50}$ x specified wages	Higher $	$65.00
WA	$\frac{1}{25}$ x specified wages	Lower $	$73.00
Annual-Wage-Formula States			
AK	4.4%–0.9% of annual wages + dependents' allowance[14]	Nearest $	$44.00–$68.00
KY	1.185% of annual wages	Nearest $	$22.00
MT	1.0% of annual wages[14]	Lower $	$54.00[6]
NH	0.8–1.1% of annual wages	Nearest $	$32.00
OR	1.25% of annual wages	Lower $	$66.00[6]
WV	1.0% of annual wages	Lower $	$24.00

Maximum Weekly Benefit Amount[2] (5)	High-Quarter Wages Required for Minimum Claim (6)	Base-Period Wages Required for Minimum Claim (7)	High-Quarter Wages Required for Maximum Claim (8)	Base-Period Wages Required for Maximum Claim (9)
$165.00	$516.01	$1,032.00	$3,948.01	$12,868.51
$265.00[16]	$965.99	$965.99	$6,095.00	$12,190.00
$185.00	$900.00	$1,350.00	$4,625.00	$19,238.01
$235.00–$311.00[2]	$1,424.00	$1,600.00	$6,142.50[2]	$12,285.00[2]
$181.00[16]	$800.00	$1,200.00	$4,525.00	$17,427.77
$282.00	$581.00	$2,323.98	$7,332.00	$21,996.00
$232.00	$1,118.00	$2,795.00	$6,032.00	$19,302.40
$185.00	$780.01	$1,560.02	$4,810.01	$19,240.00
$209.00	$1,163.00	$1,628.20	[10]	$9,405.00
$208.00	$1,625.00	$3,250.00	$5,200.00	$20,800.01
$340.00	$1,825.00	$1,825.00	$8,500.00	$30,600.00
$212.00–$284.00	—	$1,000.00	—	$22,250.00
$229.00	—	$1,500.00	—	$19,282.72
$217.00	—	$5,400.00	—	$21,700.00
$196.00	—	$2,800.00	—	$24,500.00
$285.00	—	$1,000.00	—	$22,720.00
$280.00	—	$2,200.00	—	$26,500.00

State (1)	Method of Computing Weekly Benefit Amount[1] (2)	Amount Is Rounded to Higher, Lower, or Nearest $ (3)	Minimum Weekly Benefit Amount[2] (4)
Average-Weekly-Wage-Formula States			
FL	50% of average weekly wage	Lower $	$10.00
MI	70% of average weekly wage[15]	Lower $	$42.00
NJ	60% of average weekly wage + dependents' allowance	Lower $	$69.00
NY	50% of average weekly wage	Nearest $	$40.00
OH	50% of average weekly wage + dependents' allowance[1]	Lower $	$42.00

1   When state uses weighted high-quarter, annual wage, or average-weekly-wage formula, approximate fractions or percentages are taken at midpoint of lowest and highest normal wage brackets. When additional payments are provided for claimants with dependents, fractions and percentages shown apply to basic benefit amounts. In Indiana, benefit amounts of $170–$192 are available only to claimants with 1–2 dependents and high-quarter and base-period wages in excess of those required for maximum basic weekly benefit amount. In Ohio, benefit amounts above maximum are generally available only to claimants in dependency classes whose average weekly wages are higher than those required for maximum basic benefit amount.

2   When 2 amounts are given, higher figure includes dependents' allowance. Augmented amount for minimum weekly benefit amount includes allowance for 1 dependent child. In Indiana, to claimants with high-quarter wages in excess of those required for maximum basic weekly benefit amount. Augmented amount for maximum weekly benefit amount includes allowances for maximum number of dependents. In District of Columbia, Maryland, and New Jersey, maximum is same with or without dependents. In Indiana, wage credits shown apply to claimants with no dependents. With maximum dependents, Indiana requires $4,500.00 in high quarter and $15,785.71 in base period.

3   For claimant with average weekly wages in excess of $66, weekly benefit amount is computed at $\frac{1}{52}$ of 2 highest quarters of earnings, or $\frac{1}{26}$ of high quarter if claimant has no more than 2 quarters of work.

4   Weekly benefit amount is expressed in law as percentage of average weekly wages in high quarter. In Colorado, it is 60% of $\frac{1}{26}$ of 2 highest quarters. In Illinois, it is 49.5% of wages in 2 highest quarters divided by 26. In South Carolina, it is 50% (average weekly wage is defined as $\frac{1}{13}$ of high-quarter wages). Colorado provides an alternate method of computation for claimants who would otherwise qualify for weekly benefit amount equal to 50% or more of statewide average weekly wage if this yields a greater amount—50% of $\frac{1}{52}$ of base-period wages with maximum of 60% of statewide average weekly wage in selected industries.

5   There is separate benefit schedule for agricultural workers with payments, based on annual earnings, ranging between $10 and $40.

6   In New Mexico, minimum is computed annually at 10% of average weekly wage. In Arkansas, at 12%. In Montana, Oregon, and Washington, at 15%. In Kansas, minimum is computed annually at 25% of maximum weekly benefit, and in Wisconsin, semiannually at 19% of maximum weekly benefit amount. In Rhode Island, flexible qualifying requirement results in flexible minimum weekly benefit amount.

Maximum Weekly Benefit Amount[2] (5)	High-Quarter Wages Required for Minimum Claim (6)	Base-Period Wages Required for Minimum Claim (7)	High-Quarter Wages Required for Maximum Claim (8)	Base-Period Wages Required for Maximum Claim (9)
$250.00	—	$400.00[8]	—	$26,000.00[8]
$293.00	—	$1,340.00[8]	—	$19,810.00[8]
$347.00[2]	—	$2,460.00[8]	—	$20,241.90[8]
$300.00	—	$1,600.00[8]	—	$11,980.00[8]
$238.00–$319.00	—	$1,702.00[8]	—	$12,376.00[8]

7 Amount shown for high-quarter wages is $\frac{1}{4}$ base-period wages needed to qualify for maximum benefit. Determination of maximum benefit is based on 50% of $\frac{1}{52}$ of claimant's base-period wages with no specified amount of high-quarter wages required.

8 In Florida, Michigan, New Jersey, New York, and Ohio, required base-period wages are 20 x lower limits of minimum and maximum average weekly wage brackets; in Wisconsin, 17 x average weekly wage. In Wisconsin, since benefits are determined separately for each employer, some claimants with base-period wages less than that shown may qualify for either the minimum or maximum weekly benefit amount with respect to a given employer.

9 Or weekly benefit amount may be 50% of full-time weekly wage, if greater.

10 In Vermont, amount is computed as wages in 2 highest quarters divided by 45 (but not more than maximum weekly benefit amount). In Indiana, it is computed as 5% of first $1,000 in high-quarter wages and 4% of remaining high-quarter wages. In Georgia, it is computed as $\frac{1}{25}$ of high-quarter wages when alternative qualifying wages are used.

11 In Delaware, weekly benefit amount is computed as $\frac{1}{46}$ of wages earned in highest 2 quarters if trust fund balance is at least $90 million, or as $\frac{1}{52}$ of wages earned in 2 highest quarters if trust fund balance is less than $90 million. In Illinois, it is computed as 49.5% of claimant's wages in highest 2 quarters divided by 26. In Louisiana, as $\frac{1}{25}$ of 4 quarters of base period. In North Dakota, as $\frac{1}{65}$ of total wages earned in highest 2 quarters and $\frac{1}{2}$ of total wages in third quarter.

12 Wages in 2 high quarters are used unless otherwise indicated.

13 In Pennsylvania, weekly benefit amount will be reduced by 5% or by reduction determined by trigger mechanism, but weekly benefit amount may not be reduced to less than half maximum weekly benefit amount. In Maine, during period of April 1, 1993, through December 31, 1994, claimant's weekly benefit amount will be reduced by $6; therefore, maximum weekly benefit amount will be $192–$288.

14 In Alaska, computation of claimant's weekly benefit amount and duration will vary depending on distribution of wages over base period. Claimant who is paid 90% or more of his wages in current quarter will not use that quarter of wages but will have base-period wages determined using wages earned in other 3 quarters, multiplied by 10. Claimant who is paid less than 90% of his wages in one current quarter uses all wages paid in base period. In Montana, 1% of base-period wages or 1.9% of wages in 2 high quarters of base period.

15 Weekly benefit amount is 70% of after-tax earnings up to 58% of state average weekly wage.

16   In Louisiana, weekly benefit amount reflects 7% decrease and 5% discount from computed
     maximum of $205. In Delaware, if trust fund balance is less than $165 million but more
     than $150 million, maximum weekly benefit amount will be $245. If trust fund balance is
     less than $150 million but equal to or greater than $90 million, maximum weekly benefit
     amount will be $225. And if trust fund balance is less than $90 million, maximum weekly
     benefit amount will be $205.
17   Claimant will not be eligible for benefits if base-period earnings outside high quarter are
     less than the lesser of 6 x weekly benefit amount or $900.
18   If high-quarter wages exceed $4,955.99, maximum weekly benefit amount will be 39% of
     these wages divided by 13.

that pay a dependents' allowance. This is an important fact to remember if you have worked in more than one state and can choose the state you will file against. While the rate of compensation may be the more crucial factor at low or moderate salary ranges, the maximum weekly benefit limit is of greater importance when higher salaries are involved.

THE MAXIMUM POTENTIAL BENEFIT AMOUNT

Perhaps you've now computed your weekly benefit amount. If so, you probably would like to know exactly what your *maximum potential benefit amount* is. In other words, what is the potential sum of the benefits you can receive?

Often, people explain the maximum potential benefit amount of a claim in terms of duration—usually, twenty-six weeks. It's true that in all but two states, Massachusetts and Washington, the maximum benefit amount cannot exceed twenty-six times the weekly benefit amount of the claim. And if a claimant's maximum benefit amount is twenty-six times the weekly benefit amount and he or she draws full benefits each week, the claimant will receive UI benefits for twenty-six weeks. However, if a claimant's weekly benefit amount is reduced because of earnings from part-time employment, the number of weeks he or she can draw benefits will be increased. You see, the maximum potential benefit amount is not really a number of weeks. It is the total amount of money, often expressed as a multiple of the weekly benefit amount, that the claimant can receive on his or her claim. A few states have a uniform maximum benefit amount for all claims that qualify in that state. But the majority of the states base the maximum benefit amount on a percentage of the claimant's base-period wages or a fraction of the number of weeks worked by the claimant in the base period. Claimants who earned more wages or worked for more weeks during the base period qualify for a greater maximum benefit amount than do those who earned less or worked fewer weeks. Because the duration of base-period employment and the amount of base-period wages vary from claimant to claimant, the maximum benefit amount can vary from five to thirty times the weekly benefit amount, depending on the state against which the claim is filed.

Table 6.5 shows how the maximum potential benefit amount is computed in each of the fifty-three states and jurisdictions. The second column shows the formula used to compute the maximum benefit amount. The third column shows the minimum number of weeks for which the claimant can receive benefits. The fourth column shows the maximum number of weeks for which the claimant can receive benefits.

When reading through the second column, you'll see that nine states—Connecticut, Hawaii, Illinois, Maryland, New Hampshire, New York, Puerto Rico, Vermont, and West Virginia—have uniform maximum benefit amounts of twenty-six times the weekly benefit amount. In the remaining forty-four states, the amount varies according to earnings or weeks of employment. This amount is most often expressed as a percentage of the base-period wages. In a few states, though, the formula is somewhat more complex. For instance, in Alaska, the maximum benefit amount is based on a variable schedule that takes into account the ratio of base-period wages to high-quarter wages. In cases such as this, the staff of your local unemployment office should be able to explain the schedule used in that state.

When calculating your maximum benefit amount, be aware that in no case can the potential benefit amount exceed the maximum amount allowed in each state. Similarly, it is impossible to qualify for less than the minimum number of multiples of the weekly benefit amount if you have the sufficient base-period wages, weeks of employment, and wage distribution to qualify for a claim. Also be aware that calculations can result in fractional final payments, since fractions of base-period wages may not be even multiples of the weekly benefit amount.

THE DEPENDENTS' ALLOWANCE

Our discussions of weekly benefit amounts and maximum benefit amounts were based on *basic entitlement*—that is, entitlement resulting from length of employment, wages earned, and wage distribution. Dependents' allowances were not included in these calculations. However, if you live in one of the fourteen states that provide a dependents' allowance, your weekly payment may be increased because of the dependents you support.

The states that provide dependents' allowances include Alaska, Connecticut, the District of Columbia, Illinois, Indiana, Iowa,

Table 6.5 Maximum Benefit Amount

State (1)	Method of Computing the Maximum Potential Benefit Amount (2)	Minimum Multiple of Wkly Benefit Amount (3)	Maximum Multiple of Wkly Benefit Amount (4)
AL	33.3% of base-period wages.	15	26
AK	Variable schedule based on ratio of base-period wages to high-quarter wages.	16	26
AZ	33.3% of base-period wages.	12	26
AR	33.3% of base-period wages.	9	26
CA	50% of base-period wages.	14	26
CO	33.3% of base-period wages.	13	26
CT	26 x weekly benefit amount.	26	26
DE	50% of base-period wages.	24	26
DC	50% of base-period wages.	20	26
FL	Weekly benefit amount x 50% of weeks of employment in base period.	10	26
GA	25% of base-period wages.	9	26
HI	26 x weekly benefit amount.	26	26
ID	Variable schedule based on ratio of base-period wages to high-quarter wages.	10	26
IL	26 x weekly benefit amount.	26	26
IN	28% of base-period wages.	14	26
IA	33.3% of base-period wages.	11	26
KS	33.3% of base-period wages.	10	26
KY	33.3% of base-period wages.	15	26
LA	27% of base-period wages.	8	26
ME	33.3% of base-period wages.	21	26
MD	26 x weekly benefit amount.	26	26
MA	36% of base-period wages.	10	30
MI	Weekly benefit amount x 75% of weeks of employment in base period.	15	26
MN	33.3% of base-period wages.	10	26
MS	33.3% of base-period wages.	13	26
MO	33.3% of base-period wages.	11	26
MT	Variable schedule based on ratio of base-period wages to high-quarter wages.	8	26
NE	33.3% of base-period wages.	20	26
NV	33.3% of base-period wages.	12	26
NH	26 x weekly benefit amount.	26	26
NJ	Weekly benefit amount x 75% of weeks of employment in base period.	15	26
NM	60% of base-period wages.	19	26
NY	26 x weekly benefit amount.	26	26
NC	Variable schedule based on ratio of base-period wages to high-quarter wages.	13	26

State (1)	Method of Computing the Maximum Potential Benefit Amount (2)	Minimum Multiple of Wkly Benefit Amount (3)	Maximum Multiple of Wkly Benefit Amount (4)
ND	Variable schedule based on ratio of base-period wages to high-quarter wages.	12	26
OH	20 x weekly benefit amount plus 1 x weekly benefit amount for each additional week of base-period employment over 20.	20	26
OK	40% of taxable base-period wages.	20	26
OR	33.3% of base-period wages.	5	26
PA	Variable schedule based on number of base-period weeks of wages of at least $50.	16	26
PR	26 x weekly benefit amount.	26	26
RI	36% of base-period wages.	15	26
SC	33.3% of base-period wages.	15	26
SD	33.3% of base-period wages.	18	26
TN	25% of base-period wages.	12	26
TX	27% of base-period wages.	9	26
UT	27% of base-period wages.	10	26
VT	26 x weekly benefit amount.	13	26
VA	25% of base-period wages.	12	26
VI	33.3% of base-period wages.	13	26
WA	33.3% of base-period wages.	16	30
WV	26 x weekly benefit amount.	26	26
WI	40% of base-period wages.	12	26
WY	33.3% of base-period wages.	12	26

Maine, Maryland, Massachusetts, Michigan, New Jersey, Ohio, Pennsylvania, and Rhode Island. In each state, state law defines what a dependent is, as well as the amount of the allowance to be paid. Who qualifies as a dependent? Generally, a dependent must be wholly or mainly supported by the claimant. Dependents usually live with the claimant; if not, they must receive regular support from the claimant. All of the fourteen states just mentioned recognize minor children as being dependents, although the age limit of minors differs from state to state. All fourteen states except Maryland include older children as dependents as long as they are not able to work. Many also include older relatives in special circumstances. For instance, spouses, parents, or siblings who are not able to work, or who are not employed and not eligible for unemployment benefits due to insufficient earnings, may be considered dependents.

Table 6.6 shows who is considered a dependent by each of the fourteen states that have a dependents' allowance, and provides

Table 6.6 Dependents Included Under Provisions for Dependents' Allowance

State (1)	Age Limit of Dependent Child[1] (2)	Older Child Not Able to Work Considered Dependent[1] (3)	Nonworking Wife Considered Dependent (4)	Nonworking Husband Considered Dependent (5)	Nonworking Parent Considered Dependent[1] (6)	Nonworking Brother or Sister Considered Dependent (7)	No. of Dependents Fixed for Benefit Year (8)
AK	18[4]	Yes	No	No	No	No	No
CT	18[7]	Yes[7]	Yes	Yes	No	No	No
DC	16	Yes	Yes[5]	Yes[5]	Yes[5]	Yes[5]	Yes
IL	18	Yes	Yes[6]	Yes[6]	No	No	No
IN	23[4]	Yes	Yes[6]	Yes[6]	No	No	Yes
IA	18	Yes	Yes[6]	Yes[6]	Yes[5]	Yes[5]	Yes
ME	18	Yes	Yes[6]	Yes[6]	No	No	No
MD	16	No	No	No	No	No	Yes
MA[3]	18[4]	Yes	No	No	No	No	Yes
MI	18[4]	Yes	Yes	Yes	Yes[5]	Yes[5]	Yes
NJ	19[4]	Yes	Yes	Yes	No	No	Yes
OH	18	Yes	Yes[6]	Yes[6]	No	No	Yes
PA	18	Yes	Yes	Yes	No	No	Yes
RI	18	Yes	No	No	No	No	Yes

1 In all states except Maine and Massachusetts, child includes stepchild by statute. In Alaska, Illinois, Indiana, Maine, Maryland, Michigan, New Jersey, Ohio, and Rhode Island, includes adopted child by statute. In Massachusetts, includes adopted child by interpretation. In Connecticut, Maine, Michigan, Massachusetts, and New Jersey, includes full-time student.

2 In District of Columbia, parent includes stepparent. In Michigan, includes legal parent.

3 In Massachusetts, dependents include only individuals residing in the United States and its territories and possessions.

4 In Alaska, New Jersey, and, by interpretation, Massachusetts, child must be unmarried. In Alaska, must have received more than half the cost of support from claimant or be lawfully in the claimant's custody at the time the individual claims the allowance. In Indiana, Michigan, and Ohio, must have received more than half the cost of support from the claimant for at least 90 consecutive days, or for the duration of the parental relationship.

5 In all states marked, dependent must be unable to work because of age, physical disability, or physical or mental infirmity. In Michigan, parents must be over age 65 or permanently disabled for gainful employment, and brother or sister must be under 18 and be orphaned or have living parents who are dependents.

6 In Illinois and Indiana, spouse must be currently ineligible for benefits in the state because of insufficient base-period wages. In Ohio, spouse may not be claimed as dependent if average weekly income is in excess of 25 percent of claimant's average weekly wage. In Maine, no dependency allowance is paid for any week in which spouse is employed full-time and contributing to support of dependents. In Iowa, no dependency allowance is paid for any week in which spouse earns more than $120 gross wages.

7 In Connecticut, Federal District Court has held that "children" includes any child for whom a claimant stands in place of the parents.

other information as well. Column 2 shows the age limit beyond which dependent children are no longer considered minors. In columns 3 through 7, a *Yes* indicates that an individual with the specified relationship to the claimant—the claimant's wife, for instance—is considered a dependent in that state. Column 8 indicates whether the number of dependents claimed is fixed for the benefit year. The table includes this information because in four states—Alaska, Connecticut, Illinois, and Maine—you may add on a dependent that you did not claim at the initial filing. If a child is born after the benefit year has been established, for instance, the benefit amount will be adjusted.

The amount of the dependents' allowance is usually defined in the state law, and is usually a fixed amount. Sometimes, though, it does vary according to the class of the dependent—that is, whether the dependent is the claimant's child, spouse, parent, or sibling. The amount may also be affected by the number of dependents and by the amount of the claimant's earnings. All fourteen states place limits on the amount of the dependents' allowance that can be paid. In addition, the District of Columbia, Maryland, and New Jersey do not pay a dependents' allowance if the claimant qualifies for the maximum weekly benefit amount in basic benefits. However, when the weekly benefit amount is reduced due to earnings or other reductions, the dependents' allowance is included.

Table 6.7 shows how the dependents' allowance can affect the basic weekly benefit amount and the potential benefit amount in each of the fourteen states that have a dependents' allowance. The second column shows each state's weekly allowance for each dependent. You will note that this is not always a fixed amount, but in some states—Illinois, for instance—can vary within a given range. The third column shows the maximum weekly allowance paid by each state. Again, this is not always a fixed-dollar amount. In Indiana, Iowa, and Ohio, for instance, the allowance varies according to schedules that take into account the number of dependents as well as the amount of the claimant's earnings. The fourth column shows the state's minimum basic weekly benefit amount—in other words, the basic weekly claim *without the allowance*. The fifth column shows the maximum weekly dependents' allowance that can be added to this basic minimum claim. The sixth column shows the maximum basic weekly benefit amount—again, an amount that does not include a dependents' allowance. The seventh column shows the maximum weekly dependents' allowance that can be added to this basic maximum claim. Column 8 indicates whether a full dependents' allowance will be paid during a week of only partial benefits. Finally, the ninth column shows the maximum potential benefit amount that can be paid without dependents, and the tenth column provides the same information for a claim that includes dependents.

Table 6.7 Allowances for Dependents

State (1)	Weekly Allowance per Dependent (2)	Limitation on Weekly Allowance (3)	Minimum Basic Weekly Benefit Amount (4)	Maximum Weekly Dependents' Allowance for Minimum Claim (5)
AK	$24	$72	$44	$72
CT	$10	½ weekly benefit amount	$15	$7
DC	$5. Maximum wkly benefit amount is same with or without dependents' allowances. Claimants at lower weekly benefit amount may have benefits increased by dependents' allowances.	$20. Maximum weekly benefit amount is same with or without dependents' allowances. Claimants at lower weekly benefit amount may have benefits increased by dependents' allowances.	$50	$20
IL	$1–$30	$7–$76	$51	$15
IN	$1–$22. Allowance is limited to claimants with high-quarter wages in excess of $3,999 and 1–2 dependents.	$1–$22. Allowance varies per state's graduated schedule. Allowance is limited to claimants with high-quarter wages in excess of $3,999 and 1–2 dependents.	$50	0. Allowance is limited to claimants with high-quarter wages in excess of $3,999 and 1–2 dependents.
IA	$1–$20	$1–$48. Allowance varies per state's graduated schedule.	$30	$6

Maximum Basic Weekly Benefit Amount (6)	Maximum Weekly Dependents' Allowance for Maximum Claim (7)	Full Allowance for Week of Partial Benefits (8)	Maximum Potential Benefit Amount Without Dependents (9)	Maximum Potential Benefit Amount With Dependents (10)
$212	$72	Yes	$5,512	$7,384. This assumes maximum weeks for total unemployment. Weeks of partial unemployment could increase this amount because full allowance is paid for each week of partial unemployment.
$317	$50	Yes	$8,242	$9,542
$335	0. Maximum weekly benefit amount is same with or without dependents' allowances. Claimants at lower weekly benefit amount may have benefits increased by dependents' allowances.	Yes	$8,710	$8,710. Maximum weekly benefit amount is same with or without dependents' allowances. Claimants at lower weekly benefit amount may have benefits increased by dependents' allowances.
$235	$76	Yes	$6,110	$8,086
$170	$22. Allowance is limited to claimants with high-quarter wages in excess of $3,999 and 1–2 dependents.	No. Dependents' allowances are considered as part of weekly benefit amount.	$4,420	$4,992
$211	$48	Yes	$5,486	$6,734

State (1)	Weekly Allowance per Dependent (2)	Limitation on Weekly Allowance (3)	Minimum Basic Weekly Benefit Amount (4)	Maximum Weekly Dependents' Allowance for Minimum Claim (5)
ME	$10	½ weekly benefit amount	$35	$17
MD	$8	$40. Maximum weekly benefit amount is same with or without any dependents' allowances. Claimants at lower weekly benefit amount may have benefits increased by dependents' allowances.	$25	$33
MA	$25	½ weekly benefit amount	$14	$7
MI	Weekly benefit amount is based on average after-tax weekly wage and tax tables which take into account the number of dependents.	The weekly benefit amount is based on average after-tax weekly wage and tax tables which take into account the number of dependents.	$42	The weekly benefit amount is based on average after-tax weekly wage and tax tables which take into account the number of dependents.
NJ	$3–$16	The maximum weekly benefit amount is same with or without dependents' allowances. Claimants at lower weekly benefit amount may have benefits increased by dependents' allowances.	$66	$7

Maximum Basic Weekly Benefit Amount (6)	Maximum Weekly Dependents' Allowance for Maximum Claim (7)	Full Allowance for Week of Partial Benefits (8)	Maximum Potential Benefit Amount Without Dependents (9)	Maximum Potential Benefit Amount With Dependents (10)
$198	$99	Yes	$5,148	$7,722
$223	0. Maximum weekly benefit amount is same with or without dependents' allowances. Claimants at lower weekly benefit amount may have benefits increased by dependents' allowances.	Yes. Not more than 26 payments for dependents may be made in any one benefit year.	$5,798	$5,798. Maximum weekly benefit amount is same with or without dependents' allowances. Claimants at lower weekly benefit amount may have benefits increased by dependents' allowances.
$325	$162	Yes	$9,750	$14,610
$293	Weekly benefit amount is based on average after-tax weekly wage and tax tables which take into account the number of dependents.	—	$7,696	$7,696
$347	0. Maximum weekly benefit amount is same with or without dependents' allowances. Claimants at lower weekly benefit amount may have benefits increased by dependents' allowances.	Yes	$9,022	$9,022. Maximum weekly benefit amount is same with or without dependents' allowances. Claimants at lower weekly benefit amount may have benefits increased by dependents' allowances.

State (1)	Weekly Allowance per Dependent (2)	Limitation on Weekly Allowance (3)	Minimum Basic Weekly Benefit Amount (4)	Maximum Weekly Dependents' Allowance for Minimum Claim (5)
OH	$1–$81. Benefits paid to claimants with dependents are determined by schedule according to average weekly wage and dependency class.	$81. Benefits paid to claimants with dependents are determined by schedule according to average weekly wage and dependency class.	$42	0
PA	$5. State provides $3 for one other dependent.	$8	$35	$8
RI	Weekly dependents' allowance is greater of $10 or 5% of individual's benefit rate per dependent, up to 5 dependents.	Weekly dependents' allowance is greater of $10 or 5% of individual's benefit rate per dependent, up to 5 dependents.	$41	The weekly dependents' allowance is the greater of $10 or 5% of individual's benefit rate per dependent, up to 5 dependents.

Since so many factors are involved in the determination of the dependents' allowance, we recommend that if you have dependents and are filing against one of the fourteen states just discussed, you check with your local unemployment office to find out how your benefit amount will be affected. Certainly, if you can choose the state you'll be filing against, you should consider the amount of the dependents' allowance provided by each state. Finally, we strongly suggest that when you file your initial claim, you list all of your allowable dependents, even if you know that you will qualify for a maximum claim and that this will prevent your state from adding an allowance to your UI benefits. You can never tell what might happen during the course of the benefit year!

Maximum Basic Weekly Benefit Amount (6)	Maximum Weekly Dependents' Allowance for Maximum Claim (7)	Full Allowance for Week of Partial Benefits (8)	Maximum Potential Benefit Amount Without Dependents (9)	Maximum Potential Benefit Amount With Dependents (10)
$238	$81	Yes	$6,188	$8,294
$329	$8	Yes. Not more than 26 payments for dependents may be made in any one benefit year.	$8,554	$8,762
$310	$77	Yes	$8,060	$10,062. This assumes maximum weeks for total unemployment. Weeks of partial unemployment could increase this amount because full allowance is paid for each week of partial unemployment.

BENEFITS PAID FOR PART-TIME EMPLOYMENT

All states provide benefits for *partial unemployment*—that is, for part-time employment—assuming, of course, that it was preceded by a period of greater employment. In the majority of states, if the claimant is to continue receiving UI benefits, the employment must be less than full-time, and the part-time earnings must be less than the basic weekly benefit amount. In other states, the amount of the earnings must be less than the weekly benefit amount plus a small work allowance or incentive that is added to the weekly benefit amount. In addition, in all states, a portion of the part-time earnings is disregarded before the weekly benefit amount is reduced. The reason for disregarding a portion of the part-time

---

TIP: *If you're filing against a state that pays a dependents' allowance, be sure to list all of your allowable dependents when you file—even if you think that you won't qualify for the allowance.*

---

earnings and providing an allowance or incentive is that the states want to encourage workers to accept part-time employment while they are claiming UI benefits.

Further clarification of partial unemployment can be found in Table 6.8. In column 2, you'll find the amount below which a claimant's weekly earnings must fall if he or she is to continue receiving benefits. Often, this amount includes a work allowance or incentive. In Iowa, for instance, the amount must be less than the weekly benefit amount plus a work allowance of $15. In column 3, you'll find the amount of weekly earnings that will be disregarded before the weekly benefit check is adjusted.

The adjustment for partial compensation can best be explained through the use of examples. As you read about the following cases, keep in mind that all calculations are based on gross earnings—that is, earnings before taxes and other deductions.

John, who is filing a claim against the State of Virginia, has a weekly benefit amount of $200. During a week of partial unemployment, John receives gross earnings of $100. In Virginia, for unemployment to be considered partial, the claimant must work less than full-time, and the claimant's gross earnings must be less than his or her weekly benefit amount. Clearly, John is eligible for benefits. Virginia disregards $25 of weekly earnings when adjusting the weekly benefit amount, making the deduction $75—that is, $100 minus $25. Therefore, John's adjusted UI check for that week is $125—that is, $200 minus $75.

Mary, who is filing a claim against Missouri, receives a weekly benefit amount of $175. Mary finds temporary part-time work for which she receives gross earnings of $175 per week. In Missouri, for unemployment to be considered partial, the claimant must work less than full-time, and the claimant's gross earnings must be less than the weekly benefit amount plus a $20 allowance or incentive. Therefore, in Mary's case, the limit of her weekly earnings is $195, and the adjusted amount from which the earnings will be deducted is also $195. Missouri disregards $20 of the part-time earnings before making the deduction, making the deductible amount $155. So Mary's adjusted UI check for that week is $40— that is, $195 minus $155.

Table 6.8 Computing Weekly Benefits for Partial Unemployment

State (1)	Weekly Wages Must Be Less Than Following Amount (2)*	Earnings Disregarded In Computing Weekly Benefits (3)
AL	Weekly benefit amount.	$15.
AK	1-⅓ x weekly benefit amount + $50.	¾ wages over $50.
AZ	Weekly benefit amount.	$30.
AR	Weekly benefit amount + ⅖ x weekly benefit amount.	⅖ x weekly benefit amount.
CA	Weekly benefit amount.	Greater of $25 or 25% of wages.
CO	Weekly benefit amount.	¼ x weekly benefit amount.
CT	1-½ x basic weekly benefit amount.	⅓ x wages. Holiday pay is included in benefit computation.
DE	Weekly benefit amount + greater of $10 or 30% of weekly benefit amount.	Greater of $10 or 30% of weekly benefit amount.
DC	Weekly benefit amount + $20.	⅕ x wages.
FL	Weekly benefit amount.	8 x federal hourly minimum wage.
GA	Weekly benefit amount.	$30. Payment for jury service is excluded from benefit computation.
HI	Weekly benefit amount.	$50.
ID	Weekly benefit amount + ½ x weekly benefit amount.	½ x weekly benefit amount.
IL	Weekly benefit amount.	½ x weekly benefit amount.
IN	Weekly benefit amount.	Greater of $3 or ⅕ x weekly benefit amount from other than base-period employer.
IA	Weekly benefit amount + $15.	¼ x weekly benefit amount.
KS	Weekly benefit amount.	Lesser of $47 or 25% of weekly benefit amount.
KY	1-¼ x weekly benefit amount.	⅕ x wages.
LA	Weekly benefit amount.	Lesser of ½ x weekly benefit amount or $50.
ME	Weekly benefit amount + $5.	$25. Wages received by claimant for performing volunteer emergency medical service are excluded from benefit computation.

State (1)	Weekly Wages Must Be Less Than Following Amount (2)*	Earnings Disregarded in Computing Weekly Benefits (3)
MD	Augmented weekly benefit amount.	$35.
MA	Basic weekly benefit amount.	$\frac{1}{3}$ x weekly benefit amount. Earnings plus weekly benefit amount may not equal or exceed claimant's average weekly wage.
MI	Weekly benefit amount.	Up to $\frac{1}{2}$ x weekly benefit amount. Full weekly benefit amount is paid if earnings are less than $\frac{1}{2}$ x weekly benefit. $\frac{1}{2}$ weekly benefit amount is paid if wages are $\frac{1}{2}$ x weekly benefit.
MN	Weekly benefit amount.	Greater of $50 or 25% of wages. Up to $200 in earnings from service in National Guard or military reserves or in pay received for jury duty or as volunteer fire fighter or volunteer ambulance service personnel are excluded from benefit computation.
MS	Weekly benefit amount.	$40.
MO	Weekly benefit amount + $20.	$20. Wages from training or authorized duty in organized militia are excluded from benefit computation. Termination pay and severance pay are also excluded.
MT	2 x weekly benefit amount.	$\frac{1}{2}$ x wages over $\frac{1}{4}$ x weekly benefit amount.
NE	Weekly benefit amount.	$\frac{1}{2}$ x weekly benefit amount. Full weekly benefit amount is paid if earnings are less than $\frac{1}{2}$ x weekly benefit. $\frac{1}{2}$ weekly benefit amount is paid if wages are $\frac{1}{2}$ x weekly benefit.
NV	Weekly benefit amount.	$\frac{1}{4}$ x wages.
NH	Weekly benefit amount.	$\frac{1}{5}$ x weekly benefit amount.
NJ	Weekly benefit amount + greater of $5 or $\frac{1}{5}$ x weekly benefit amount.	Greater of $5 or $\frac{1}{5}$ x weekly benefit amount.
NM	Weekly benefit amount.	$\frac{1}{5}$ x weekly benefit amount. Payment for jury service is excluded from benefit computation.

State (1)	Weekly Wages Must Be Less Than Following Amount (2)*	Earnings Disregarded in Computing Weekly Benefits (3)
NY	Benefits are paid at rate of ¼ x weekly benefit amount for each effective day within a week beginning on Monday. Effective day is defined as fourth day and each subsequent day of total unemployment in week in which claimant earns not more than $300.	Benefits are paid at rate of ¼ x weekly benefit amount for each effective day within a week beginning on Monday. Effective day is defined as fourth day and each subsequent day of total unemployment in week in which claimant earns not more than $300.
NC	Week of less than 3 customary scheduled full-time days.	10% of average weekly wage in 2 highest quarters.
ND	Weekly benefit amount.	60% of weekly benefit amount.
OH	Weekly benefit amount.	⅕ x weekly benefit amount.
OK	Weekly benefit amount + $7.	$7.
OR	Weekly benefit amount.	⅓ x weekly benefit amount. Wages from training or authorized duty in organized militia are excluded from benefit computation. Holiday pay is included in benefit computation.
PA	Weekly benefit amount + greater of $6 or 40% of weekly benefit amount.	Greater of $6 or 40% of weekly benefit amount.
PR	Week in which wages, or remuneration from self-employment, are less than 1-½ x claimant's weekly benefit amount, or claimant performs no service for working period of 32 hours or more in a week.	Weekly benefit amount.
RI	Basic weekly benefit amount.	⅕ x weekly benefit amount.
SC	Weekly benefit amount.	¼ x weekly benefit amount.
SD	Weekly benefit amount.	25% over $25.
TN	Weekly benefit amount.	$30.
TX	Weekly benefit amount + greater of $5 or ¼ x weekly benefit amount.	Greater of $5 or ¼ x weekly benefit amount.
UT	Weekly benefit amount.	30% of weekly benefit amount.
VT	Weekly benefit amount + $15.	Greater of $40 or 30% of weekly benefit amount.
VA	Weekly benefit amount.	$25.

State (1)	Weekly Wages Must Be Less Than Following Amount (2)*	Earnings Disregarded in Computing Weekly Benefits (3)
VI	1-⅓ x weekly benefit amount + $15.	Wages in excess of $15.
WA	1-⅓ x weekly benefit amount + $5.	¼ wages over $5.
WV	Weekly benefit amount + $26.	$25.
WI	Claimant is considered partially unemployed in any week he receives any wages. No claimant is eligible for partial benefits if benefit payment is less than $5, or if employer paid claimant at least 80% of base-period wages or claimant worked for employer at least 35 hours in week at same or greater rate of pay as claimant was paid in high quarter.	$20 plus 33% of wages in excess of $20. Claimant is considered partially unemployed in any week he receives any wages. No claimant is eligible for partial benefits if benefit payment is less than $5, or if employer paid claimant at least 80% of base-period wages or claimant worked for employer at least 35 hours in week at same or greater rate of pay as claimant was paid in high quarter.
WY	Basic weekly benefit amount.	Wages in excess of 50% of weekly benefit amount.

*In addition to earning wages below the specified amount, in all states, the claimant must work less than full-time.

Bill, who is filing against the District of Columbia, receives D.C.'s maximum weekly benefit amount of $335, and has four allowable dependents. Normally, Bill doesn't get a dependents' allowance because in D.C., the maximum weekly benefit amount cannot be exceeded even with a dependents' allowance. Bill is called back to his job on a part-time basis, and receives $300 a week in gross earnings. D.C., like Missouri, requires that for unemployment to be considered partial, the claimant must work less than full-time, and the claimant's gross earnings must be less than the weekly benefit amount plus $20. Bill, like Mary, is eligible for benefits. The adjusted amount from which his earnings will be deducted is $355—that is, $335 plus $20. In D.C., 20 percent of wages are disregarded before the deduction is made, making the deductible amount $240 per week. Therefore, his resulting benefit amount would be $115—that is, $355 minus $240—*except* that D.C. pays a dependents' allowance of $5 per dependent. As Bill's benefits are now far below the maximum weekly amount, $20 per week is added to his benefit check, bringing the amount up to $135.

As you can see from these examples, unless the state you're filing against defines partial unemployment as having earnings less than the weekly benefit amount, you can earn as much or more than your weekly entitlement in wages from part-time employment and still receive partial unemployment benefits. You should also be aware that only those benefits actually paid out are deducted from the claim balance, so that while part-time employment reduces the amount of the benefit check, it does not reduce the maximum potential benefit amount. Therefore, part-time work can lengthen the period of time that benefits can be claimed. Also, if your part-time work is covered employment, you will be accumulating wages for future benefit entitlement. And, of course, in some cases, part-time work means additonal benefits such as health insurance or employee discounts. Finally, it's important to keep in mind that if you work part-time to supplement your weekly benefit amount, and your part-time employer wants you to work full-time, you could be disqualified from receiving benefits if you decline full-time employment or quit your part-time job.

QUALIFYING FOR A SUBSEQUENT CLAIM

By now, you should have a fairly clear idea of whether you are eligible for UI benefits and, if so, what you can expect to receive during the benefit year. But what happens after the benefit year is over? When a benefit year expires, regardless of whether all the potential benefits were used on the claim, you can no longer receive benefits from that claim. However, you can file a new claim—called a *subsequent claim*—meet the qualifying requirements in a new base period, and establish a new benefit year.

In states with long lag periods, it is entirely possible for your lag wages to be sufficient to meet the basic monetary requirements for a new claim. You may recall from our discussion of base periods that lag wages are wages earned between the end of the base period and the beginning of the benefit year of the initial claim. In other words, lag wages were earned before the initial claim separation, but were not used to compute the entitlement on the initial claim because they were earned too recently to fall within the base period. However, all states that have long lag periods—and nearly all of the states do—place restrictions on the use of lag wages to establish a subsequent claim. These restrictions are intended to prevent claimants from qualifying for benefits in two successive benefit years based on only one period of employment. The restrictions require the claimant to have had new employment after the filing of the initial claim. The specific requirements regarding the amount of wages earned, the length of the employment, and whether or not the employment must have been covered vary from state to state. A few states also make it necessary for the wages to have been earned in specific quarters of the first claim's benefit year or the subsequent claim's base period.

Table 6.9 shows the requirements of each of the fifty-three states and jurisdictions. The second column indicates whether that state requires covered employment. (See Chapter 3 for a detailed discussion of covered employment.) The third column shows the wage requirements needed from new employment. As you'll see, this is usually expressed as multiples of the weekly benefit amount, although it is sometimes expressed as a number of days of employment or an amount of wages. The fourth column shows any other prerequisites needed in that state.

As you can see by examining the table, the most common requirement for using lag wages to establish a subsequent claim is that the claimant must have earned, in subsequent employment, eight times the weekly benefit amount of the original claim. Perhaps the easiest way to explain the requirements for successive benefit years is to follow a claimant from initial claim to subsequent claim.

Bill worked for an auto dealer for several years, and was laid off in early December 1992. Because of severance pay and pay for unused vacation time that was still due him after his separation, Bill waited until late January 1993 to file his claim. The base period of his initial claim was the most common one—the first four of the last five calendar quarters completed at filing. Bill's base period, then, was October 1, 1991 through September 30, 1992, and Bill qualified for a weekly benefit amount of $200.

During the course of his benefit year, Bill was called back to work for six weeks on a part-time basis, and earned $3,000 in part-time earnings. Nevertheless, Bill's benefits were exhausted before his benefit year expired in January 1994. Bill then went to file a new claim, and had a new base period of October 1, 1992 through September 30, 1993. Bill had lag wages of $8,000 in his new base period's first quarter—October 1 through December 30, 1992. Thanks to severance pay and vacation pay—all of which were paid to him in January 1993—he also had lag wages of $5,000 in the first quarter of 1993. In his filing state, South Carolina, these lag wages were sufficient in amount and distribution for Bill to qualify for a new claim. That is, he had wages in two quarters of the base period, and his total base-period wages—$13,000—were equal to or greater than one and one-half his high-quarter wages—$12,000. However, Bill could not use the lag wages to establish a new claim unless he had new earnings of eight times the weekly

Table 6.9 New Employment Requirements for Subsequent Claims

State (1)	Employment Must Be Covered (2)	Wage Requirements (3)	Other Requirements (4)
AL	Yes	8 x weekly benefit amount.	—
AK	No	8 x weekly benefit amount.	—
AZ	No	8 x weekly benefit amount.	—
AR	Yes	3 x weekly benefit amount.	Wages must have been earned after establishment of last valid claim.
CA	No	Must have earned qualifying wages during preceding benefit year.	—
CO	No	$2,000.	—
CT	Yes	5 x weekly benefit amount.	Earnings must be 5 x weekly benefit amount or $300, whichever is greater.
DE	Yes	10 x weekly benefit amount.	Wages must have been earned after establishment of last valid claim.
DC	Yes	10 x weekly benefit amount.	—
FL	No	3 x weekly benefit amount.	—
GA	Yes	10 x weekly benefit amount.	—
HI	No	5 x weekly benefit amount.	—
ID	No	5.5 x weekly benefit amount.	—
IL	No	3 x weekly benefit amount.	Employment does not have to be covered, but must be bona fide.
IN	No	$300 must have been earned in last 2 quarters of new base period, with at least $500 earned overall.	—
IA	Yes	$250.	—
KS	Yes	8 x weekly benefit amount.	Wages must have been earned after establishment of last valid claim.
KY	No	8 x weekly benefit amount.	Wages must have been earned in last two quarters of new base period.

State (1)	Employment Must Be Covered (2)	Wage Requirements (3)	Other Requirements (4)
LA	Yes	6 x weekly benefit amount.	Earnings must be 6 x weekly benefit amount or $3/13$ of high-quarter wages of previous claim, whichever is less.
ME	Yes	8 x weekly benefit amount.	—
MD	Yes	10 x weekly benefit amount.	—
MA	No	3 x weekly benefit amount.	—
MI	No	—	Because of state's short lag period, it is not possible to base subsequent claim on lag wages.
MN	Yes	10 x weekly benefit amount.	—
MS	Yes	8 x weekly benefit amount.	—
MO	Yes	5 x weekly benefit amount.	If wages are not earned in covered employment, must be 10 x weekly benefit amount.
MT	Yes	6 x weekly benefit amount.	Earnings must be 6 x weekly benefit amount or $3/13$ of high-quarter wages of previous claim, whichever is less.
NE	No	4 x weekly benefit amount.	—
NV	No	3 x weekly benefit amount.	—
NH	No	—	Because of state's short lag period, it is not possible to base subsequent claim on lag wages.
NJ	No	6 x weekly benefit amount.	—
NM	Yes	6 x weekly benefit amount.	Earnings must be 6 x weekly benefit amount or $3/13$ of high-quarter wages of previous claim, whichever is less.
NY	No	—	Because of state's short lag period, it is not possible to base subsequent claim on lag wages.

State (1)	Employment Must Be Covered (2)	Wage Requirements (3)	Other Requirements (4)
NC	Yes	10 x weekly benefit amount.	—
ND	Yes	10 x weekly benefit amount.	—
OH	No	—	Earnings must be 3 x average weekly wage, and there must be covered employment in 6 weeks.
OK	No	10 x weekly benefit amount.	—
OR	No	6 x weekly benefit amount.	—
PA	No	6 x weekly benefit amount.	—
PR	Yes	3 x weekly benefit amount.	Wages must have been earned during at least 1 calendar quarter, and must not be less than $50.
RI	No	80 x minimum hourly wage.	—
SC	Yes	8 x weekly benefit amount.	Work must have been with single employer.
SD	Yes	4 x weekly benefit amount.	—
TN	Yes	5 x weekly benefit amount.	—
TX	No	6 x weekly benefit amount.	—
UT	Yes	6 x weekly benefit amount.	—
VT	No	4 x weekly benefit amount.	—
VA	No	30 days.	—
VI	No	6 x weekly benefit amount.	Earnings must be 6 x weekly benefit amount or $3/13$ of high-quarter wages of previous claim, whichever is less.
WA	No	6 x weekly benefit amount.	—
WV	Yes	8 x weekly benefit amount.	—
WI	Yes	5 x weekly benefit amount.	—
WY	Yes	8 x weekly benefit amount.	—

benefit amount of the initial claim. Because Bill earned well over the $1,600 needed when he performed the part-time work, he qualified for a subsequent claim. Note that Bill would qualify even if the part-time earnings did not fall within the new base period, because he had lag wages in the new base period.

It's important to recognize that it isn't necessary for new wages to be from full-time employment or from employment that is believed to be permanent. Nor is it necessary for the new employment and the employment used to establish the initial claim to be in the same state. Of course, if the two periods of employment took place in different states, a combined wage claim might be possible if the subsequent wages were covered and fell within the base period of the state against which you're filing. Be aware that if you file a subsequent claim as a combined wage claim, and the state you're filing against is different from the one against which you filed the initial claim, you do not have to meet the requalification requirements of the first state, as that state will only be transferring wages to your new filing state. Of course, whether you're filing your initial claim or a subsequent claim, the filing state's basic monetary qualification requirements must be met. Now you understand why we advised you to accept any suitable employment—even if it is only part-time or temporary in nature— when receiving UI benefits!

We hope that any period of unemployment you might experience will be of short duration, and that you won't need to worry about exhausting your first claim, much less establishing a subsequent claim. But we know that this can occur, and that it is to your benefit to have a clear idea of your state's requirements. If your filing state is one that has relatively complex requirements, you may wish to consult with your state's unemployment office staff for verification of the information presented here. It is often easier to explain requirements when using concrete data regarding wages and employment history.

In this chapter, we have discussed the calculation of basic benefits, and have clarified the relationships between various wage and employment requirements. We have tried to provide you with an understanding of the state-to-state variations and to suggest strategies that may allow you to maximize your UI benefits. Certainly, any discussion involving numbers and formulas can be difficult—and, perhaps, a little intimidating. We hope that this chapter has minimized the difficulty and, at the very least, will help you better formulate any questions you might have about your own situation or your state's laws and regulations. Should you have questions, we do encourage you to seek assistance from the appropriate unemployment office.

In the next chapter, we'll complete our picture of the UI system by telling you about state and federal programs that, in special situations, can provide benefits above and beyond regular entitlement. We'll also look at training programs, job-search assistance, and other services that may be available to you.

7. EXTENSIONS, ASSISTANCE, AND OTHER SPECIAL PROGRAMS

Throughout the preceding chapters, most of our discussions have centered on basic unemployment insurance (UI) benefits. But there are various related programs that can extend your benefits, provide job training, or furnish other types of assistance. In this chapter, we will briefly look at each of these programs. We do not intend to examine each program in great detail, but only to give you basic information so that if you are interested, you can contact the appropriate source.

EXTENDED BENEFITS

The term *extended benefits* is applied to any type of benefits paid during sustained periods of high unemployment to claimants who have exhausted their benefits under regular state programs. Extended benefit programs were established when it was recognized that during periods of prolonged high unemployment, claimants have more difficulty finding work. These programs may be state-financed, jointly financed by the state and the federal government, or completely financed by the federal government. Those that are partially or wholly financed by the state usually become effective when the unemployment rate in that state reaches a "trigger point." Those programs that are wholly financed by the federal government are usually triggered by the national unemployment rate.

To qualify for extended benefits, claimants must have had valid claims for which they exhausted benefits within specified periods of high unemployment. Usually, benefits under extension programs are paid at the same weekly benefit rate as they are under regular, or "stem," claims. While general eligibility requirements are also largely the same as those of regular claims, there may be additional employment or wage requirements, and work-search requirements are likely to be more stringent.

State Extended Benefits

Several states—Alaska, California, Connecticut, the District of Columbia, Oregon, and Minnesota, for instance—have state-financed extended benefit programs that are triggered by high unemployment rates. Still other states have programs based on other factors that may influence unemployment rates. In Puerto Rico, for example, extended benefits can be paid to claimants who become permanently displaced from their regular employment as a direct result of the permanent termination of an industry, factory, or occupation, or the reduction of sugarcane-crop areas. And Hawaii provides thirteen additional weeks of benefits when a natural or man-made disaster results in unemployment of a substantial number of people or families. Generally, eligibility and work-search requirements for claimants receiving state-financed extended benefits are the same as those for claimants receiving regular benefits.

Because of the changeable nature of state economies and the many factors that affect them, legislation designed to establish new extended benefit programs or to continue existing ones may be pending even as we write. So regardless of whether your state is mentioned within this discussion, we recommend that you contact your unemployment office if your regular benefits have been exhausted or are soon to be exhausted—especially if there is a high unemployment rate in your state. The unemployment staff should be able to help you determine if you are eligible for extended benefits, and to explain any requirements that must be satisfied in your state.

Federal-State Extended Benefits

The federal-state extended benefit program is financed equally by state and federal funds. However, the benefits are triggered by the unemployment rate in the state you are filing against, and are paid through the state's regular UI system. The formula for this trigger is so complicated that we are not going to attempt to explain it here. Fortunately, if such an extension is in effect during your period of unemployment, your state unemployment office should notify you before or immediately after your benefits become exhausted. If you exhaust your UI benefits some time before the program triggers on and you are eligible for extended benefits, the state will notify you at your last address of record.

Be aware that if you are filing on an interstate claim basis, you may be eligible for only two weeks of benefits unless the agent state—that is, the state where you filed your claim—is also on extended benefits. The trigger is linked to the unemployment situation in the state where the claim is filed because it is felt that if the claimant resides in and is seeking work in a labor market in which jobs are more readily available, the extended benefits are not as necessary. Also note that the law which provides for federal-state extended benefits requires a more active work search than may be required by state laws, and that it also demands that the states verify contacts with potential employers. In addition, "suitable work" is defined as any work that the claimant is physically able to perform.

Federal Extended Benefits

Solely federal extensions are enacted by Congress, and are based on national unemployment conditions. In previous years, these benefits were called Federal Supplemental Benefits and Federal Supplemental Compensation. The extension that was finally enacted in November 1991 was entitled the Emergency Unemployment Compensation Act (EUCA). Although financed by the federal government, the benefits are administered by and paid through the state agencies. Like extended benefits that are partially funded by the federal government, those that receive all funding from the federal government require that the claimant make a more active work search than that necessary under regular programs, and that the state agencies verify contacts with prospective employers. Similarly, the definition of "suitable work" is extended to include any work that the claimant is physically able to perform.

EUCA has been extended four times since November 1991, and each time, the benefit entitlement and eligibility requirements have been modified. For the most recent extension, the trigger point for EUCA was a 7-percent unemployment rate.

If you believe that you might be entitled to EUCA benefits and you were not contacted by your unemployment office when your regular benefits were exhausted, by all means, contact your local office.

Keep in Touch!

As we've already discussed, if and when you become eligible for extended benefits, you should be contacted at your last address of

record. Clearly, this is a good reason to advise your state unemployment office of any change of address—even if you have stopped claiming UI benefits. Of course, information on extension programs is usually printed in local newspapers and announced over television and radio. However, if you have exhausted your regular UI benefits and have not yet regained employment, we strongly recommend that you visit your local office to learn about any programs that might be available to you.

THE TRADE ADJUSTMENT ACT

The Trade Adjustment Act of 1974 was amended in 1988 and was scheduled to expire on September 30, 1993, but was extended at that time. This act established a federal program that provides assistance to workers who become unemployed as a direct result of increased imports due to trade adjustments. Assistance can include allowances above and beyond regular state benefit entitlement, relocation and work-search allowances, and subsistence and transportation allowances during referred remedial—that is, corrective—job training. The program is federally funded, but payment is made through the state unemployment agencies.

To be eligible for assistance under this act, affected workers must have been certified by the Secretary of the Department of Labor. The Secretary makes the certification determination on request of three or more workers, the employer, or the authorized representatives of either the workers or the employer, and then notifies the applicable state agency. Claimants may be notified of potential eligibility by their state unemployment office or their former employer.

If your employer has closed his or her business or laid off workers because imports have diminished the demand for your work product or service, be sure to contact your employer or your union representative to see if a petition for certification has been filed under the Trade Adjustment Act. You may also contact the central office of your state unemployment agency or the Department of Labor to determine if there are any programs for which you might qualify.

TIP: *If your benefits have been exhausted but you're still unemployed, be sure to let your unemployment office know about any change of address so that they can contact you if you become eligible for extended benefits.*

DISASTER UNEMPLOYMENT ASSISTANCE

Under the Disaster Relief Act of 1974, the President of the United States may authorize appropriate assistance, including the payment of benefits, to individuals who are unemployed as a result of a "major" disaster, whether natural (such as floods or an earthquake) or man-made (such as an oil slick or a civil disturbance that destroys property). Benefits are paid through state unemployment offices, but are financed by the Federal Emergency Management Agency through cooperation with the Secretary of Labor. These benefits are comparable to regular UI benefits.

We hope that you won't ever need disaster relief, but if a disaster does occur, you should be contacted by your state unemployment agency, the State or National Guard, or other authorized emergency workers.

TRAINING ASSISTANCE PROGRAMS

In many states, employment training programs are available to help workers who need training in order to gain employment or improve work-search techniques. Such programs are usually voluntary, although training in work-search techniques may be required as part of the eligibility review program, particularly if it is determined that a claimant's work-search efforts have been inadequate.

Workers who qualify for UI benefits through the regular state unemployment program may continue to receive benefits while obtaining training from this program. Workers who do not qualify for benefit payments may receive transportation and subsistence allowances. Certainly, there are tremendous variations from state to state, and programs may continue to be modified as the needs of unemployed workers change. If you are unemployed or underemployed and are interested in job training or are simply in need of assistance with your work search, we recommend that you contact your local unemployment office to learn about the programs available in your state. Whether or not you are eligible for UI benefits, you may be referred to an employment counselor for an assessment of your training needs.

DISPLACED WORKERS PROGRAMS

Several states have programs that provide job-search assistance and job training to workers who have been permanently displaced due to discontinuation of their customary occupations or technological improvements within an industry. While these programs are not financed by UI funds, assessment and referral may be made through local unemployment offices.

If you have become or are about to come unemployed because your occupation has become obsolete, there is every probability that your state Employment Security Agency will contact you. If you are not contacted, by all means get in touch with an office of the agency to see if you qualify for this assistance.

In this chapter, we have outlined special programs that may be available to you through contact with your state unemployment office. This is an area that's constantly changing and expanding in response to the changing nature of our economy and work place. For this reason, we have not gone into detail about any one program. If you feel that you may be eligible for any of the assistance discussed in this chapter, we suggest that you make your initial contact with your local unemployment office—unless, of course, the central or administrative office is equally accessible. If your initial contact does not have the desired result, we urge you to seek further assistance.

CONCLUSION

It has been said that a recession occurs when a specific number of people are out of a job. A depression occurs when *you* are out of a job. Unfortunately, this joke has a strong ring of truth. The important thing to remember is that you are not alone. There are millions of people out there in the same situation.

Our country has set up a system to help you and your family get through this period of unemployment. It is a system financed by employer-paid taxes based on payrolls. No matter how impersonal, frustrating, or confusing the system may sometimes be, you still should receive all the benefits that are rightfully yours. Don't let the system intimidate you and stop you from claiming those benefits.

This book was specifically written to help you understand the process, language, and rules and regulations of the unemployment insurance system. It points out those errors most often made by claimants so that you can avoid these common pitfalls, and it explains in detail what you need to know to get the largest benefit check possible. In the course of using this book, if there is more information that you would like to see added, or if there is a comment that you wish to make, we would very much like to hear from you. Please write to us in care of the publisher at the following address:

UI Benefits
c/o Avery Publishing Group, Inc.
120 Old Broadway
Garden City Park, NY 11040

GLOSSARY

Italicized words are defined elsewhere in the glossary.

Abandonment of position. Walking off the job or failing to go to work without prior notice. Considered *misconduct,* abandonment of position can be reason for *disqualification.*

Ability to work. An eligibility requirement in all states, ability to work requires that the claimant be physically able to work "without undue restrictions." Some states also specify that claimants must be mentally able to work. Inability to work is considered a reason for *ineligibility.*

Absence without leave. Failure of an employee to obtain the employer's permission to take leave during regular working hours. Considered *misconduct,* absence without leave can be reason for *disqualification.*

Additional benefits. See *Extended benefits.*

Additional claim. The reopening of an existing claim following a period of one or more weeks of employment. The filing of such a claim is necessary after a claimant returns to full-time employment—making him or her ineligible for unemployment benefits—and then again becomes unemployed during the same *benefit year.* The additional claim "restarts" the continued claim process, allowing the claimant to again receive benefit checks. If there is a balance remaining in the claim, the benefit year, *weekly benefit amount,* and other determinations are the same on the additional claim as they were on the original claim.

Adjudicator. A staff member of an unemployment office who is responsible for obtaining information, examining and weighing documents and testimony, and making a determination of eligibility on an unemployment claim. An adjudicator may interview claimants, former employers, witnesses, and other involved parties to obtain necessary information. This term is sometimes used interchangeably with the terms *appeals examiner, claims examiner,* and *fact-finder.*

Agent state. In the case of an *interstate claim,* this is the state in which the claimant files for compensation against the *liable state,* also called the paying state, which is the state in which the wages were earned. The agent state is so called because it acts as an agent by accepting the claim application and transmitting it to the paying state for processing.

Allowance. See *Dependents' allowance.*

Annual-wage-formula states. States that base their computation of the *weekly benefit amount* on the claimant's total *base-period* wages.

Appeals examiner. The staff member of the unemployment office who conducts and controls the first-level *appeals hearing* and issues the written appeals decision. The appeals examiner states the order of the proceedings at the start of the hearing, and reserves the right to ask questions or otherwise expedite an orderly and fair process. This examiner is sometimes referred to as a "referee" or *adjudicator*.

Appeals hearing. A formal hearing, requested by either the claimant or a former employer, designed to review a *determination* made at the claims-examining level. An appeal may call into question either the amount of benefits being provided for the claimant or the eligibility of the claimant to collect benefits. Both parties—claimant and employer—are notified of an appeals hearing and are allowed to bring legal counsel and witnesses to the hearing. The hearing may reverse, affirm, or modify the original determination. The decision must be issued within thirty days of the hearing, and can be appealed through a second-level appeal.

Availability for work. An eligibility requirement in all states, availability for work requires that the claimant be willing and ready to work. Normally, this must be demonstrated by an active in-person work search. Lack of availability is considered a reason for *ineligibility*.

Average-weekly-wage-formula states. States that base their computation of the *weekly benefit amount* on the average weekly wage earned during all or part of the *base period*.

Backward disqualification. Imposed only in certain states, a so-called "backward" disqualification has to do with the particular job *separation* that is considered when determining whether a claimant will be disqualified from receiving unemployment benefits. Usually, *disqualifications* are based on a claimant's separation from his or her last job. In the case of a backward disqualification, a claimant is disqualified for leaving or being fired from a job other than his or her last one.

Base period. A fifty-two-week period defined by state law and determined by the filing date of the *initial claim application*. It is the earnings from *covered employment* paid within this base period that determine the unemployment benefits paid to the claimant. Each state uses one of five possible base periods, with the most common base period including the first four of the last five calendar quarters completed before the establishment of a valid claim.

Basic entitlement. The claimant's entitlement resulting from length of employment, wages earned, and wage distribution, before being augmented by *dependents' allowance* or being reduced by *deductible income*.

Basic weekly benefit amount. See *Weekly benefit amount*.

Benefit year. The period of time during which a claimant may draw his or her *maximum potential benefit amount*. In most states, the benefit year is the fifty-two-week period that begins the week the claimant files a valid *initial claim application*.

Bona fide employment. "Bona fide," meaning "in good faith," is used to describe employment in which there was a genuine employer-employee relationship. In some states, the employment must have been covered, but the term may also be used to indicate that the employment was of a specified duration, or that at the time of the hiring, the intent of the employer and claimant was that the employment would be continuous. The determination as to whether employment was bona fide is important in determining the employer's coverage liability and in deciding whether a *separation* from a particular job should be considered the cause of a claimant's unemployment.

Cash wages. Actual salary payments made by an employer, as distinguished from the value of room and board or other goods and services given in exchange for labor. "Cash wages" do not have to be hard currency. This term is often used when determining whether an employer must provide unemployment insurance coverage for his or her employees. For instance, employers of agricultural workers must cover their employees if cash wages of $20,000 or more were paid for labor in any calendar quarter of the current or preceding year.

Casual labor. Services that are not part of the employer's regular course of business, and are not performed by an individual regularly employed by the employer. For instance, the shoveling of snow from an employer's premises performed by someone other than a regular employee may be considered casual labor. This labor is excluded from unemployment insurance coverage in most states.

Claim. A request for benefit payment. See *Additional claim; Combined wage claim; Consecutive claims; Continued claiming; Initial claim application; Interstate claim; Interstate combined wage claim; Unemployment Compensation for Ex-Servicemembers (UCX) claim; Unemployment Compensation for Federal Employees (UCFE) claim.*

Claimant's handbook. Known by different names in different states, this booklet or pamphlet explains the claims process, benefit rights, and claimant responsibilities under a particular state's laws and regulations. Each unemployment office should be able to provide each claimant with this booklet. It is important to ask for a copy of the booklet during the first visit to the unemployment office, and to request clarification of any confusing terms or policies.

Claims examiner. A staff member of an unemployment office who is responsible for interviewing claimants, employers, and witnesses to obtain information; and for examining and weighing documents and testimony to make *determinations* of *eligibility* on unemployment insurance claims. The examiner writes and issues determinations. This term is sometimes used interchangeably with the terms *adjudicator* and *fact-finder.*

Combined wage claim. An unemployment claim based on *covered employment* in two or more states during the *base period* of the *filing state*—the state in which the claim is filed. Claimants may combine wages earned in more than one state to maximize their *weekly benefit amount* or the duration of their entitlement. Generally, all *determinations* regarding the amount of the benefits or the claimant's *eligibility* are made by and under the regulations of the filing state.

Consecutive claims. Separate claims, filed against separate states, one after the other. Claimants who have worked in more than one state sometimes choose to file consecutive claims instead of a *combined wage claim,* as consecutive claims can maximize the length of time during which benefits are received. In order to file consecutive claims, the claimant must qualify for a claim in each of the states. The benefits provided in the first claim must be exhausted before the second claim is filed.

Continued claiming. The process through which the claimant applies for subsequent weeks of benefit payments after the filing of the *initial claim application.* Most of the time, each claim form allows the claimant to apply for two weeks of benefits. In states with automated mail-in claim systems, continued claim forms are sent to the claimant by mail. In other states, continued claim forms are completed in-person during visits to the unemployment office. In some states, claimants are now able to file continued claims via their touch-tone telephones.

Covered employment. Employment on which the employer is required to pay state and/or federal unemployment insurance taxes. It is estimated that 97 percent of wage and salary employment is covered employment.

Covered wages. Payment for services performed in *covered employment.*

DD-214. The official document given to a servicemember of the United States Armed Forces at the time of discharge. This form, which contains the information on which the determination of eligibility is made, should be submitted to the unemployment office by the claimant at the time the *initial claim application* is filed.

Deductible income. Income received by a claimant that results in total or partial *ineligibility.* Deductible income can include earnings from *partial unemployment,* pensions, worker's compensation, severance pay, holiday or vacation pay, and back pay.

Dependent. Defined differently by each of the fourteen states that provide *dependents' allowances,* a dependent usually must be wholly or mainly supported by the claimant. All of the fourteen states recognize minor children as being dependents, and some states also include older children who are unable to work, as well as nonworking spouses, parents, and siblings.

Dependents' allowance. A special allowance provided under some state unemployment compensation laws to claimants with family support responsibilities as defined by that state. The amount of the dependents' allowance is usually defined in the state law, and is normally a fixed amount.

Determination. A decision made by the unemployment office regarding either a claimant's *eligibility* for benefits or the amount of benefits that a claimant is entitled to receive. All notices of determination must include instructions for filing an appeal. The *Notice of Monetary Determination* is perhaps the most common notice of determination.

Discharge for misconduct. Involuntary separation from employment resulting from actions of or omissions by the worker that are harmful to the employer's interests. Examples of misconduct range from irregular attendance to theft and assault. See also *Gross misconduct; Misconduct.*

Disqualification. A penalty imposed on the basis that the claimant is responsible for his or her condition of unemployment, disqualification is the postponement or cancelation of benefits for a specific period of time or until a particular condition is met. Actions that can result in disqualification include quitting employment without *good cause*, discharge for *misconduct*, discharge for *gross misconduct*, refusing *suitable work*, involvement in labor disputes, and *fraudulent misrepresentation*. See also *Backward disqualification; Durational disqualification; Term disqualification.*

Distribution requirement. A basic requirement of *monetary eligibility*, a distribution requirement specifies the period of time during which wages from *covered employment* must have been earned to qualify the claimant for benefits. In many states, a claimant's wages must have been paid in at least two quarters of the *base period*, and at least half of the total base-period wages must have been paid in a quarter or quarters other than the *high quarter.*

Domestic employment. Service performed in people's homes or in other residences such as boarding houses, fraternities, and sororities. Included among domestic workers are housekeepers, maids, cooks, butlers, nannies, baby sitters, companions, personal chauffeurs, and gardeners.

Durational disqualification. A type of disqualification that prevents payment of benefits until the claimant regains employment for a specified period of time and/or earns a specified amount of wages, and then again becomes unemployed for reasons that are not disqualifying. See also *Disqualification; Term disqualification.*

Duty station. For civilian employees of the United States, the duty station is the site from which the employment is controlled and directed. Usually, it is the state in which the worker's services are performed. The federal personnel office designates the duty station when a position is posted. An unemployment insurance claim based on civilian employment for the United States Government generally must be filed against the state of the claimant's last duty station.

Eligibility. The condition of meeting all requirements to receive unemployment benefits. See also *Ineligibility; Monetary eligibility; Nonmonetary eligibility.*

Eligibility review program. A review conducted by the unemployment office to determine the *eligibility* of a claimant who is already receiving unemployment benefits. When called for an eligibility review, claimants are required to report to their unemployment office at a specified time. Nearly every claimant is called for at least one eligibility review, and in most cases, these reviews result in the continuation of benefit payments.

Extended benefits. Unemployment benefits paid during sustained periods of high unemployment to claimants who have exhausted their benefits under regular state programs. An extended benefit program may be state financed, federally financed, or financed equally by state and federal funds.

Fact-finder. A staff member of a local unemployment office who interviews both claimants and former employers during *fact-finding interviews* in order to get the information upon which the final *determination* is based. Because the fact-finder is often also the *adjudicator* or *claims examiner,* these terms may be used interchangeably.

Fact-finding interview. An interview conducted by the unemployment office staff in order to resolve a question regarding the claimant's eligibility to receive unemployment benefits. Such a question may arise as the result of the claimant's responses on the *initial claim application* or continued claims forms, an eligibility or quality control review, or an employer inquiry. During the interview, both the claimant and the former employer may be questioned in order to find the facts necessary to determine the claimant's *eligibility.* See also *Predetermination fact-finding proceeding.*

Federal Unemployment Tax Act (FUTA). The 1939 act that codified the current unemployment insurance program on the federal level. FUTA defines the various categories of *covered employment* and provides the general framework with which all state unemployment insurance laws must comply.

Filing state. The state in which an *initial claim application* is submitted by a claimant. On an *interstate claim,* the filing state acts as an agent by accepting the claim for the state in which the claimant worked. On a *combined wage claim,* the filing state is also the *liable state*–the state that makes both the determination of eligibility and the payment of benefits.

Fraudulent misrepresentation. Used to describe the actions of a claimant, this term refers to the willful misrepresentation or withholding of facts that are material to *eligibility* for unemployment benefits. To establish fraudulent misrepresentation, it must be shown that the claimant deliberately concealed information or gave false information in order to obtain benefits to which he or she would not have been entitled had the fraudulent action not occurred. This act may be committed on the *initial claim application* or accompanying documentation, on continued claims forms, or at any other point at which the claimant supplies information that could affect *eligibility.* Fraudulent misrepresentation is considered a reason for *disqualification.*

FUTA. See *Federal Unemployment Tax Act.*

Good cause. Often defined as "compelling cause," this term is most often used to describe a claimant's reason for quitting his or her employment, but is also used to describe a claimant's reason for refusing a job offer. When determining if a claimant had good cause to leave employment, *claims examiners* consider a number of factors: whether the reason for leaving would have caused a prudent person to resign, what the potential harm would have been if the claimant had remained, and what steps were taken to solve the work problem. Similar factors are considered when examining job refusals. Both quitting without good cause and refusing employment without good cause can result in *disqualification.*

Gross earnings. Sometimes referred to as "before-tax earnings," these are total earnings before deductions are made for income tax, Social Security and Medicare contributions, health insurance, etc.

Gross misconduct. Used to describe the actions of an employee, gross misconduct—which is cited in the laws of thirty-one states—refers to the commission of a crime in connection with work, and can include theft; fighting on the job; assault; intoxication, including use of illegal substances; arson; sabotage; and willful disregard of safety regulations. Discharge for gross misconduct is considered a reason for *disqualification.* See also *Misconduct.*

High quarter. The quarter of the *base period* during which the claimant earned the highest amount of wages. This may be any one of the four quarters that make up the base period.

High-quarter-formula states. States that base their computation of the *weekly benefit amount* on wages paid during the *high quarter* of the *base period.*

Industrial misconduct. See *Misconduct.*

Ineligibility. A condition based on a claimant's failure to meet one or more eligibility requirements, ineligibility can be total, resulting in the denial of benefits, or partial, resulting in the reduction of benefits. Factors that may cause ineligibility include lack of *ability to work,* lack of *availability for work,* alien citizenship status, and the receipt of *deductible income.*

Initial claim application. The first application for unemployment insurance benefits filed by the claimant after becoming separated from his or her job.

Insubordination. The deliberate failure or refusal of an employee to follow the order or instructions of a superior. Considered *misconduct,* insubordination can be reason for *disqualification.*

Internet System. A computerized interstate information-exchange system begun in 1983, the Internet System has increased the processing speed of *combined wage claims* and *interstate claims.*

Interstate claim. A type of claim application usually filed by a claimant who has worked in one state and then moved to another state. The interstate claim is filed in the new state of residence (the *agent state*) against the state in which the work was performed (the *liable state*). This type of claim may also be filed by a claimant who has worked in more than one state, but who chooses to file against only one state—usually the state with the highest *weekly benefit amount*—rather than combining wages in a *combined wage claim.* The rules governing such a claim are those of the state in which the work was performed.

Interstate combined wage claim. A claim application filed in one state against another *liable state* based on wages earned in *covered employment* in two or more states during the liable state's *base period.* An interstate combined wage claim is relatively rare because a *combined wage claim* can be allowed on an interstate basis only in instances in which the claimant does not qualify for a regular combined wage claim against the state in which he or she is filing.

Lag period. The time between the end of the *base period* and the effective date of the unemployment claim. The wages paid during this lag period are not used for computation of the claim because they were not paid during the base period, but can sometimes be used to establish a subsequent claim.

Lag wages. See *Lag period.*

Liable state. Also referred to as the "paying state," this is the state against which a claim is filed through the facilities of another state, called the *agent state.*

Mail claim. A continued claim form filed by mail instead of being filed in person at an unemployment office. See also *Continued claiming.*

Maximum potential benefit amount. The highest amount of benefits for weeks of *total unemployment* that a claimant can receive during a *benefit year* under unemployment compensation law.

Maximum weekly benefit amount. The highest *weekly benefit amount* that a claimant can receive for a week of *total unemployment* under unemployment compensation law.

Minimum potential benefit amount. The smallest amount of benefits for weeks of *total unemployment* that a claimant can receive during a *benefit year* under unemployment compensation law.

Minimum weekly benefit amount. The lowest *weekly benefit amount* that a claimant can receive for a week of *total unemployment* under unemployment compensation law.

Misconduct. Sometimes called "industrial misconduct," this term—used to describe the actions of an employee—refers to the willful and deliberate violation or disregard of accepted standards of on-the-job behavior, or the intentional or substantial disregard of an employer's interests or an employee's duties and obligations. Usually work-connected—that is, occurring in the course of work or on the work premises—misconduct can include attendance violations, *insubordination*, rudeness to clients or co-workers, theft or misuse of an employer's property or time, fighting, the use of controlled substances, and the falsification of records. Discharge for misconduct is considered a reason for *disqualification*. See also *Gross misconduct.*

Monetary eligibility. The claimant's eligibility for unemployment benefits as determined by the wages earned by the claimant or the length of time the claimant was employed during the *base period*. In some states, the claimant learns of his or her monetary eligibility during the initial visit to the unemployment office. In most states, the claimant learns of his or her monetary eligibility through the *Notice of Monetary Determination*—a notice issued by mail or in person after the initial visit. The term "monetary eligibility" also refers to the amount of the entitlement. See also *Nonmonetary eligibility.*

Monetary qualification. See *Monetary eligibility.*

Moving party. This term, which refers to the individual who initiated or was in control of a job *separation*, may be applied to either the claimant or the employer. When the claimant is the moving party, the claimant bears the burden of demonstrating that he or she had *good cause* for leaving employment. When the employer is the moving party, he or she bears the burden of establishing that the claimant was fired for *misconduct.*

Multi-quarter-formula states. States that base their computation of the *weekly benefit amount* on wages paid in more than just the *high quarter* of the *base period*. Usually, the two highest quarters are used.

Net earnings. Sometimes referred to as "take-home pay," these are a worker's earnings after deductions are made for income tax, Social Security and Medicare contributions, health insurance, etc.

Nonmonetary eligibility. The claimant's eligibility for unemployment benefits as determined by nonmonetary factors such as the cause of the *separation* from employment, *ability to work, availability for work,* and residency status. See also *Monetary eligibility.*

Notice of Monetary Determination. The statement that informs the claimant of his or her *monetary eligibility*—in other words, whether or not the claimant has earned sufficient wages and worked for a sufficient amount of time to qualify for unemployment benefits—and shows the claimant's *weekly benefit amount* and *maximum potential benefit amount,* as well as the wages used to make these determinations, any *dependents' allowance* the claimant is entitled to receive, and the *base period* for which the claim was computed. This statement may be sent to the claimant by mail, or may be hand-delivered to the claimant on a return visit to the unemployment office. It is important that the claimant review this notice for accuracy and request a reconsideration or *appeals hearing* if any information is incorrect.

Partial benefits. Unemployment benefit payments of less than the full *weekly benefit amount* resulting from reductions for part-time earnings or other *deductible income.*

Partial unemployment. The "less than full-time" employment of a claimant. Defined differently in different states, this usually refers to employment of less than forty hours per week and/or employment that provides earnings less than the *weekly benefit amount* of the claim. All state laws specify the amount of earnings from partial unemployment that will result in the reduction of benefit payments.

Paying state. See *Liable state.*

Potential benefit amount. See *Maximum potential benefit amount.*

Predetermination fact-finding proceeding. An interview conducted by the unemployment office staff to resolve a question of *eligibility* that arises during the filing of the *initial claim application.* A specific type of *fact-finding interview,* this proceeding takes place before any determination of eligibility is made.

Pro forma resignation. Literally a resignation "as a matter of form," this type of resignation is requested or required by the employer, and therefore is not considered voluntary. A pro forma resignation usually does not result in *disqualification* for unemployment benefits.

Quality control program. A program, conducted by both the Department of Labor and each state, designed to insure that applications for unemployment insurance are being correctly processed. In this program, claims are selected at random by computer, and the selected claimants are asked to fill out detailed questionnaires and to meet in-person with a quality control investigator. Only a small fraction of claimants are selected for quality control interviews.

Quitting without good cause. See *Good cause.*

Separation. The loss of employment, whether permanent—as occurs when a worker leaves or is fired from his or her job—or temporary—as occurs during layoffs.

Standard Form 8. A form given by the personnel office to civilians employed by the United States Government at the time of *separation* from their job. This federal form, which shows the address to which the unemployment office must send claim inquiries, should be submitted to the unemployment office by the claimant at the time the *initial claim application* is filed.

Standard Form 50. A form given to civilian employees of the United States Government each time there is a personnel action, such as a job *separation.* This federal form, which shows the pay rate of the employee, should be submitted to the unemployment office by the claimant at the time the *initial claim application* is filed.

Statutory exception. A citation in a state's unemployment laws or regulations that either allows benefits or results in *disqualification* in the case of specific situations or occurrences.

Suitable work. Used most often when the unemployment office considers the refusal of work by a claimant, this term is defined differently by different states. When deciding the suitability of work, claims examiners usually consider if the employer made a bona fide job offer; if the work was in keeping with the claimant's prior employment history, salary rate, educational attainments, and physical capabilities; and if the claimant had "good"—meaning "compelling"—cause to refuse the job. Refusal of suitable work is considered a reason for *disqualification.* See also *Bona fide employment; Good cause.*

Tax base. The amount of wages subject to taxation for each employee within a specific calendar year. The federal unemployment insurance tax base now amounts to the first $7,000 of each employee's wages in each calendar year.

Tax rate. The percentage of the *tax base* that must be paid as taxes. The federal unemployment insurance tax rate is now 6.2 percent. State tax rates vary according to the experience rating of each employer's account and the condition of that state's unemployment insurance fund.

Term disqualification. A penalty imposed on a *separation* or work-refusal *determination,* a term disqualification postpones benefits for a specific period of time, such as ten weeks. The penalty may begin with the week the disqualifying action occurred, or with the effective date of the claim. In some states, a term disqualification includes a reduction of the *maximum potential benefit amount.* See also *Disqualification; Durational disqualification.*

Total unemployment. A week of total unemployment is one in which the claimant performs no services for which he or she receives payment, or earns an amount that is less than the deductible amount specified in the respective state's definition of *partial unemployment.*

UCFE claim. See *Unemployment Compensation for Federal Employees claim.*

UCX claim. See *Unemployment Compensation for Ex-Servicemembers claim.*

Unemployment Compensation for Ex-Servicemembers (UCX) claim. A type of unemployment claim based on services performed for the United States Armed Forces, as distinguished from claims based on employment taxed and covered by the regular state unemployment insurance systen.

Unemployment Compensation for Federal Employees (UCFE) claim. A type of unemployment claim based on civilian services performed for the United States Government, as distinguished from claims based on employment taxed and covered by the regular state unemployment insurance system.

Wage credits. Wages earned by employees working in *covered employment.*

Wage record states. States in which the unemployment office should have records of wages from all *covered employment* performed in that state. In wage record states, employers are required to report wages to the state unemployment office at the end of each quarter. When the claimant files the *initial claim application,* he or she need provide only the name and address of the last employer.

Wage request states. States in which the unemployment office must request specific wage data from the appropriate employers in order to process an *initial claim application.* In wage request states, when the claimant files the initial claim application, he or she must list every employer worked for during the *base period.*

Waiting period. A week of unemployment for which the claimant receives no compensation, but during which he or she must be otherwise eligible for unemployment benefits. In most cases, the waiting period is the first week of the claim. All but eleven states have a one-week waiting period that must be served before benefits can be paid for *total unemployment.*

Weekly benefit amount. The benefit amount payable to the claimant for one week of *total unemployment* without the addition of any *dependents' allowance* or deductions made for *deductible income.* This amount, which is nearly always based on gross wages earned during the *base period,* can be computed in four different ways. See *Annual-wage-formula states; Average-weekly-wage-formula states; High-quarter-formula states; Multi-quarter-formula states.*

INDEX